CLOSE TO JESUS

Close to Jesus

ISBN 978-0-9848586-1-3

All scripture references are from the King James Version.

Categories:

Christian Spiritual Growth

Christian Faith

Christian Inspiration

Printed in the United States of America for World Wide Distribution

Copyright © 2026 by Sean Mize

All rights reserved. No part of this book may be reproduced in any manner whatsoever without written permission except in the case of brief quotations embodied in critical articles and reviews.

First Printing, 2026

Close to Jesus

Sean Mize

Behold, I stand at the door, and knock: if any man hear my voice, and open the door, I will come in to him, and will sup with him, and he with me. (Revelation 3:20)

Contents

PART 1: THE JOURNEY TO CLOSE TO JESUS		1
1	Invitation to Draw Close to Jesus	3
2	My Life Journey of Growing Close to Jesus	11
3	Why I Wrote This Book	23
4	Why Draw Close to Jesus?	29
PART 2: THE SPIRITUAL FOUNDATION		41
5	God: Father, Son, and Holy Spirit	43
6	Your New Life in Christ	57
7	Righteous by Faith	65
8	The Holy Spirit	71
PART 3: CONNECTING WITH JESUS		89
9	Introduction to Presence and Practices	91
10	Praise and Worship	103
11	Reading the Bible	141
12	Prayer	155
13	Hearing His Voice	167
14	Conversations With Jesus	187
15	Journaling	209
16	Praying in the Spirit	217
17	Praying in Tongues	237

PART 4: WALKING WITH JESUS	259
18 Time With Jesus	261
19 Community	277
20 Walk in the Spirit	289
21 Rivers of Living Water	307
PART 5: DEFEAT SIN AND ADDICTION	319
22 Defeat Sin	321
23 Addiction	343
24 When You Sin and Fail	351
PART 6: FEAR, ANXIETY, AND OTHER EMOTIONS	363
25 Anxiety and Worry	365
26 Unwanted or Negative Thoughts	385
27 Fear, Feelings, and Emotions	395
PART 7: MATURITY IN JESUS	411
28 Where Are You, Lord?	413
29 Maturity With Jesus	429
30 Always in His Presence	451
31 Stay Close to Jesus for Life	483
A Personal Note	497
Additional Reading	501
About the Author	503

Lord Jesus,

I pray that You connect closely with the readers of this book as You have connected with me.

Your love is abounding, and Your Spirit is all-encompassing.

Thank You for Your Presence in my life, and the life of those who embrace You.

– Sean

To Cricket:

You taught me to truly feel love. You gave me a deeper understanding of Jesus' unconditional love for me. Your body wore out before our story was finished, and I cherish every thought and memory of you. I am looking forward to skiing the mogul fields you are making for me now. Remember, the moguls don't need to be in perfect lines, we can ski the wonky, oval moguls too! Tell Jesus I'll see Him soon too. Invite Him to ski with us!

I love you forever!

That they all may be one; as thou, Father, art in me, and I in thee, that they also may be one in us: that the world may believe that thou hast sent me.

And the glory which thou gavest me I have given them; that they may be one, even as we are one:

I in them, and thou in me, that they may be made perfect in one; and that the world may know that thou hast sent me, and hast loved them, as thou hast loved me. (John 17:21-23)

PART 1: THE JOURNEY TO CLOSE TO JESUS

1

Invitation to Draw Close to Jesus

Do you want to be closer to Jesus, but no matter how hard you try it feels like there's always something missing?

Do you want to have a deeper relationship with Him, but it feels like you aren't quite able to connect?

Do you possibly feel like He's close to you when you draw close to Him, but as soon as you mess up, He's gone again?

Do you yearn for a deeper, more personal relationship with Jesus, but the reality is you don't feel it?

Have you been crying out to heaven but it feels like there are no answers?

You've been faithful to pray, and read, and talk to Jesus, but you feel like He's not talking with you?

Or maybe He replies, but it doesn't feel close, it doesn't feel personal, or it doesn't feel like He's really here?

I get it.

For years I prayed and worshiped and read my Bible and helped other people . . . but I never felt like my relationship with Jesus was truly intimate and close.

Jesus was my Savior, and He answered my prayers sometimes, and I felt like I was walking with Him, even somewhat close to Him at times, but I didn't feel like He was close to me consistently. He was there as my Savior, as a promise, or as a "source" but I wasn't sure how close He was!

I thought it was just something that over time, with more and more work and effort, you eventually kept getting closer to Jesus.

You see, I knew of this passage in the Word where Jesus invites us to abide in Him and Him in us, and He said that abiding would bring forth much fruit:

Abide in me, and I in you. As the branch cannot bear fruit of itself, except it abide in the vine; no more can ye, except ye abide in me.

I am the vine, ye are the branches: He that abideth in me, and I in him, the same bringeth forth much fruit: for without me ye can do nothing. (John 15:4-5)

Such a powerful verse, and it carries great depth and meaning. If we abide with Him, we can produce much fruit, but without Him I can do nothing. I desperately wanted to abide more deeply with Him, more frequently, more closely.

I considered "to abide" an active verb, something we actively do (and I still believe that). But I had this mental map that said that as long as I actively abide in Him, then He abides in me. And that meant to me the inverse would be true: if I don't abide in Him, He doesn't abide in me.

Yes, He dwells in me, I knew that. But even though He lives in me, if I'm not abiding, He isn't abiding. That was my mental map.

So as long as I worked and strived and was actively walking in Him, He was abiding in me.

I always felt as though I had to continue to work for my relationship with Him. My relationship with Him was labored; I was frequently frustrated with my inability to not sin, to not grieve His heart, to not do the things He didn't want me to do.

Paul's discussion about "I do what I don't want to do and the things I don't want to do, I do," (Romans 7:15-20) was very real to me.

I had a very deep belief in His presence in my heart, and I trusted that He would abide in me when I abided in Him. But human nature being what it is, and sin rearing its ugly head from time to time, would break my abiding.

Although I was saved and knew He lived in my heart, I was laboring and working for my relationship (abiding) with Him!

For over 40 years of my life, it was a deeply vexing, challenging part of my walk with Him, never feeling like I could quite live up to His standard, and never feeling like I could constantly walk in His presence.

Then I discovered this passage in Jesus' prayer for His disciples before His crucifixion:

That they all may be one; as thou, Father, art in me, and I in thee, that they also may be one in us: that the world may believe that thou hast sent me.

And the glory which thou gavest me I have given them; that they may be one, even as we are one:

I in them, and thou in me, that they may be made perfect in one; and that the world may know that thou hast sent me, and hast loved them, as thou hast loved me. (John 17:21-23)

Now, mind you, that passage has always been there. And I had read it before, but I had either skimmed over it, skipped it because I didn't understand it, or intentionally ignored it.

Given my conservative denominational background, I believed the concept of "that they all may be one" and "that they also may be one in us" was sacrilegious; that it was a concept that might lead people to believe that they could be god.

My heart was closed to the possibility that He could not only be in me, but I could also be in Him, and that we might be one, as They are one.

So I glossed over the passage, thinking, I just don't understand it; thinking that Jesus didn't mean exactly that; or that His meaning was obscured in translation. And my temperament is that I'm okay with not knowing things, so I was perfectly comfortable not knowing, consigning it to His sovereignty and accepting that it was something I didn't understand.

But once the Holy Spirit had highlighted that passage to me, He continued to bring me back to it. I began to dig deeply into that verse (and the entire context of John 14-17).

I became open to the idea that Jesus meant exactly what He said, word for word what the disciples recorded (imagine that!). I began to ponder, what would that look like in real life, "I in them, and thou in me, that they may be made perfect in one?"

If Jesus is in me, and the Father is in Jesus, then not only does "Christ live in my heart" but God the Father lives there as well, and of course the Holy Spirit lives in me too.

But it also held a wider interpretation of what it meant for Christ to live in me than I had believed for over 40 years. I had this mental picture of Christ in my heart, inhabiting my heart. And then mentally I would give Him - or not give Him - access to the other parts of me, at will. And that was part of the process of actively submitting to Him, daily picking up my cross. If I didn't pick up my cross today, if I didn't give Him access today, if I didn't abide with Him today, He wasn't abiding either. He was close, His Spirit lived in my heart, but His active work in me was on the sidelines, like a co-pilot, waiting to be included in my life.

So when I prayed more, He was more active. When I spent more time in quiet time, He was more active. When I prayed about decisions, He helped out. But if I wasn't actively abiding and praying, neither was He!

This may feel highly literal and religious to you as you read it, and I admit that it is/was, but it's exactly the way I processed it. And that mental processing held me back from fully accepting His complete life in me and the wholeness of the Spirit living within me.

But when I continued to contemplate this phrase: "I in them, and thou in me, that they may be made perfect in one," I realized that was Him living completely in me, all of me, and that meant the Father was in me as well, and "that they also may be one in us" indicates that even as they are in me, I am in them.

After a crushing trial over about 18 months, and at least a decade prior to that of deep emotional and relationship struggles, I began to experience a closeness with Jesus that is nothing short of amazing to me, feels completely encompassing to me, and includes an incredible peace that I believe is the "peace that passes all understanding." I began to realize that it's a deep connection with God Himself, Jesus Christ, and the Holy Spirit - all at once, and completely engulfing me with His Presence and His Love.

And now that I have truly experienced it - although with stumbles and falls and disappointments and struggles - I know it to be true. And once I had a taste of it, it became a reality to me that I could simply lean into Him more, and experience His closeness more frequently.

I have realized that Jesus wants to be close to me, He wants to be close to you, but sometimes we block Him because we are doing, doing, doing, trying to make it happen, or we are focused on something other than Him.

I realized that when we draw close to Christ in this way that He intended, it becomes so much easier to communicate with Him, to understand His ways and His intention for our lives, and to hear His Voice clearly.

When we are no longer working constantly to keep Jesus close and abiding, we have the freedom to simply exist in Him and He in us.

I have discovered that although there's time, intention, awareness, and communication needed to fully embrace His Presence, the prayer and time with Him doesn't feel like work - it's spending time with the King of the Universe, the Savior of the world - and it's not a weight at all; it's freeing, and it's a wonderful thing to spend time with Jesus.

It's a wonderful thing to lean on Jesus, to trust Him, to learn His ways, and to feel comfortable in His presence.

In a moment, I'll share my personal journey of growing close to Jesus over the course of my life, but first let's picture together what close with Jesus could be like for you.

Imagine for yourself now:

You have a deep connection with God Himself, Jesus Christ, and the Holy Spirit - all at once, and completely engulfing you with His Presence and His Love.

You walk with Him every hour, you sense Him every moment, and His Spirit connects with you from the time you wake up until the time you fall asleep at night. And of course He's right there through the night watches as well.

In the pages of this book, I'll share how God has created us for that closeness, and how we can follow Jesus so closely that we have access to everything He offers. I'll share with you the primary components of the time, activities, and postures I've had with Him that have aided me in drawing close to Him, and the deep reliance I've developed in Him.

2

My Life Journey of Growing Close to Jesus

When I was 15, I nearly died from starvation, and I was in a hospital for several months. I don't remember much of that experience, but it leads to the one I do remember vividly: being driven to a children's group home by a social worker.

When I was shown my new digs, which was a twin sized bed with a dresser next to it, and next to the dresser was a twin sized bed with another boy with no parents, and next to his bed was a dresser, and next to that dresser was another bed, with a boy with no parents, or abusive parents, or parents in jail; I was the most alone I have ever been in my entire life.

For the first time since my grandmother died when I was about six, I remember crying deeply, feeling horribly forsaken in life and having no idea how I could make it through.

When the social worker dropped me off and introduced me to my new caretakers, people with huge hearts that spend their time making sure children with no parents have a place to sleep and a meal to eat, I was so alone.

Just me and Jesus. And for months, as I interacted with other children with unknown, incapable, or missing parents, with caretakers who cared but were overwhelmed and stressed, with no spiritual guidance except my Bible and a guy by the name of Moses who took me to church on Sundays, I grew in reliance on Jesus, Jesus Himself.

I spent the next 2 ½ years in a foster group home during high school, and drew deeply closer to Jesus during that experience.

Prior to that, my parents had divorced, and I had drawn near to Jesus, relying on Him for comfort during the incredibly lonely and trying period of being a teenager living in a broken home, with no model of secure and effective communication or mature love. That was also the time period during which I began my lifelong journey of studying His Word.

I did my level best to rely on Jesus and draw on His power during those difficult years as a teenager facing emotional distress. I wouldn't have made it through those years without deeply relying on Him. I developed an intensely deep trust in Jesus.

I considered my experience in a broken home as a "light suffering," compared to the genocide of the Holocaust, the sexual abuse and human trafficking I prayed against in high school, and the lost souls who didn't have Jesus the way I did. Because of that perspective, I downplayed the negative effect on my emotional state and attachment development as I matured into an adult.

As I wandered through life for the next 15 years after graduation, I wandered from the Lord some, aimless and bored, and not knowing what I know now, that unknown trauma from the earlier years had been hidden and buried because it was easier to have no emotion than to cry or get angry, and having Jesus right by my side actually made it easier for me to ignore the hidden pain. My relationship with Him then was mostly me talking, and not hearing Him clearly, but He was still an incredible comfort to me, and I believed I could carry any load if He were there.

My favorite verse in high school and the years following was Philippians 4:13:

I can do all things through Christ which strengtheneth me.

In addition to relying on Him for strength to get through it all, I felt like I did everything I knew to be closer to Him, to have actual true relationship with Him. But for years I felt like I was missing something. I felt like I couldn't hear His voice. I even turned it off for a while. I allowed other things to speak much louder than He was speaking. Jesus was still there, but my relationship with Him was missing the depth of closeness I write about in this book.

My marriage of 17 years struggled deeply partly because I had put my own fears and desires ahead of Him, partly because I had unresolved, deeply buried, and unacknowledged pain from my teenage years, partly because I tried to be a god in my own life instead of submitting to Him and waiting for His perfect plan, and partly because I worshiped people and their opinion of me over my loyalty to Jesus.

I treaded water emotionally for years, and although I talked with Him frequently, most of the time it was cries for help in my then-current situation. I could no longer pretend that I could fix my marriage by being god in my own life, and I could no longer do it on my own.

For years I relied on His presence to get me through everyday. I drew closer to Jesus.

Nearly two years before I wrote this, my stressful, anxious, painful and disconnected life came to a screeching cataclysmic explosion and it got acutely worse. The marriage that was unknowingly set up to fail from the very beginning, not for love lost but for the intense unresolved childhood trauma in my life, that had been stuffed and buried for decades, unknown in its nuclear toxicity, finally surfaced and became a great external battle that ultimately destroyed my marriage.

The relationship that I thought was supposed to last for all eternity had come crashing down.

When my marriage blew up, I struggled to focus on the rest of life, my understanding of human emotions was completely upended, and I was desperate, horribly riddled with shame and guilt at failing and hurting the person I thought I was doing my very best to provide for.

Out of desperation, guilt and shame, and a feeling of helplessness, I started spending significantly more time with Jesus. I attended multiple worship services, began a practice of talking and walking with Him for hours on end, and He became the primary focus of my attention and my life.

Crying deep, deep tears for every mistake I had made, experiencing deep regret, and yet, crying out to Him, "God, I did the best I knew how." One of the hardest things for me to wrap my mind around was that I trusted Him deeply, I had done the best I knew how at the time, and yet I had fallen horribly short of His ideal as a husband, as a child of God, and as a human.

I grew deeply dependent on Him for my sanity, resources, wisdom, and staying power. Even though I had made mistakes that had consequences and deep pain associated with them, He was always not just there, but closely there.

I had taken things to Jesus in the past, but once the situation would resolve, my communication with Him would go back to the status quo.

But the difference this time was that things were so bad, my emotional health so low, and my deep state of regret, sorrow and pain the worst of my entire life.

After months of hours and hours of tears and crying out to God, I finally came to the very end of myself and said to Him, "God, please burn away the wood, hay, stubble, and chaff. I want to be free of anything that is not You."

That was the scariest prayer I've ever prayed, because I envisioned that He would take me through a painful, revealing, cleansing, and crushing process that would be worse than anything I had ever been through.

And He did.

The next 12 months were the hardest months of my entire life. I identified (or He revealed) (hopefully every) sinful thought, attitude, selfish posture, and idolatry in my life, and I experienced deep tears and incredible remorse over it all. The depth of my angst over hurting Him, disappointing Him, and hurting those who were affected by my irresponsibility, was nearly impossible to carry. Perhaps impossible, and I only carried it by the grace of Jesus.

He took me through multiple challenges, the hardest days of my life, the hardest emotional and tactical relationship decisions I've ever made in my life, and He was right by my side all the way through.

God continued a process of revelation, peeling back and opening the hidden places, the hurting places, and ultimately burning away the desire to hide from the truth about my pain.

I realized that there was sin in my life: idolatry; placing others ahead of Him; being dishonest to avoid the deep pain of other people seeing my broken places, and out of fear of hurting others; and treating my life as if I were the only one who could run it, instead of Him. As I discovered that sin, there were layers of pride, idolatry, and selfishness that took months to uncover and dismantle, and I entered a prolonged period of deep shame and guilt.

Through most of that first full year, I spent intense time with Jesus, communicating with Him deeply, much in praise and worship, walking and talking with Him, and knowing that He would take me through it all.

But during most of that time, my experience was much like in every major life event prior:

I still didn't feel like I was getting much closer to Him! I desperately wanted to clearly hear His voice and differentiate it from my own and from the enemy's voice. I had also fixated on my mistakes, loss, and grief, wallowing in shame and guilt. I knew I was saved, I knew He loved me, but I was still in a place of striving and working for my standing with Him as a Son, rather than simply accepting His complete redemption. And I feel like that posture of striving, and my intense sense of shame before Him, was blocking a completely deep and close connection with Him.

I went through an intense period of classes and spiritual mentoring that taught me about vulnerability, the value of the community of saints around me, my identity in Christ, and the true meaning of His blood sacrifice, and I had a fresh awareness that His redemption was complete and it fully covered my current shame and mistakes.

Although I knew that intellectually His sacrifice is complete and final, I realized that my entire 40+ years of following Jesus was based on an achievement model of Christianity: I had to work and strive for everything I did for Him, and He only loved me in accordance with how well I performed.

If I messed up, I had to get forgiveness anew - and that might have been repeated multiple times in a day, begging for forgiveness anytime I said a cross word, thought a mean thought, or didn't respond to another human's request with love and a quick "yes."

I was bound by religiosity that kept my mind in a constant turmoil, and this deeply affected my relationships and not in a good way! I loved Jesus devoutly, but I had no freedom in Him, and my relationship and communication with Him was horribly deficient because of it.

Nearly a year into the devastating crisis, the Lord began to lead me to people who one by one introduced me to the concepts of the true nature of His blood sacrifice, the deep meaning of the verse "there is therefore now no condemnation to them who are in Christ Jesus," the real freedom that Jesus provided at the cross, not just for heaven, but right here, right now on earth, the true "abundant life," and our proper identity in Christ as a Son or Daughter of the Risen King, as well as showing me what unconditional love and acceptance truly looks like.

Once I realized the deep life-giving nature of His blood sacrifice as a complete solution, not just a "ticket to heaven," I began to let go of the deep guilt and shame I had been holding onto.

During about the same time period, He was also revealing the hidden hurt and pain from my childhood that had driven the patterns of thought and behavior that had made it so hard for me to communicate vulnerably, transparently, and safely with those near and dear to me.

Simultaneously I was engaging in a deep effort to hear His voice and differentiate it from my own voice and the voice of the enemy.

I felt like I was going through three grueling transformational experiences at one time: the removal of systemic shame and guilt in my life, navigating the emotional insecurity deeply engrained in me from childhood, and learning to hear His Voice clearly.

During that time, as He comforted me deeply, He showed me how to hear His voice; He shepherded me through complete reliance on Him; He helped me break patterns of worshiping those around me, and their view of me; He showed me the freedom He bought and paid for with His sacrifice; and He taught me submission to His Kingship in my life.

He gave me places of vulnerability and security to model His love for me, and showed me His overwhelming love. I discovered the value of emotional security, complete submission to His will, and complete willingness to lay every single thing in my life down, no matter the cost.

With the help of human counselors and His continued guidance in my life, He taught me new ways to deal with my old coping patterns that included distraction, avoidance, and people pleasing.

He's taught me to live a secure life that starts with dependence on Him and is fueled by His love and acceptance of me the way He originally created and designed me. All along He was showing me, teaching me, and guiding me to not only rely on Him 100%, but also to communicate with Him as deeply (or more so) than I do with any human on this earth.

As those transformations were occurring I began to hear the voice of Jesus in my life more clearly than ever before, commune with Him in a way that's inexpressible in words, experience a peace in Him - and in life - that truly "passes understanding," and have a truly unspeakably satisfying abundant relationship with Him.

During that process, and in the midst of that pain as I was spending as much as 5 hours a day in His Presence, both corporately and privately, He became more real to me than at any other time during my life.

Exponentially more real.

I began to rely on Him for everything.

Every solution.

Every answer.

Every need for peace.

Everything.

And He gave me a sense of calm and peace that I had never experienced before.

Sure, I had been through trouble in the past, and He was there, and He had given me peace.

But nothing like this.

Through it all, He drew me closer and closer to Him.

I am His and He is mine.

I rely on Him intensely more than I did 18 months prior to writing this. And that's not to say that I didn't rely on Him significantly then, it's just increased. And the enemy can't take it away.

I am closer to Jesus than I ever imagined prior to this experience. The level of closeness I have with Jesus is accompanied with a deep, deep trust that mirrors the Hebrew boys when they said that even if He doesn't [save us] we will not bow (Daniel 3:18) and Job when he says, "Though he slay me, yet will I trust in him:" (Job 13:15).

When I look back at the entirety of my life, I can see a thread of Him drawing me closer to Him through each experience. Giving me several years of depth with Him even as I developed codependent caretaking behaviors as a teenager, navigating living in a hospital, a foster home, and then a group home for my last two years of high school, and showing me His comfort through it all. Being with me through financial success and failure. Being with me through a marriage that was founded on my false expectation of being able to provide completely for the emotional needs of someone else, when I was broken, insecure, and "playing God" myself, instead of relying on Him for relational security.

He was by my side for years as I tried to live life in my own power, even as I trusted and followed Him.

But He never left me. And He has never left you. No matter what others did to you, or what you have suffered, He has never left you.

No matter how you may have treated others, He has never left you. And no matter what coping mechanisms you used as a response to how others have treated you, or your own internal trauma, He has never left you.

Without the pressure, without the hours and hours with Him, without the guidance He sent me in sane, wise advisors, without communicating with Him intensely the way I've shared in this book, and without His explicit guidance, direction, and actions, I wouldn't have made it through.

Now that He has taken me all the way through, I know there will be new storms in my life - but I have His presence in a way I never had. No one can take from me my new, deep, intense relationship with the Lord.

3

Why I Wrote This Book

About 6 months prior to writing this book, people who had seen me at the very worst depths of my despair began to comment to me things like, "you seem to have more peace now," and "you are like a different person." One man asked me if things in my circumstances had improved. I told him they hadn't, and at that time, if anything, they were worse. His response was that it would be no great feat if I were calmer and more at peace if things were better, but if they were worse maybe there was something to my increased peace with Jesus.

People who had seen the depth of my despair were now seeing me carrying a fresh level of His presence and peace.

I told them what Jesus had done for me, and how He had transformed my view of His sacrifice, how I was walking with Him in a new level of communication, and how I was beginning to hear and understand His voice.

As I talked with people, I realized that not only had this level of peace and communication with Him been elusive for me, but that many people were struggling with some of the same disconnects I had previously had in my relationship with Jesus.

They might not have had the same dysfunctional family roots or specific sin issues, but the outcome was the same in their lives: they weren't living in the full freedom and peace that Jesus had bought and paid for with His blood sacrifice and with His loving day-to-day abiding presence.

Many people I talked with wanted to know more about how Jesus had transformed my life from one that strived to earn His approval, was filled with shame and guilt, and that often prioritized others' opinions or perceived judgments over my loyalty to Him; to a walk with Him that's intimately close, accepts His love and forgiveness completely, and makes a sincere effort to prioritize Him in everything, resulting in a significant level of peace and trust in Him.

I'd like to say it was a booming voice or a burning bush that led me to write this book. Instead, over time I realized that not only had I lived 40+ years walking and talking with Jesus but had never entered this level of intimacy with Him, but that many others were apparently in the same situation.

Because the transformation and the drawing nearer to Jesus occurred during a relatively short period of time (less than 18 months, and most of it in the latter 12 months), I could specifically recall and identify the actions I took, the thoughts I had, and the path He's led me on to grow closer to Him.

I believe we are called to be a light on a hill, to edify and help others in their time of need, and that the fruit of our own suffering should be to help others with their similar suffering. One way we can do that, day in, day out, as Christian brothers and sisters, is to share Christ's transformation in our own lives, so that others can grow closer to Him through our testimony.

I began sharing my story of transformation in small groups and with individuals one-on-one who were going through similar situations. I realized that I was sharing very similar thoughts with each person, and that it took hours to share even a part of what's in this book.

Some would ask me about particular elements I've written about herein, and due to time constraints, I would share only a glimpse, knowing that if we had a few hours together, I could more clearly elucidate what Jesus had done for me.

I realized that if I were to write out the key elements that I was sharing with others, and focus specifically on what I believed had made the most difference for me, a written form of my story and His transforming work in me could help many more people than I ever could in small groups or one-on-one.

Because much of what I share experientially in this book has been deepened or added in my relationship with Jesus in the last year, I suspect that if I were to write this or document my future-current relationship with Jesus 10 years from now, it might look somewhat different, as I continue to grow and mature with Him.

But I believe there's a deep value in fellow Christians being able to see - as close to real time as possible - the activities and process that Jesus used to draw me infinitely closer to Him and instill a level of peace, reliance on Him, and communication with Him that frankly "passes all understanding" to me. I could not fathom feeling this close to Jesus prior to this period of rapid growth with Him, and in fact, it feels unreal to me when I contemplate how close I feel to Him, and how much peace accompanies that closeness.

I pray that God uses the message in this book to transform your relationship with Him, increase your ability to hear and communicate with Him, and aid you in entering a level of the expression of the fruit of the Spirit that you could never have imagined.

May God bless you richly as you read and implement the message contained in the following pages!

This Is My Journey

What you are reading in the pages of this book is like a mirror of my own relationship with God and with Jesus. I'm not sure there's any other person who has this exact relationship with Jesus, and I'm also not sure anyone else has the exact relationship with Jesus as any other person on earth.

God is infinite, and He created each of us as unique as our fingerprints and our psychological makeup. As much as we try to codify fingerprints by the presence of swirls or loops and the length or shape of them, they are unique to every single one of the billions of us inhabiting earth today! And as much as we try to codify psychological traits or personality styles with attachments or emotional processing patterns, we each have a singularly unique personality and communication pattern.

So since God is infinite, and we each, out of billions of people living, have unique personalities and communication patterns, then the interactions between an infinite God and totally unique personalities, must be infinite in nature!

What this means is that it is impossible to create the perfect blueprint for relationship with God and Jesus in your life, based on my life experiences. The Bible itself is infinite in nature, and although no scripture is of private interpretation, I do believe that Scripture can have unique meaning to us, depending on the crisis, battle, life event, or life stage we are going through, and that He specifically highlights to us the exact healing pathway we uniquely need for our unique situation.

Consider this one man's journey and a current snapshot of a life walked with Jesus. It's not an ideal; it's my own journey. Take what you want and what Jesus shows you is right for your relationship with Him. Leave what doesn't feel right, or doesn't feel inspired from Jesus for your relationship with Him.

This book has been birthed out of a life spent with Jesus, in the midst of trial, trauma, sin, mistakes, consequences, pain, codependency, vulnerability, rediscovery, and finally complete freedom in Jesus.

My journey isn't complete. A year ago this would have looked different, and certainly wouldn't include the deep realizations of the freedom in Christ. A year from now it should be written from a place of more experience with Him. It's a storyline of suggestions to help you grow closer to Jesus, inspired by the Word of God, and informed by my own personal experience with Christ. Read at your own risk, and apply as you process it with Jesus!

4

Why Draw Close to Jesus?

Who Jesus is to Me

I think of Jesus as friend, Savior, and healer.

He was not only the friend of the disciples, He was a friend of people who didn't follow God, and He was a friend to those were "sinners of the time:" drunks, cheats, adulterers, and others who weren't accepted or respected.

He healed repeatedly during His days on earth.

He loved His disciples intently, and He loved the entire human race that would come after.

He loved so much that He finished what He came to do, He allowed the people of the day to place Him on a cross and beat Him, and He suffered a gruesome death of most likely asphyxiation from hanging on the cross with no support to His lungs. He was literally gasping for His last breaths, and then He speaks the words: "Father, forgive them for they know not what they do." (Luke 23:34)

Even in gruesome, excruciating earthly pain, suffering for crimes He never committed, He held on and went through it, to redeem us today, and not only connect us back relationally to the Father, but leave us His Spirit, the Holy Spirit, to live in us on this earth, until we join Him in heaven forevermore.

That's the Jesus I think of when I think of drawing close to Jesus.

He's the Jesus who was with me during my parents' divorce, as I endured the effects of their toxic relationship, neither realizing the pain they were allowing to be inflicted on their children.

He's the Jesus who was with me as I comforted my mother during that dreadful time.

He's the Jesus who was with me when I nearly died of starvation as a side effect of that drama.

He's the Jesus who was with me in the children's home, when I desperately would have rather been at home taking care of my mother.

He's the Jesus who was with me for the next 30 years of life as I fumbled and bumbled and unknowingly lived out a reaction to that upbringing, but just thinking I was carefree and independent and couldn't figure out life the way others did.

He's the Jesus who was with me through a 17 year marriage to someone I loved deeply, and yet hurt her intensely because I couldn't express or deal with emotions I learned to completely suffocate during my teenage years.

He's the Jesus who was with me every step of the way during the brutal separation and death of the marriage I expected would live until we both died, no matter how hard or painful or dysfunctional.

And He's the Jesus who has nurtured in me such a deep, abiding sense of His presence that as I have emerged from this journey so far, I have a complete, abiding trust and reliance on Him and His place in my life, such that the fruit of it is peace and calm in Him that literally surpasses all understanding.

I can't fully explain it. It's both a knowing and a feeling. It's rooted in a deep sense of His sovereignty and existence in my life. It's bolstered by the deep awareness that I can rely on Him completely, no matter my circumstances, no matter how much I have hurt those I love, no matter how much others have hurt me, and no matter what messes I have made that He has helped to clean up.

And it's anchored in a deep faith that knows without a shadow of a doubt that He is closer to me than my life itself, even as I am typing these words in utter disbelief that this message makes sense, as it's been packed in my mind for months, and much of it for years, but I've been unable heretofore to verbalize it so it can be shared.

Why I want to be close to Jesus

So much of my life I've wanted closeness to Jesus for different reasons. At times to relieve pain, to fill a hole of loneliness caused by early childhood experiences. To feel loved. To be a part of ... something. And Jesus was safe.

To cover for my shame when I wasn't picked to play ball when other kids didn't accept or understand me; to deal with my mother's demands before I understood they were more about her own pain than my inadequacy.

I wanted to be close to Him for years, but the cares of this world, my own selfish desires, and hidden idolatry dimmed the way for me to grow close to Him. When my life hit rock bottom, I started crying out to God, "I don't know what to do," and "help me."

Even last year, it was partly to be there for me when everything fell apart, a deep feeling of disappointment in myself that I had let my God down. And yet not understanding the real source of the earthly pain.

Over time I began to enjoy His presence for His presence alone, not just for the desperation He could relieve, the pain He could balm, or the mistakes He could fix.

But it didn't start out that way.

Now, although I admittedly want Him to continue to relieve pain, to help me continue to understand and deal with loneliness, and I want to be close to Him because I know that only His way produces life; I believe I can finally say, I want Him for . . . Him . . . His very Presence.

Not just His life giving Presence, not just His peace giving Presence, not just His strong arm of comfort.

But because I want to personally be close to Him.

Somewhere inside of me there is a deep comfort in knowing that if Jesus said, "I in them, and thou in me, that they may be made perfect in one," that must be His perfect way.

It's an awesome sensation to finally know that not only am I loved with theological love that accepts me based on the merit of Christ's sacrifice, but that I am also loved unconditionally by a Father who simply wants every prodigal son back in His arms, willingly.

He sent me help to grow close to Him. He gave me safe places to spend in His presence.

I leaned in. He leaned back to me. He gave me more than I gave Him.

He'll do the same for you. He loves you; He created you for intimacy with Him. I encourage you to lean into His presence no matter what you are going through or why you want to draw closer to Him.

Jesus Wants to Be Close With Us

Jesus wants to be close with us. He loves us and cares for us. He calls out and sends us nudges, speaking in our spirits, whispering quiet words of connection and direction. This is Jesus:

Behold, I stand at the door, and knock: if any man hear my voice, and open the door, I will come in to him, and will sup with him, and he with me. (Revelation 3:20)

Sometimes we resist what we hear in our spirit.

Maybe we don't believe it's Him, we aren't sure it's for us, or we just don't hear Him clearly.

The world - and the enemy - arrange it so it's hard to pursue intimacy with Him.

Speaking to His disciples, and referring also to those who would believe on Him in the future, Jesus prays that He would be in us, and the Father would be in Him:

That they all may be one; as thou, Father, art in me, and I in thee, that they also may be one in us: that the world may believe that thou hast sent me.

And the glory which thou gavest me I have given them; that they may be one, even as we are one:

I in them, and thou in me, that they may be made perfect in one; and that the world may know that thou hast sent me, and hast loved them, as thou hast loved me. (John 17:21-23)

Jesus is speaking of an intimate relationship between believers and the Father and Jesus and the Holy Spirit.

He is saying, "I in them, and thou (Father) in me, that they may be one in us."

That's what Jesus wants for us; that's His prayer for us.

His prayer was that the glory that God the Father gave Jesus . . . may be in us.

Not part of it.

Not like it.

THE SAME GLORY.

You (the Father) loves them (me and you) as You (the Father) has loved me.

That's the SAME love the Father has for His Son Jesus -

He loves me (Sean) and you - yes YOU - with that same love.

Not a love like it.

Not a partial love.

But the SAME love.

This amazes me, it overwhelms me.

Same glory, same love.

That same glory, that same love, is what makes possible the communion I have with Jesus, even with the Father.

The realization of what I've written in these last two pages has occurred through the process of what's written in this book, experientially over about a year and a half. The more time I've spent with Him, the more He has shown me His unconditional love, love that reaches out to me even when I did nothing to earn it, the more He has shepherded me through a period of intense trial, both of my own making, and as a side effect of others' actions, the more I've realized His Presence around me, within me, and walking alongside me.

The more I've embraced His Presence in that way, the more I realize how immersive and all-encompassing is His Presence and His love, the easier it has become to simply walk in it, and walk with Him.

I genuinely hope and pray that as you read the pages of this book, and you dig deep with Him, perhaps even testing the activities and words and postures I share with you, that He will become so real to you that you know His Presence and His love completely fills you. So much so that it flows out to those around you in an abundant and bountiful way!

Introducing Connection Spaces

I feel inspired to write what I'll call Connection Spaces at various points in the book. These are designed to make it easy to stop reading and simply connect with Him, and they model so much of my own time with Him.

Allow these Connection Spaces to be time when you are open to His Presence, and to spending time with Him.

I believe these Connection Spaces will help you experientially draw closer to Him much faster than if you read the book through quickly, and then try to apply things later.

Here's the first Connection Space:

> **Connection Space:**
>
> Consider why you want to draw closer to Him.
>
> What has compelled you to want to draw closer to Jesus?
>
> Why do you want to draw closer to God?
>
> What would it mean to you to draw closer to Jesus?
>
> What would it maybe mean to Jesus for you to be closer to Him?
>
> What would it mean for you to have a deep, abiding relationship with the Holy Spirit?
>
> What would it mean for you to be closer to Him?

I encourage you with each Connection Space to take the time to go through it experientially.

As you continue to spend time with the Lord in these breaks, in your own quiet times, and incrementally though the day, you will draw closer to Him!

Why do you want to draw closer to Jesus now?

Just as we each have a unique personality and a unique friendship with Jesus, we each have a unique starting point in our growth in our relationship with Him.

In my own case, I came to the end of myself, and although I had followed Jesus for many years, I wasn't as close with Him as I wanted or needed.

My renewed growth and closeness to Jesus was precipitated by spending a lot of time in His presence. Much of that time, for months, was a time of surrender, tears, regret, sorrow, and a recognition that my own works were like "filthy rags." But to say that anyone else's journey has to start that way would be amiss.

Perhaps for you something has drawn you to grow closer to Him. There is an aching, a seeking in your heart and you yearn for more of Him. It's a positive pull, sensing there's a deeper and closer relationship possible with the Almighty.

Perhaps for you it is "the end of yourself," as it was with me. Perhaps for you it is a sin that you realize has to go. Perhaps for you it is seeing someone else come to the end of themselves, and that leads you to want to come close to Jesus. Perhaps it was a message you heard, or a book you read. Maybe it was a gradual leaning in towards Jesus, for any number of reasons.

The initial circumstances that led you to spend time with Jesus might influence the way you initially spend that time.

Your heart posture might be different based on where you are in your journey with Him.

Connection Space:

Pray with me:

Jesus, thank You for loving me, even before You created me.

Thank You for wanting me to be close to You.

Thank You for caring for me, loving me, and wanting me to be safe.

Thank You for reaching out first, and for drawing me to You.

Add some of your own words, tell Jesus something meaningful from you:

_____

_____

If you've had a realization about how much He loves you, share that with Him now.

And if you have a response to Him - and it's okay if you don't - share that with Him.

Thank You, Lord!

Amen

PART 2: THE SPIRITUAL FOUNDATION

5

God: Father, Son, and Holy Spirit

Jesus, the Son of the Father, God Himself, is full of majesty and power and the image of God:

Who is the image of the invisible God, the firstborn of every creature:

For by him were all things created, that are in heaven, and that are in earth, visible and invisible, whether they be thrones, or dominions, or principalities, or powers: all things were created by him, and for him:

And he is before all things, and by him all things consist. (Colossians 1:15-17)

He is the image of the invisible God . . . by Him were all things created . . . He is before all things and by Him all things consist.

The majesty of Jesus is incredible . . . and He is seated at the right hand of God (Majesty on high).

Who being the brightness of his glory, and the express image of his person, and upholding all things by the word of his power, when he had by him-

self purged our sins, sat down on the right hand of the Majesty on high: (Hebrews 1:3)

But we also know that the Father sent the Son to redeem mankind:

And we have seen and do testify that the Father sent the Son to be the Saviour of the world. (I John 4:14)

The Father sent the Holy Spirit after He ascended to heaven:

But the Comforter, which is the Holy Ghost, whom the Father will send in my name, he shall teach you all things, and bring all things to your remembrance, whatsoever I have said unto you. (John 14:26)

Paul, writing of Jesus:

Let this mind be in you, which was also in Christ Jesus:

Who, being in the form of God, thought it not robbery to be equal with God:

But made himself of no reputation, and took upon him the form of a servant, and was made in the likeness of men:

And being found in fashion as a man, he humbled himself, and became obedient unto death, even the death of the cross. (Philippians 2:5-8)

Jesus specifically refers to the Father as giving us to Him; He states that He gives eternal life, and then that He and the Father are one:

And I give unto them eternal life; and they shall never perish, neither shall any man pluck them out of my hand.

My Father, which gave them me, is greater than all; and no man is able to pluck them out of my Father's hand.

I and my Father are one. (John 10:28-30)

It's clear that the Father is the Son is the Holy Spirit, yet they each have different roles in our lives, our salvation, and our ongoing abiding.

In my own life, I talk with God the Father, God the Son Jesus, and God the Holy Spirit, at various times and circumstances.

Sometimes it feels more personal and intimate to communicate with Jesus Himself, perhaps because He came to earth in the form of a man, so I can visualize myself speaking with a man.

When I walk, I can visualize Him walking with me. Of course, I can also sometimes visualize Him as a King on a throne, literally sitting in my heart.

> **Connection Space:**
>
> Question for you:
>
> How do you relate to the Father?
>
> How do you relate to the Son, Jesus?
>
> How do you relate to the Holy Spirit?
>
> Do you want to relate deeper with the Father?

Do you want to relate deeper with Jesus?

Do you want to relate deeper with the Holy Spirit?

Let's lean into this and pray:

Father, Son, and Holy Spirit, please guide me in Your way, in my life, and even as I read this book.

Draw me closer to You and show me more of Who You are.

Thank You Father, Son, and Holy Spirit for Your Presence, for Your Love, and for Your Intimacy with me!

I love You Lord!

Creation and Free Will

When God created man, He created us in His image, with thoughts and feelings and intelligence and will. He gave us dominion and power over the earth.

So God created man in his own image, in the image of God created he him; male and female created he them.

And God blessed them, and God said unto them, Be fruitful, and multiply, and replenish the earth, and subdue it: and have dominion over the fish of the sea, and over the fowl of the air, and over every living thing that moveth upon the earth. (Genesis 1:27-28)

God didn't create us as His robots or servants, forced to follow Him or be in relationship with Him.

In order to create beings that could fully love Him with their own hearts, He created us with free will. And with free will comes free choice and the freedom to love and the freedom to leave. Free choice to "do good things," and free choice to "go our own way."

He created us with perfect free will. We have the will and the choice to follow and love the God who created us, or to choose not to. We have the will and the choice to love and treat our fellow humans well, or to choose not to.

If He had created a perfect world with perfect humans and no pain, it would be a world with no choice and freedom on our part. I would be perfect, I would never hurt anyone, I would never make mistakes - and I would also have no freedom to choose, no freedom to willingly love, and no freedom to appreciate personal happiness!

The downside to that freedom is that I have made mistakes that miss the mark with God, and that miss the mark with fellow humans. I have chosen not to trust God completely, out of the free will that He has given me; and I have hurt others, I have done things that have hurt myself, and I have been hurt by others. Because the others in the world have that same freedom, with varying levels of compassion and care for each other, we ultimately have a world with an incredible level of pain and hurt.

We go through life with pain, struggles, difficulties, relational trauma, our mistakes and consequences and hurts. Our journey is unique to us, and yet the commonality across human nature is that we all go through struggles and pain, both of our own making, and through the faults of others.

Sin

The Bible calls our inherent tendency to hurt each other and turn away from God, "sin," which is literally "missing the mark." The Greek word translated "sin" is "hamartona" which means "to err," "to miss the mark," or "the one who keeps missing the mark with God;" and the word in Hebrew for "sin" is "chattaah" and means "an offense" and is actually derived from the word "chata" that has a primary meaning of "to miss the way."

The Word tells us this is common to all people:

For all have sinned, and come short of the glory of God; (Romans 3:23)

That sin, missing the mark with God, and inflicting pain on others, separates us from the very God who created us so that we could love Him willingly. (Romans 6:23)

Knowing ahead of time that as humans we could not live a life without sin and pain and hurt, He prepared in advance the sacrifice of Christ to bring us into fellowship with Him:

According as he hath chosen us in him before the foundation of the world, that we should be holy and without blame before him in love:

Having predestinated us unto the adoption of children by Jesus Christ to himself, according to the good pleasure of his will, (Ephesians 1:4-5)

Although I've read that passage so many times over the years, I never fully comprehended the richness of His love and His overarching plan to make us "holy and without blame before Him in love."

You see, even as a Christian, for years and years I would daily beg for God's forgiveness for anything I had done wrong that day, from the big sins down to a cross look at someone (as if sins have a rating system). Day after day, for some years hour after hour. A tiring, draining ritual of confessing my faults before God, eventually leading me to a compulsive confessing behavior that was extremely frustrating and draining.

Maybe you can relate. Maybe you follow Jesus but you are constantly struggling with sin or mistakes or the feeling that no matter what you do, you can never be free of the condemnation and shame. Or maybe you don't follow Jesus (yet!) and you live with constant shame and guilt and pain, and it feels like it will never end. Or maybe your situation is different than this, but you still want a deeper relationship with Jesus.

Jesus Our Redeemer

In the midst of our sin and pain, Jesus Himself, as God, chose to separate Himself from God the Father, and come down from Heaven, to live on earth with us humans, experience the same pains, traumas, temptations, and betrayals that we experience, and yet somehow live a life without sin, without any deviation or mistakes.

But made himself of no reputation, and took upon him the form of a servant, and was made in the likeness of men:

And being found in fashion as a man, he humbled himself, and became obedient unto death, even the death of the cross. (Philippians 2:7-8)

So often we hear about the salvation of Jesus as being a "ticket to heaven" or a "stay out of hell" option. But Jesus came to earth to redeem us not just for eternity, but to give us a full restoration for our entire current life as well:

Our pains
Our hurts
Our sins
How we hurt others
How other hurt us
To heal our sickness
To heal us when we are brokenhearted

He not only came to "save us" in eternity, He came to give us an abundant life, right here, right now.

God lovingly created us; we in our humanity and in the past required laws to approach God, but Jesus is now our peace with God.

He has made a way for us to be reconciled with God through the cross, and now we have access to the Father by the Spirit!

Jesus Brings Healing and Salvation

Jesus quoted Isaiah, referring to Himself:

The Spirit of the Lord is upon me, because he hath anointed me to preach the gospel to the poor; he hath sent me to heal the brokenhearted, to preach deliverance to the captives, and recovering of sight to the blind, to set at liberty them that are bruised, (Luke 4:18)

The message Jesus brought to earth was one not only of salvation, but of healing from sickness, healing from being brokenhearted, freedom from the sin that binds us, and liberty from the hurts and traumas in our relationships.

He came to restore us to original relationship with God, to relieve us of the religious necessity to keep all the rules and regulations, and instead to have peace with God by faith instead of works and our own sacrifice.

So how can we enter into a relationship with Jesus where He restores us, heals us, and saves us completely, such that we can have the close and intimate relationship with Him about which He prayed to the Father, "I in them, and thou in me, that they may be made perfect in one;"?

Jesus, talking with Nicodemus, said that the way we enter into that relationship with Him is by becoming "born again":

Jesus answered, Verily, verily, I say unto thee, Except a man be born of water and of the Spirit, he cannot enter into the kingdom of God.

That which is born of the flesh is flesh; and that which is born of the Spirit is spirit.

Marvel not that I said unto thee, Ye must be born again.

The wind bloweth where it listeth, and thou hearest the sound thereof, but canst not tell whence it cometh, and whither it goeth: so is every one that is born of the Spirit. (John 3:5-8)

Jesus is saying that we must be born again, born of the Spirit and not just of the flesh, to be close with Him.

Finally, in Romans we read:

That if thou shalt confess with thy mouth the Lord Jesus, and shalt believe in thine heart that God hath raised him from the dead, thou shalt be saved. (Romans 10:9)

Just that simple: confess that the Son of God, Jesus Christ Himself, is Lord; and believe in our heart that God raised Him from the dead (as the victory over the death of sin that He died to overcome for us).

Instead of having to constantly repent over and over again, offering sacrifices or repeated apologies, and yet still living a life that fights for autonomy and control, Jesus made it possible for us to live a life of freedom in Him, one in which there is no condemnation or separation from God.

When we accept that gift of His salvation, repent from our past, confess Him with our mouth, and accept Him as our Lord and Master, we then get unfettered access to God the Father, Jesus the Son, and the Holy Spirit.

That's the full and complete relationship with Jesus, which allows me complete access to not just "talk to Jesus," but to have complete connection with God, Jesus, and the Holy Spirit.

We lay down our own form of righteousness, earning and working our way to a peace that never culminates; and we accept that His sacrifice on the cross, and His subsequent resurrection, is the doorway through which we pass to have peace with God.

Once we pass through that doorway into peace with God, all the promises of Jesus become available to us, including, "I in them, and thou in me, that they may be made perfect in one."

If you want to be "born again" and enter that relationship with Jesus so you can be a part of that union of "I in them and You in Me," genuinely draw close to Jesus, have that deep access to God, and have the infilling of His Holy Spirit; you can confess Him with your mouth, ask Him to become Lord of your life, and believe in your heart God raised Him from the dead for your salvation.

You might pray something like this, with your own heart and decision of intimacy with the Lord of all:

Dear Jesus, I realize that I have made my own desires into idols in my life, and I have lived my life for myself. I have sinned against You and against my fellow man, and I realize I cannot work myself out of this on my own.

I repent and turn from my sin, and I am ready to follow You as Lord and Master of my life, whatever that entails.

Please forgive me of my past sin, and enter me into covenant with You such that my entire sin nature is under Your blood and cancelled, and make me your Son or Daughter.

I confess with my mouth that You are my Lord and Savior, I believe on You for eternal salvation, I believe that God raised You from the dead after dying for my sins, and that Your death and resurrection made it possible for me to enter that union with You. You are my Lord and Savior.

In Jesus name, Amen

If you've just offered your heart to God in this way for the first time, I want to be the first to personally welcome you into the Kingdom of Heaven.

And whether you've just given your life to Christ, or you've been following Him for many many years, everything in this book is available to you as a follower and Son or Daughter of the King.

Everything in His Kingdom is available to you. Consider this:

Blessed be the God and Father of our Lord Jesus Christ, who hath blessed us with all spiritual blessings in heavenly places in Christ:

That the God of our Lord Jesus Christ, the Father of glory, may give unto you the spirit of wisdom and revelation in the knowledge of him:

The eyes of your understanding being enlightened; that ye may know what is the hope of his calling, and what the riches of the glory of his inheritance in the saints,

And what is the exceeding greatness of his power to us-ward who believe, according to the working of his mighty power, (Ephesians 1:3,17-19)

and

In this was manifested the love of God toward us, because that God sent his only begotten Son into the world, that we might live through him. (I John 4:9)

We live through Him.

His life is in us.

Everything in His life is available to you and me.

Connection Space:

If you've just given your heart to Jesus, I commend you . . . and welcome to the Kingdom!

If you've followed Jesus for years, I trust that seeing this laid out like this is a refresher of His love and our responsive love!

And if you aren't ready yet, I encourage you to continue to talk with Him about entering His Kingdom and communion with Him!

Let's all pray this together:

Father, thank You for Your love and Your desire for intimacy.

Jesus, thank You for bridging the gap in the heavenlies!

Thank You for paying the price for my sins, so that I can live abundantly, and in Your righteousness!

Thank You God for creating us, for being You, and for our shared life together!

Amen

6

Your New Life in Christ

Your New Life in Christ

Once you are "born again" - born into the Kingdom of God - your old self, the "old man," your old nature, has been symbolically crucified with Jesus on the cross:

Knowing this, that our old man is crucified with him, that the body of sin might be destroyed, that henceforth we should not serve sin.

For he that is dead is freed from sin. (Romans 6:6-7)

The Word tells us that as a result of His death and resurrection, when we accept His free gift, we are crucified with Him, and our old man - including our old lifestyle, our old desires, our old traumas, our sinfulness - is placed under the blood so that we no longer serve sin.

Likewise reckon ye also yourselves to be dead indeed unto sin, but alive unto God through Jesus Christ our Lord. (Romans 6:11)

This new life with Him is the very thing that informs and empowers our relationship with God.

Not only does He give us life, but He actually gives us His Spirit to live within us, so He is as close as our breath:

But ye are not in the flesh, but in the Spirit, if so be that the Spirit of God dwell in you. Now if any man have not the Spirit of Christ, he is none of his.

And if Christ be in you, the body is dead because of sin; but the Spirit is life because of righteousness.

But if the Spirit of him that raised up Jesus from the dead dwell in you, he that raised up Christ from the dead shall also quicken your mortal bodies by his Spirit that dwelleth in you. (Romans 8:9-11)

Once we are born again, we are not in the flesh, and our "old man," our old spiritual body, is dead.

Candid admission: although I was born again many many years ago, and fully accepted His life in me, it's just during this last trial and fresh intimacy with Him that I've realized that His blood sacrifice was not just a symbolic thing that a holy Father sitting on a jewel-encrusted throne accepts because His Son performed a sacrifice - but instead that blood sacrifice was fully loving, His blood completely washed over me, and that He sees me as Holy in His sight. I'm totally washed clean. Not only are my sins separated as far as the East is from the West, but my old man, my old identity, is too.

I no longer have to walk in sin and shame and guilt, constantly begging for His daily and hourly forgiveness; instead His blood has completely covered me and there is no condemnation in my life. There are no mental gymnastics needed, no positive thinking needed, no hoping that it is so.

Friend, in the last year or so, Jesus has revealed to me the true cleansing and forgiving power of His blood, what the Bible really means when it says there is no condemnation to those who follow Him, true freedom in Christ and in being a Son or Daughter of the Risen King, and what truly abiding in Him and walking in the Spirit looks like.

Once I realized what Jesus really did for me - and does for me daily - it immediately became exponentially easier for me to connect with Him. You see, it's really hard to draw close to someone when your primary activity with Him is apologizing for every cross word or stumble, day in and day out. You feel like a servant or even a slave, not someone worth Jesus abiding with and living in. Once I positionally understood exactly what the blood did for me, and the freedom He has given me in Him, I was instantly able to start connecting with Him better.

This was a huge personal realization, and an important part of my journey to being able to commune with Him so deeply. Prior to this, I understood it theologically, but I simply didn't accept it for myself.

The picture someone gave me, which I spent several days deeply contemplating, that shifted everything for me, was this:

Each time you recall any sin from the past that He has paid for and separated as far as the east is from the west, it's like you are reaching into the river of blood that flowed from His body for you.

Honestly, I was offended at first, and felt it was sacrilegious to talk about His sacrifice in that way. He didn't literally have a river of blood flowing out of Him, and I focused on that. But symbolically I realized that His sacrifice for me was so complete, that it might as well have been a river of blood, because His sacrifice was complete. It wasn't partial. It was complete.

And each time I picked up my old sin, an old rumination of a fault that was placed under the blood already, I was essentially saying, "I don't accept Your death for me. I don't accept Your blood sacrifice for me."

It's become very clear to me that He intended His sacrifice to be "once for all," and that His one sacrifice completely covers my sin - past, present, and future.

Consider Hebrews 10:10, 12, and 14:

By the which will we are sanctified through the offering of the body of Jesus Christ once for all.

But this man, after he had offered one sacrifice for sins for ever, sat down on the right hand of God;

For by one offering he hath perfected for ever them that are sanctified.

He has perfected me forever, completely sanctifying me once for all!

This was the single greatest realization and the largest key to unlocking my ability to fully allow His sacrifice, His death, and His subsequent resurrection, to completely atone for my mistakes, great and small.

Without that realization, I would likely not be writing this book.

No Condemnation

The next key was fully embracing the concept of "no condemnation."

There is therefore now no condemnation to them which are in Christ Jesus, who walk not after the flesh, but after the Spirit. (Romans 8:1)

I have read that verse many many times in the past, and somehow I must have just glanced over it, thinking it meant something theological but it didn't really apply to me.

But it's now very clear to me what it means.

You see, "There is therefore now no condemnation to them which are in Christ Jesus, who walk not after the flesh, but after the Spirit" is a statement: no condemnation.

Not "some condemnation."

Not "mostly no condemnation."

But "no condemnation."

It's emphatic.

If that verse is true as written, there is no way I can get around the fact that there is no condemnation to me when I am walking in the Spirit.

This doesn't give us an excuse to sin, the specific qualifier is that we "walk not after the flesh, but after the Spirit." Paul addressed this and concludes that although there is no condemnation, that should not be used as an excuse for continuing to sin:

What shall we say then? Shall we continue in sin, that grace may abound?

God forbid. How shall we, that are dead to sin, live any longer therein? (Romans 6:1-2)

I know I sin daily, but I don't purposely sin because there's no condemnation, and I suspect you don't either. I don't use "no condemnation" to intentionally sin, or I wouldn't be walking in the Spirit and not in the flesh!

But it still doesn't change this fact:

There is therefore now no condemnation to them which are in Christ Jesus, who walk not after the flesh, but after the Spirit. (Romans 8:1)

If you are covered by the blood and walking in the Spirit, there is no condemnation.

An expectation to repent and make things right when you do fail and sin, and to not intentionally sin, yes.

Condemnation. No.

This powerful truth - and the full acceptance in my life - has been radically transformational for me, and has practically eliminated all of my ruminating and worrying about my sin, offending God, and so on. But I don't believe it has led to any increased sin in my life. I don't want to sin. I do sin but I don't want to.

If you are following Jesus, my guess is that's the case with you: you don't want to sin. Now, there may still be areas in your life that you wrestle with and maybe you give in more than you should ... but in your deepest truest heart, you don't want to sin, you don't want to violate God or offend Jesus!

Stop worrying about whether accepting His full sacrifice and offer of "no condemnation" will lead to more sin in your life!

Instead, accept His full sacrifice, lean deeply into the Lord's salvation and ongoing abundant life, and live the fully abundant life He bought and paid for!

Connection Space:

Take a moment to reflect on your new life in Christ, where there is no longer any condemnation for not only what you have done in the past, but for who you are now.

Jesus loves you just as you are.

You are righteous in His sight.

You are made righteous in Him.

If you never did anything else for Him, He loves you as a Son or Daughter.

You are His and He is yours!

7

Righteous by Faith

We are the Righteousness of God

Now that we have Christ dwelling in our hearts, we have no condemnation, no shame, and no guilt because our sins are completely covered by the blood. Our sins are separated from us as far as the east is from the west, and we enter into a new level of freedom in Christ!

By the which will we are sanctified through the offering of the body of Jesus Christ once for all. (Hebrews 10:10)

Christ's sacrifice for us was once and for all. We are forever covered by the blood of Jesus, and there is no condemnation.

Now that we have been made new in Christ there is no condemnation towards us, and we are made into His righteousness:

Therefore if any man be in Christ, he is a new creature: old things are passed away; behold, all things are become new.

And all things are of God, who hath reconciled us to himself by Jesus Christ, and hath given to us the ministry of reconciliation;

To wit, that God was in Christ, reconciling the world unto himself, not imputing their trespasses unto them; and hath committed unto us the word of reconciliation.

Now then we are ambassadors for Christ, as though God did beseech you by us: we pray you in Christ's stead, be ye reconciled to God.

For he hath made him to be sin for us, who knew no sin; that we might be made the righteousness of God in him. (II Corinthians 5:17-21)

This passage summarizes our entire freedom in Christ! We are a new creature! We aren't just repaired or fixed; we are a new person in Christ! God has completely reconciled us to Himself by the death of Christ, because He was made sin for us.

The new righteousness in Christ is by faith:

But the righteousness which is of faith speaketh on this wise, Say not in thine heart, Who shall ascend into heaven? (that is, to bring Christ down from above:)

Or, Who shall descend into the deep? (that is, to bring up Christ again from the dead.)

But what saith it? The word is nigh thee, even in thy mouth, and in thy heart: that is, the word of faith, which we preach; (Romans 10:6-8)

Notice Paul specifically says that it's not about bringing Christ down from above (in the physical, that we might commune with His body), and it's not about bringing Christ back from the dead (again, in His physical body).

He concludes that the way we have this righteousness by faith is by the word of faith that is so near that it's in our mouth and our heart!

The next verse states what is that word of faith:

That if thou shalt confess with thy mouth the Lord Jesus, and shalt believe in thine heart that God hath raised him from the dead, thou shalt be saved.

For with the heart man believeth unto righteousness; and with the mouth confession is made unto salvation. (Romans 10:9-10)

The righteousness that is by faith comes specifically through the word of faith that is confessing Jesus as Lord! When we believe on Him, we are believing unto the righteousness that He imputes on us and culminates in us being *made the righteousness of God in him.* (II Corinthians 5:21)

This results in us being made the righteousness of God in Him. This righteousness is by faith, it is not earned. Our old level of attempted righteousness was by works, but it was impossible for us to do.

That the righteousness of the law might be fulfilled in us, who walk not after the flesh, but after the Spirit. (Romans 8:4)

We have the full righteousness as if we fully obeyed every law forever; it's completely fulfilled in us who walk after the Spirit!

And if we want to take this even deeper, not only have we been declared the righteousness of God by faith, we have actually been adopted as Sons and Daughters into the Kingdom:

For as many as are led by the Spirit of God, they are the sons of God.

For ye have not received the spirit of bondage again to fear; but ye have received the Spirit of adoption, whereby we cry, Abba, Father.

The Spirit itself beareth witness with our spirit, that we are the children of God:

And if children, then heirs; heirs of God, and joint-heirs with Christ; if so be that we suffer with him, that we may be also glorified together. (Romans 8:14-17)

He has made us the righteousness of God. We walk by faith, not by sight. We walk not after the flesh, but after the Spirit. His Spirit dwells in us. And now we are the Sons (and Daughters) of God! He refers to this new creation state as being that of adoption. In the natural the one adopted has the full rights and responsibilities of a child who was born into the family. In the same way, we are adopted into the family of God, where we are fully His Sons and Daughters!

He goes on to say that if we are children, we are heirs. We are heirs of God (as His children) and joint-heirs with Christ (as His brother or sister in Him), we have already suffered with Him in His sacrifice, as we were sacrificed with Him in the Spirit (Galatians 2:20), and now we are glorified together (as the righteousness of God!).

To review, we are saved by grace through Christ's sacrifice and our acceptance of that gift. He dwells in our hearts by faith. His living Spirit lives and abides in us. All our sins are under the blood, there is no condemnation to us, and we are considered righteous in the sight of God. And in that new creation state of righteousness, we are now living by the Spirit, and not by the flesh.

Connection Space:

Father, thank You for loving me.

Thank You for putting my past firmly behind me and leading me down a powerful path of love and acceptance!

Thank You that Your Spirit lives in me, and that I don't have to go anywhere to experience You!

Jesus, thank You for Your sacrifice that was so complete that not only are all my sins covered, past, present, and future, but my sin nature is atoned for as well.

Thank You that I no longer live in shame and guilt, constantly worrying that I am offending You by doing something wrong.

Thank You that I have been made righteous before You, not for anything I do, but simply because You see me as righteous.

Thank You for making me a Son or Daughter and loving me just as if I had never rebelled or turned away.

Thank You for giving me all the rights of a natural Son or Daughter, and for embracing me in Your eternal embrace.

Thank You for the new life You have given me.

I love You, Lord Jesus!

8

The Holy Spirit

Holy Spirit, Spirit of Jesus

Jesus said He would send the Holy Spirit to always be with all of us who follow Him, once He had ascended back to the Father:

And I will pray the Father, and he shall give you another Comforter, that he may abide with you for ever;

Even the Spirit of truth; whom the world cannot receive, because it seeth him not, neither knoweth him: but ye know him; for he dwelleth with you, and shall be in you. (John 14:16-17)

Paul called Him both the Spirit of God and the Spirit of Christ:

But ye are not in the flesh, but in the Spirit, if so be that the Spirit of God dwell in you. Now if any man have not the Spirit of Christ, he is none of his. (Romans 8:9)

Again he references the Spirit of Christ:

For I know that this shall turn to my salvation through your prayer, and the supply of the Spirit of Jesus Christ, (Philippians 1:19)

Jesus also said:

That they all may be one; as thou, Father, art in me, and I in thee, that they also may be one in us: that the world may believe that thou hast sent me.

And the glory which thou gavest me I have given them; that they may be one, even as we are one:

I in them, and thou in me, that they may be made perfect in one; and that the world may know that thou hast sent me, and hast loved them, as thou hast loved me. (John 17:21-23)

And He said:

I and my Father are one. (John 10:30)

Taken together, we see that Jesus and the Father are one, the Spirit of God is referred to as the Spirit of Christ, and Jesus said "that they may be one, even as we are one."

It's clear that although the Father, the Son, and the Holy Spirit have different manifestations and roles, they are one and the same God, the same Spirit!

When I'm talking with Jesus, I'm talking with the Holy Spirit. And when I'm nudged by the Holy Spirit, when He speaks something into my soul, it's Jesus talking with me.

When I pray, I typically address Jesus, and I know in my heart that when I hear His Voice, when I sense a nudge to do something, speak to someone, or when I receive instruction, it's from His Spirit within me.

As followers of Christ, we have the Spirit of Christ, the Holy Spirit, inside of us.

It's the same Spirit that raised up Jesus from the dead. He placed all of our sin on His shoulders and allowed Himself to carry that.

In order for Him to fully pay the price, He had to have been fully dead, and the Spirit made Him go from fully dead to fully alive.

Imagine that you have that same exact Spirit inside of you that made Jesus go from fully dead to fully alive!

We're not talking about just a Spirit that can make things better, not just a Spirit that can put a cheer on my smile, not just a Spirit that can fix my soul or things in my life; but the same Spirit that raised Jesus Christ from the dead after he bore the sin of all of us.

The Spirit of Christ, the Holy Spirit, lives in us, and we have access to the fruit of the Spirit.

But the fruit of the Spirit is love, joy, peace, longsuffering, gentleness, goodness, faith,

Meekness, temperance: against such there is no law. (Galatians 5:22-23)

If that Spirit is inside of us, we therefore have all of the fruit of the Spirit, we have the characteristics of the Spirit, and we have all of the power that Jesus Christ had that raised him from the dead.

In fact, Jesus even said we shall do greater works than He did:

Verily, verily, I say unto you, He that believeth on me, the works that I do shall he do also; and greater works than these shall he do; because I go unto my Father. (John 14:12)

He was speaking of that power given to us through the Holy Spirit living in us! We have all the power of Christ living in us, but most of the time we don't tap into it.

Not only has Jesus made it clear that He is in the Father and the Father is in us, and Jesus is in us, and we are one in Him, but He very specifically indicates that the Holy Spirit will live in us, guide us in all truth, speak to us, and remind us of things Jesus said.

He dwells in us!

We can live with Him, Him in us, us in Him, completely connected with Him, every day of the rest of our lives!

This realization - the deep, internal, visceral understanding of it - has transformed my relationship with Him:

He is in me, with me, I am in Him, I am loved by Him. He doesn't see my sin anymore, He has washed away my shame and my guilt, not just by winking, but purely forgetting it, completely accepting me in Him. Then He chooses to have continuous, 24-7 communion and conversation with me. I can be completely guided by Him, nudged by Him, led by Him - and yet, still have complete free will and autonomy to choose. Yet I continue to submit to His presence - and it's not binding at all; it's completely freeing and glorious to be led by Him and in constant communication with Him!

His transforming presence in my life, His guidance, His word in the Word, His word through people, and His abiding word and presence in my life, have brought those truths to a living reality in my life!

I'm forever grateful to Him, and it's awestriking to me that no one can take it away, that He has given me an unspeakable gift, and He loves me and I love Him!

One of the greatest realizations for me has been His Spirit living in me. I am talking with Jesus, but I know that His Spirit is right in me. I can sense Him. I can feel Him. His nudges are real.

You can have that same connection with the Spirit. You can sense Him. You can feel Him. You can learn the way He speaks through nudges, words, people, and circumstances. You can learn to hear His still, small voice!

Connection Space:

Let's take this time to reflect on His Spirit living in you!

This might be a new concept for you, and that's okay.

Lean into the fact that He lives in you.

If Jesus is your Lord, the Holy Spirit lives in you.

He's as close as your heartbeat.

He's as close as your thoughts.

In fact, you can close your eyes and in a split second be completely connected with Him, simply by focusing your attention on Him.

(I recall when I first realized I could close my eyes and mentally connect with Him and He was right there, there was some effort and time lag involved. Now, I can simply think, with my eyes closed or even wide open, how close He is . . . and I can sense His complete Spirit within me, immediately, right here, right now.)

Perhaps just sit in His Presence for a moment.

Just knowing that He is in you.

Imagine He completely envelops your entire body, every cell of your body.

It's like His spirit is a shadow - an essence - that completely fills and engulfs your body, all at the same time!

Sit in that for a moment.

Embrace His Presence.

Embrace His Spirit.

Sit in this . . . .

Enjoy His Presence.

Let's pray:

> Holy Spirit, I love You.
>
> Thank You for Your Presence.
>
> Please continue to enlighten me with Your Presence.
>
> Continue to make me more aware of Your abiding Presence.
>
> I love You, Holy Spirit!

Characteristics of the Holy Spirit

The Holy Spirit has a wide array of characteristics: friendship, counsel, comfort, power, patience, the ability to guide us into all truth and reveal hidden things to us, and much more.

When we seriously draw close to Jesus and to His Spirit, we begin to experience a much fuller expression of His characteristics.

When Jesus was introducing the Holy Spirit, He called Him a Comforter:

And I will pray the Father, and he shall give you another Comforter, that he may abide with you for ever; (John 14:16)

Paul suggested there could be fellowship of the Spirit that would give us the ability to have love and be in one accord with each other:

If there be therefore any consolation in Christ, if any comfort of love, if any fellowship of the Spirit, if any bowels and mercies,

Fulfil ye my joy, that ye be likeminded, having the same love, being of one accord, of one mind.

Let nothing be done through strife or vainglory; but in lowliness of mind let each esteem other better than themselves. (Philippians 2:1-3)

The grace of the Lord Jesus Christ, and the love of God, and the communion of the Holy Ghost, be with you all. Amen. (II Corinthians 13:14)

The Greek word translated as "fellowship" in Philippians 2:1 above is the same word that's translated "communion" in II Corinthians 13:14: "koinonia." Koinonia has a meaning of fellowship, sharing, participation, and partnership.

The Holy Spirit can fellowship with us, have communion with us, have partnership with us, share with us, and participate with us.

He will also guide us into all truth:

Howbeit when he, the Spirit of truth, is come, he will guide you into all truth: for he shall not speak of himself; but whatsoever he shall hear, that shall he speak: and he will shew you things to come.

He shall glorify me: for he shall receive of mine, and shall shew it unto you.

All things that the Father hath are mine: therefore said I, that he shall take of mine, and shall shew it unto you. (John 16:13-15)

Jesus said that the Spirit of truth, the Holy Spirit, would guide us into all truth. All truth is a pretty wide statement. Everything that is true. That is every admonition in the Word. That is every wise thing in the Word. That is every wise thing that exists, even if it's not in the Word.

He goes on to say that all things that the Father has are His, Jesus'. Everything. And then that the Holy Spirit will take from that store of knowledge, and show it to us:

But as it is written, Eye hath not seen, nor ear heard, neither have entered into the heart of man, the things which God hath prepared for them that love him.

But God hath revealed them unto us by his Spirit: for the Spirit searcheth all things, yea, the deep things of God.

For what man knoweth the things of a man, save the spirit of man which is in him? even so the things of God knoweth no man, but the Spirit of God.

Now we have received, not the spirit of the world, but the spirit which is of God; that we might know the things that are freely given to us of God. (I Corinthians 2:9-12)

This tells us that eye has not seen, nor ear heard, nor even entered into the heart of man, the things which God has prepared for us already. That's pretty vast! That's things that have not been seen or heard before, they haven't even been in any man's heart, these are new things that God has prepared for us who love Him.

God reveals those things to us by His Spirit. It goes on to say the Spirit searches everything - all things - including the deep things of God. We have received the Spirit of God so that we can know the things that are freely given to us by God.

In the context of all the other verses right here, He will guide us to all truth and all wise things; the Holy Spirit will take from all the knowledge and access in God and shall show us deep and new things that God has prepared for us. He reveals them to us by His Spirit. And all these things are "freely given to us by God!"

He shows us what we need for our own growth or for others' growth, but I believe He may not show us things from His store of knowledge that are not relevant to us, our mission, or our communities' needs.

I also believe it is given to us over time, as we draw closer to Him. How can we receive from a faucet or a stream if we are not plugged in? We receive more over time, as we draw closer to Him.

A few verses later:

For who hath known the mind of the Lord, that he may instruct him? but we have the mind of Christ. (I Corinthians 2:16)

Paul states that we have the mind of Christ! So far he's been talking about how we have the Holy Spirit Who has access to all the deep knowledge of God, but now Paul says we actually have the mind of Christ! We have access to this knowledge and information through connecting with Him and His Spirit Who lives within us.

To tightly summarize, He will guide us in all truth, wise things, new things, and deep things that have never entered the heart of man; and we have the Spirit of Christ and the mind of Christ, and we can know the things that are freely given to us by God!

For Our Edification

This access to the deep things of God and the mind of Christ is for the church's edification. By the church, I mean the people in the church. You. Me. Your Christian brothers and sisters.

We should use that knowledge to edify others, to edify ourselves, and to become more like Christ.

Paul, in a deep conversation about love, charity, praying in tongues, and prophecy talks about the end point of it all, edification:

For he that speaketh in an unknown tongue speaketh not unto men, but unto God: for no man understandeth him; howbeit in the spirit he speaketh mysteries.

But he that prophesieth speaketh unto men to edification, and exhortation, and comfort.

He that speaketh in an unknown tongue edifieth himself; but he that prophesieth edifieth the church.

I would that ye all spake with tongues but rather that ye prophesied: for greater is he that prophesieth than he that speaketh with tongues, except he interpret, that the church may receive edifying. (I Corinthians 14:2-6)

He's comparing the different uses of the gift of tongues and the gift of prophecy. When we speak in tongues, we are speaking to God, we are speaking mysteries (the deep things of God), and we are edifying ourselves. I'm a firm believer we must be edified ourselves before we can consistently edify others!

Then he says that those who prophecy are edifying, exhorting, and comforting others. So we gain access to the deep things of God, the knowledge, and the mind of Christ, through communing with the Spirit, but its end purpose is to edify others through prophecy, or psalms, or doctrine (teaching), or tongues, or revelations, or interpretations (of tongues):

How is it then, brethren? when ye come together, every one of you hath a psalm, hath a doctrine, hath a tongue, hath a revelation, hath an interpretation. Let all things be done unto edifying. (I Corinthians 14:26)

So we have this huge body of knowledge that's really deep, and new, and even things to come, and we have access to it. And we have access to it so that we can edify each other. In short, so we can help each other.

When do we need help? When we are hurting, when we are in trouble, when we are confused, when we need help, when we need clarity, when we make decisions.

Based on all the things the Word tells us that we have access to, including the mind of Christ, should there be any situation where someone needs help, or you need help, or I need help, where we can't get access to the deep things of God?

We have incredible access to the deep things of God, and the mind of Christ, the fruit of the Spirit, and His fellowship, and sharing, and participating, and all for the glory of God, and to edify ourselves and those around us.

Connection Space:

Consider what it would mean for you to be more intimate with Jesus through His Spirit.

What would more intimacy with Jesus do for you?

How would it feel to have more intimacy with the Holy Spirit?

Let's pray:

Father, thank You for Your call to intimacy.

Thank You for sending Your Son, Jesus.

Thank You for Your Spirit to live within me.

Thank You that You want to be close to me.

Give me the ability to let my walls down if they are up,

To become open to being closer to You

Without fear

Without worry of being burned

To come closer to You!

Guide my journey, please.

Amen

Connecting With His Spirit

The deep underlying principle to growing close to Jesus is interacting with the Spirit. The more we interact with the Spirit - both in time and in depth - the closer we are to Jesus.

The closer we are to Jesus, and the more frequently and deeply we actively walk in His Spirit, the more like Christ we become, the more like Christ we act, the more we hear from the Spirit, the more we can pour from His Spirit into others, the more we walk in the Spirit, the more access we have, the more peace we have, and the more calm we have.

He wants to connect with us and commune with us. He is in us, and we are in Him. He wants an intimate relationship with us. We were created for intimate relationship with Him.

This is only possible through Jesus Christ - I in you, you in Me. His Spirit lives in me. This deep union of Christ in me and me in Him - and the Holy Spirit of Christ.

This is not something we attain, it is a gift from Him.

It's something every believer has access to, and yet hardly any know or step into it. I followed Jesus for over forty years, most of those years with intensity and drive and desire, loving Him, following as many rules as I possibly felt I could, mostly in my own strength, but begging for His strength, and yet failing again and again. I was born again. I was saved. I loved Jesus with all my heart. And yet I didn't have this understanding of the union with Him.

Imagine that all of those efforts to love Him by doing things for Him are efforts from our physical body and mind, but we are attempting to draw near to a Spiritual God. God is Spirit, and if we are attempting to access Him through physical and mental means, there is a disconnect between our effort and His Spirit nature.

Paul talks in this next passage about how he's been teaching things not that man's wisdom teaches, but what the Holy Spirit teaches:

Which things also we speak, not in the words which man's wisdom teacheth, but which the Holy Ghost teacheth; comparing spiritual things with spiritual.

But the natural man receiveth not the things of the Spirit of God: for they are foolishness unto him: neither can he know them, because they are spiritually discerned. (I Corinthians 2:13-14)

He goes on to say that the natural man - the flesh - cannot receive these spiritual truths, because they are foolishness to the natural man.

They are spiritually discerned. So how do we get access to them?

We connect with the Holy Spirit through our spirit!

We are spirit; He is Spirit:

God is a Spirit: and they that worship him must worship him in spirit and in truth. (John 4:24)

We connect with God through our spirit. We are spirits. Our true self is our spirit. We are spirits living in a flesh body.

Imagine if we connect with Him spirit to Spirit. Our spirit talking with His Spirit. One language. One communication. We aren't translating from flesh to Spirit.

As I was going through this transformation, I drew closer to Him one day at a time, one step at a time, and I had realizations through that time.

One of the keys has been that over time, I began connecting with Him more and more from my spirit, and less from my flesh. As I connected with Him more from my spirit, I connected more deeply. That was reflected back to my flesh.

We are spirit, He is Spirit, and when we connect with Him it must be not just in the natural, but also at the spirit level!

And as we connect with the Spirit through our own spirit, we participate in the characteristics of the Holy Spirit:

Fellowship, partnership, sharing, participation, knowledge, deep things of God, and the mind of Christ!

This allows us to live out the fruit of the Holy Spirit, and edify ourselves and others:

But the fruit of the Spirit is love, joy, peace, longsuffering, gentleness, goodness, faith,

Meekness, temperance: against such there is no law. (Galatians 5:22-23)

This is truly the manifestation of not just living in the Spirit, but walking in the Spirit:

If we live in the Spirit, let us also walk in the Spirit. (Galatians 5:25)

And we live this out through connecting to His Spirit with our spirit!

Connection Space:

Talk with the Lord for a moment about how you feel about your spirit being.

Does this feel far-fetched to you, or does it help make other things make sense?

God is Spirit . . . and connects with you as spirit.

Tell the Lord how this feels for you.

Tell Him if you have reservations about it.

If this has been revelatory for you, tell Him that as well.

Let's pray:

Father, we come to You with varying levels of understanding or acceptance of our spirit self.

We know that You have created us, body, mind, soul, and spirit, and we thank You for creating us.

We are so thankful to be alive here in Your world!

Thank You for loving me and being here with me!

In Jesus name,

Amen

PART 3: CONNECTING WITH JESUS

9

Introduction to Presence and Practices

Let's Pray

I'm so very excited for the next phase of this book, as we move from this foundation of who God and Jesus and the Holy Spirit is and how He dwells in us and intimately communicates with us, to the practices and activities we can do that help us deepen our intimacy with Him, even as He draws closer to us!

Let's pray before we begin this journey.

Just imagine your eyes are closed, and I'm right here with you, I'm praying personally for you:

> Dear Father, I come before You so grateful for this time with Your child (Your Name) and I am grateful for Your work in their life. I'm so thankful that You are here with them, no matter how good - or bad - or disastrous - the circumstances in their life are right now.

Father, You have given them Your Spirit, Your Holy Spirit - and instead of (Your Name) having to reach out and have Your Presence come from afar, millions of miles away in some distant heaven - and touch them from afar, I know that Your Spirit is actually right inside them.

Not just in a corner of their heart, not just in their whole heart, or their chest, or their mind - but in ALL of them - that Your Spirit is right there, right now, You are already there, filling them with Your Presence.

You are with them, beside them, filling them with Your Presence. Completely You, completely God, Your complete calm, peace, and comfort is right here, right now. You are wrapping Your arms of peace and calm around them now, comforting them and loving them.

So I ask that (Your Name) would simply lean into Your Presence that's already there, and immediately connect with You.

Not waiting for a touch from Heaven, but connecting with the very Spirit from Heaven that's inside them now.

Oh! Might You comfort them, knowing Your Spirit is right here, right now, may they - right now - have a deep sense of knowing that You are right there with them.

You are fully complete, fully filling them, their mind, their heart, their desires, their pains.

Wrap Your arms around them completely, filling them with Your Calm, Your Peace, a perfect knowing that no matter how rough the storm, no matter how hot the fire, no matter the shame or the guilt, no matter how they were wronged by others, no matter their pain . . . that You are simply there.

You are right there, right now, comforting them.

When they are ready, You are healing them.

When they are ready, You are giving them the words and the plan to help others with what they've survived.

You have made them for such a time as this.

Your Son said: *I in them, and thou in me, that they may be made perfect in one.*

I believe they can sense Your Spirit right now, a oneness with you that is only supernatural in power, supernatural in form, and only because they have Your Spirit, fully alive, fully complete.

May they walk in deep calm and peace today, Your Calm, Your Peace, and may You bless them richly, in Jesus mighty name, Amen

Reflection:

That prayer embodies the concept that His calm, His Peace, and His Self is in us always. Because He is always here, immediately when we remember that and recognize it we immediately begin to feel calm; because He is already here, we simply have to touch Him. But because He is Spirit we don't touch Him with our hands like we might touch a pumpkin pie, we touch Him in our spirit, with our mind . . . the very thought and remembrance of His Presence is an active connection with Him.

"I am with you always," Jesus said. (Matthew 28:20)

There's no time delay.

It's instantaneous.

He simply says "I am with you always."

He didn't say "when you connect with Me," or "activate this or that."

Instead He simply commands us to not be afraid nor dismayed - BECAUSE He is with you always.

He is right here, right now.

Now is part of always.

Tomorrow is part of always.

Next minute is part of always.

This exact second is part of always.

He's right here, right now, and not only is His calm and peace right here, every other facet of God Himself is right here: power, strength, compassion, giving, caring, being loved, loving . . .

I may go into a prayer time with the Lord with great fear, or unrest, or anxiety, and immediately when I recall His presence, I begin to calm. In fact, I know instantly that He has given me His perfect peace - but it might take half an hour or more of simply walking and talking with Him, of praying in the Spirit, or of just singing to Him, etc., before my entire body - the physical manifestation of my self (because I am actually spirit with a skin and bone shell) - completely feels the calm.

Even when you don't feel it, as soon as you immediately tap into His Spirit in you and you sense that first ray of calm or peace, He is immediately and fully infusing you with the full measure of Himself and His peace.

Presence and Practices

There is no closer that we can be than for Him to completely fill us with His presence.

That closeness implies a deep relationship with that presence, the Spirit of Jesus. It's not just the presence of the Presence, and it's not just our awareness of His Presence, but it's a deep relationship itself.

It's a spiritual relationship, but because we live in a physical body, some of the outward communication and the framework for connecting with Jesus occurs with both spiritual communication and earthly communication, through time with Him, intention, and fellowshiping with Him, both in the Spirit and in the body.

When Jesus was talking with the woman at the well, she referenced the activities and practices that they did to be close to God:

Our fathers worshipped in this mountain; and ye say, that in Jerusalem is the place where men ought to worship. (John 4:20)

She is saying that historically the way people approached God was with a physical act of worshiping in the physical place of Jerusalem.

But then Jesus replies:

Jesus saith unto her, Woman, believe me, the hour cometh, when ye shall neither in this mountain, nor yet at Jerusalem, worship the Father.

Ye worship ye know not what: we know what we worship: for salvation is of the Jews.

But the hour cometh, and now is, when the true worshippers shall worship the Father in spirit and in truth: for the Father seeketh such to worship him.

God is a Spirit: and they that worship him must worship him in spirit and in truth. (John 4:21-24)

The word translated "truth" is "aletheia" which has an original meaning not just of truth, but of objectiveness and reality. This could have been translated as "worship Him in spirit and in objective reality."

Jesus knows that while we are constrained to this earthly body, even though we will now worship and relate to Him spiritually, we will still be worshiping in a physical and reality-based body.

Paul specifically directs us to glorify God in our bodies and our spirits:

What? know ye not that your body is the temple of the Holy Ghost which is in you, which ye have of God, and ye are not your own?

For ye are bought with a price: therefore glorify God in your body, and in your spirit, which are God's. (I Corinthians 6:19-20)

We communicate with Him in spirit because we have a spirit and in truth (reality), because we still live in a flesh body.

In addition to praying in the Spirit at the spirit level, we use our flesh, our body, our mind, our mouth, and the praises that emote from our lips, to be the instrument of the words in our understanding that we use to communicate with Him.

But it's not the words themselves, it's the meaning and the depth of the spirit connection behind the words that connects with the Holy Spirit.

We receive revelation in our spirit, through spirit to Spirit communion with Jesus. Then we use our words to speak edification, exhortation, and comfort to others!

For example, in this moment, I am sharing with you these spiritual truths using words which I am forming in this book, much as Paul formed the words that made his letters to us.

But between segments of writing, I am walking around, I am praying, I am communing with the Spirit to determine the right words to write. I am receiving these words (or the meaning and the connections behind them) through the Spirit, and then I am using my words (my earthly body and communication ability) to transform those Spirit thoughts into words that can edify and share the concepts.

We receive inspiration and revelation at the spirit level, but we speak it out on earth, either privately to God, or to others, using our words!

But while our spiritual communication with the Spirit is in our Spirit, the tangible way that we activate our own interaction with the Spirit, and the way we can share that interaction with others, is through earthly activities and practices such as praise, worship, thanksgiving, prayer, reading His Word, and praying in tongues.

To do all of that, we use words in praise and worship and thanksgiving and prayer to lay the foundation of our communication with the Holy Spirit, in a way that we understand it.

When I engage with Him deeply in the Spirit, I am connecting with my thoughts and my spirit, and I may also use my words, I may also use my mind, I may also use my own flesh presence to form the thoughts and the words to initiate that conversation with Him.

It culminates in my spirit, at its deepest level the interaction is with my spirit, but the conduit through which it happens is the practices I'll write about next.

The practices alone won't create intimacy; in fact I would argue that any one of them isn't necessary. But without some practices, without actively engaging with His Presence in our physical bodies and through our minds, we won't develop the intimacy because we won't have a framework with which to enter into the spiritual plane, to enter into the spiritual conversation!

The practices are the meeting space between our flesh and the expression of our spirits. Jesus Himself said:

Watch and pray, that ye enter not into temptation: the spirit indeed is willing, but the flesh is weak. (Matthew 26:41)

So we will use the practices to lay the foundation, to soften our heart, to open the gates of heaven so to speak, but the deepest level of communication with God, with Jesus, with the Holy Spirit is in our spirit.

The Purpose of it all is Relationship

Even as we are communicating with Jesus through the practices of praise, prayer, Bible Study, and even talking with Him and hearing His voice, it's important for us to recall that we are cultivating a relationship with Him through it all.

Jesus wants our heart first and foremost.

Jesus said in Revelation:

Behold, I stand at the door, and knock: if any man hear my voice, and open the door, I will come in to him, and will sup with him, and he with me. (Revelation 3:20)

When He was dining at the home of Martha and Mary, where Martha was working hard to provide a meal for Jesus, and Mary was sitting at His feet, talking with Him, Jesus says of Mary:

But one thing is needful: and Mary hath chosen that good part, which shall not be taken away from her. (Luke 10:42)

Even though Martha was doing the necessary work, Jesus highlighted the value of the fellowship and communion with Jesus that Mary was having with Him.

Jesus wants us to have a deep, personal relationship with Him, where we are talking with Him and He with us. We must take care not to be so engaged in the work of the kingdom, and doing work for Him, that we don't engage in conversation and relationship with Him!

Even though we have His Presence at salvation, we must commune with Him, draw close to Him, and actively communicate with Him!

The practices of praise and worship, Bible reading and study, talking with Him, seeking His voice, and praying in the Spirit are all activities that aid us in communing, drawing close, and communicating with Him, but the practices themselves are not the things that actually bring us closer to Him.

While the practices are aids in our relationship with Him, they are not the focus of our relationship with Him. Jesus is the focus of our relationship. Time with Him, trust on Him, reliance on Him, and deep intimacy is far more important than the activities themselves!

Connection Space:

Consider how you have interacted with God and Jesus in the past.

When have you felt closest to Him?

When have you felt like it was mostly "work and striving" instead of just loving on Him?

How have you most enjoyed spending time in His Presence?

What are you most looking forward to about spending deeper time with Him?

Tell Him your heart, in your own words!

Lord, I love You, and I'm glad to be here, I'm glad to grow closer to You.

Lord, _____

Lord, _____

Lord, _____

Amen

10

Praise and Worship

I've chosen to open the practical advice with praise and worship because this is usually the first place I spend in my quiet time, and also because so much of my own breakthrough and healing occurred in the context of praise and worship. Praise and worship not only opens our hearts up to God quickly, but it also blesses His heart, and it puts us in a mindset of humility and submission to Him. It draws us closer to Him quickly.

Paul advised us to spend time in psalms and hymns and spiritual songs:

Speaking to yourselves in psalms and hymns and spiritual songs, singing and making melody in your heart to the Lord;

Giving thanks always for all things unto God and the Father in the name of our Lord Jesus Christ; (Ephesians 5:19-20)

And:

Let the word of Christ dwell in you richly in all wisdom; teaching and admonishing one another in psalms and hymns and spiritual songs, singing with grace in your hearts to the Lord. (Colossians 3:16)

I believe it should be normal to spend time singing and humming and worshiping. Paul assumed the early Christians would do just that, and they didn't have online streaming to make it easy for them!

When we praise God, and when we delight in Him, we are setting our love upon Him.

Because he hath set his love upon me, therefore will I deliver him: I will set him on high, because he hath known my name.

He shall call upon me, and I will answer him: I will be with him in trouble; I will deliver him, and honour him.

With long life will I satisfy him, and shew him my salvation. (Psalm 91:14-16)

That is written from the perspective of God, that because we have set our love upon Him, He will set us on high, He will be with us in trouble, He will deliver us, and He will honour us. He will give us a long life, and give us salvation.

God loves us so very much.

He created us for communion with Him in the garden.

He wants to have a personal relationship with us.

He sent His Son to make it possible.

And He gave us His Holy Spirit - God Himself - so that we have God inside us.

This is the God we serve.

This is the God we know.

This is the God we draw near to and He draws near to us (James 4:8)

God is an awesome, Holy God, and when we praise and worship Him we immediately create an awareness of His presence and His greatness.

As we are actively aware of His presence and greatness, we connect more deeply with His presence within us. Praise and worship was a significant component of the posturing before God that allowed me to grow close to Him, and even access and develop the deeper levels of communication with Him.

Jesus made it so that we can commune with Him anytime, we can worship Him and draw close to Him, and He lives in us as the Spirit of Christ, the Holy Spirit.

When we praise, it draws us so much closer to Him. Our awareness shifts as we set our minds on Who He is and what He's done for us. It reminds me of my place in the kingdom as a created son, and yet it also reminds me of His great love for me and how He cherishes me as a redeemed son!

The time I've spent in praise and worship has paved the way to my much deeper intimacy with Him, it's softened my heart for Who He is and how much He loves me, and it's also made it easier for me to step into the spiritual and talk with Him, listen to Him, and commune with Him, all such critical components of growing close to Jesus!

Private Praise and Worship

With private praise and worship, we can intimately and personally praise and worship Him, enter an awareness of His presence, and immerse ourselves in His Spirit, even when there is no leader or service available. With our words and our voice we can create an atmosphere of praise and worship right in our homes, right in a local park, right in our cars, or anywhere we worship. We don't need a prayer leader; we can use words of praise and worship and glorify Him with our lips!

I might enter into this time of private praise and worship with some statements of praise:

You are worthy!

You are worthy of my praise!

You are worthy of my time, You are worthy of my effort.

The Rocks cry out in praise of You!

I love You!

I praise You!

I worship You!

I encourage you to stop right now - say those words to God.

Read them aloud.

Maybe say them again, with your eyes turned to heaven.

Can you begin to sense an awareness of His awesomeness, perhaps even of His presence right here, right now?

There are no perfect words or sequences. God hears your heart, and over time you will become more comfortable making statements of praise.

I encourage you to intently practice private praise and worship. It might just be a few short phrases at first, and that's okay.

Sometimes when we begin our praise time, we have to make an effort that's not natural or comfortable, but once we've been praising for a few moments, our hearts warm up and we become more spontaneous.

Praise with me:

Lord Jesus, I worship You, I praise You!

Thank You for Your sacrifice, Your complete gift to me so I can have relationship with You.

You bore the shame of the cross for my pain.

You are my Redeemer, the King of Kings and Lord of Lords.

Oh! Lord, I worship You!

I worship You!

You are a mighty God and a mighty King!

Thank You for Your love for me!

When we worship in that way, we are coming before Jesus as our Redeemer and Saviour, and before God as the King, as the Father that He is, with all due respect.

There's a very real difference in our mentalities between seeing God as a far away God and a personal, very real God to me right now.

I might specifically call out to Jesus:

Lord Jesus, You are worthy!

You are worthy before the creation of the world to be praised!

I am so grateful for Your love and sacrifice for me.

I worship You, Lord Jesus!

We can model Paul's worship in Ephesians:

For this cause I bow my knees unto the Father of our Lord Jesus Christ,

Of whom the whole family in heaven and earth is named,

That he would grant you, according to the riches of his glory, to be strengthened with might by his Spirit in the inner man;

That Christ may dwell in your hearts by faith; that ye, being rooted and grounded in love,

May be able to comprehend with all saints what is the breadth, and length, and depth, and height;

And to know the love of Christ, which passeth knowledge, that ye might be filled with all the fulness of God.

Now unto him that is able to do exceeding abundantly above all that we ask or think, according to the power that worketh in us,

Unto him be glory in the church by Christ Jesus throughout all ages, world without end. Amen. (Ephesians 3:14-21)

Modeling it:

We love You Lord Jesus!

You are able to do exceedingly abundantly above all that we ask or think!

Your love passes knowledge,

And Your love allows us to be filled with all the fulness of God!

You dwell in our hearts by faith!

We love You, Lord Jesus!

And of course, I will often worship both the Father and Jesus!

I particularly like praising with some of the phrases from this passage:

And they sung a new song, saying, Thou art worthy to take the book, and to open the seals thereof: for thou wast slain, and hast redeemed us to God by thy blood out of every kindred, and tongue, and people, and nation;

And hast made us unto our God kings and priests: and we shall reign on the earth.

And I beheld, and I heard the voice of many angels round about the throne and the beasts and the elders: and the number of them was ten thousand times ten thousand, and thousands of thousands;

Saying with a loud voice, Worthy is the Lamb that was slain to receive power, and riches, and wisdom, and strength, and honour, and glory, and blessing.

And every creature which is in heaven, and on the earth, and under the earth, and such as are in the sea, and all that are in them, heard I saying, Blessing, and honour, and glory, and power, be unto him that sitteth upon the throne, and unto the Lamb for ever and ever. (Revelation 5:9-13)

This might look like, in my own words of worship:

You are Worthy!

You are so Worthy!

Jesus, You are worthy!

You are the Lamb!

Worthy is the Lamb that was slain to receive power, and riches, and wisdom, and strength, and honour, and glory, and blessing.

Blessing, and honour, and glory, and power, be unto him that sitteth upon the throne, and unto the Lamb for ever and ever.

Here is an example when I worshipped on a group faith livestream:

Father, You are worthy and You are worthy of my praise and You are worthy of my time. You're worthy of the time that You've given me.

You are worthy of all of our praise. You are worthy of this next hour. The rocks cry out when we don't.

The trees and the mountains worship You. I worship You. My friends worship You.

I love You, Lord. I praise You. What a mighty God.

I worship You.

I worship You. I love You, Lord. I love You, Lord.

We worship You. We worship You. We're so grateful to be here right now.

Father, I'm so thankful to be here in Your presence. I humble myself in Your presence. I worship You.

I worship You. I'm grateful for what You've done in my life. I'm grateful for who You are to me.

I'm grateful that You've placed Your spirit in me so that I don't have to remain fallen, so that I don't have to remain in pain, so I don't have to remain in that state of the first Adam. I'm so grateful, Lord, for what You've done. I worship You.

I worship You. I worship You. Even as I'm taking this time right now, I want to draw closer, Lord.

I want to draw closer. I want to lean into this time with You. I want out of this time whatever it is that You want.

I want to give You whatever You desire out of this time. I want to delight in You.

This is very personal. These don't need to be your words. You can tell Him how much you love Him, what He means to you, how thankful you are to Him.

You can praise Him for His goodness, His power, His majesty, His life-giving power.

You can thank Him for your redemption, for the journey He's taking you through, for past victories, for future successes.

You can thank Him for drawing you close to Him, for being in your life, for revealing His Holy Spirit to you in your life.

There is no end to the words of praise, worship, and even thanksgiving that we can offer during these times of praise and worship.

> **Connection Space:**
>
> Let's take some time to practice just praising God:
>
> Father, I worship You!
>
> You are worthy of my praise!

You are worthy of my time!

    You are worthy that I slow down and give You my attention!

    Thank You for Your Presence!

    You are a good, good God!

    Thank You for Your awesomeness in my life!

    I love You Lord!

    Ah! Lord God - I worship You!

    The rocks cry out - and I cry out!

    I love You!

    I love Your Presence!

    I love being in Your Presence!

    I love Your Presence in me, Oh! Holy Spirit!

    Oh! Lord, I love You, I worship You!

    I worship You, I worship You, I worship You!

    Great and mighty God, I love You!

    You are so worthy, You are my King!

King of Kings, Lord of Lords, I worship You!

Take a moment to ad lib . . .

Just worship the Lord in your own words . . .

Then come back . . .

. . .
. . .
. . .

Lord, I worship You!

You are worthy of all praise!

You are King of Kings and Lord of Lords!

Powerful God, Mighty God, I worship You!

Almighty God, Almighty King!

I love You and adore Your Presence!

Keep going if you want!!!

In Jesus name,

Amen

Intentionally Praising

There is a component of focus and attention that is necessary during our praise time.

Thoughts arrive and distractions occur.

We can take our thoughts captive (control them), so that we are in control of them, and they are not in control of us. Paul instructed us:

Casting down imaginations, and every high thing that exalteth itself against the knowledge of God, and bringing into captivity every thought to the obedience of Christ; (II Corinthians 10:5)

This verse indicates that we can purposefully choose what to think on:

Finally, brethren, whatsoever things are true, whatsoever things are honest, whatsoever things are just, whatsoever things are pure, whatsoever things are lovely, whatsoever things are of good report; if there be any virtue, and if there be any praise, think on these things. (Philippians 4:8)

These verses are about our attention. We can choose to allow our attention to be on the things we worry about, and on things that distract and bother us; or we can choose to place our attention on things that are true, honest, just, etc., including Him and His Presence.

When you make this attempt to focus more attention, if you spend 15, 20 minutes, 30 minutes worshiping the Lord, and you do this on a regular basis, your attention will increase, and you'll be able to step into that place of attention faster because you know what it feels like.

Tune out the social media, the phone, the texts, the demands, the obligations, the fears, the other people, what people are demanding, and what you have to do. The sooner you can tune that noise out, the sooner you can just be like you're one-on-one with Jesus, and so you can literally step into that time and sense His presence right away.

Lord, You're so worthy, and I'm so thankful to be right here with You.

I'm so thankful that the rocks don't have to cry out today because I'm crying out.

I'm so thankful that I'm able to be here with You.

I love You, Lord, and I worship You, and I'm so thankful for Your presence, and You're a great and mighty God, and You're bigger than anything that's in my life, and You're bigger than any stress that's in my life, and You're bigger than any worry, and You're bigger than any enemy.

You're an amazing God. Thank You for being right here with me. Thank You for being in me.

Thank You that I don't even have to take 30 seconds to get to this place, but I can literally just connect with You immediately as You wrap Your arms around me.

As you are reading that, or if you are praising it out loud, if you can't sense that closeness yet, I challenge you to take the time and the effort to continue to step into that level of communication with him. The more time you spend with Him, the easier and faster it will be that you can sense you are truly in His Presence and connected with Him.

Connection Space:

Imagine right now that you are stressed, that you don't feel like praising.

(Maybe that's even true right now!!)

And just . . . praise anyhow!

Let's imagine you just don't have the energy to think up your own words . . .

Turn to a Psalm . . .

Choose one:

Psalm 8

Psalm 24

Psalm 29

Psalm 33

I'll print Psalm 33:1-8:

Rejoice in the Lord, O ye righteous: for praise is comely for the upright.

Praise the Lord with harp: sing unto him with the psaltery and an instrument of ten strings.

Sing unto him a new song; play skilfully with a loud noise.

For the word of the Lord is right; and all his works are done in truth.

He loveth righteousness and judgment: the earth is full of the goodness of the Lord.

By the word of the Lord were the heavens made; and all the host of them by the breath of his mouth.

He gathereth the waters of the sea together as an heap: he layeth up the depth in storehouses.

Let all the earth fear the Lord: let all the inhabitants of the world stand in awe of him. (Psalm 33:1-8)

Praise some of that in your own words:

Rejoice in the Lord!

Praise the Lord with the harp!

Praise the Lord with my own voice!

I'll sing unto You a new song!

You made the heavens

And You made the earth!

And I am Your creature . . .

Even though I am tired

Even though I don't have the perfect words!

Even though I am tired,

And even though this is a sacrifice of praise!

I worship You and I praise You!

Praise the Lord!

In Jesus name,

Amen

How does that feel, friend?

You enter the time of worship out of sacrifice, out of tiredness, not knowing the words . . . and yet with just a few minutes in His word, singing out a praise from the Bible . . .

Do you feel more of Him?

Perhaps you aren't as tired?

Or perhaps you aren't as weak?

Reflect on how even a few minutes taken away, reading a Psalm, adding a few lines . . . can change your perspective . . .

And offer Him thanksgiving and praise at the same time!

Sacrifice of Praise

The phrases "the sacrifice of praise" and "the sacrifice of joy" are mentioned a few times in the Word:

*By him therefore let us offer the **sacrifice of praise** to God continually, that is, the fruit of our lips giving thanks to his name.* (Hebrews 13:15)

*And now shall mine head be lifted up above mine enemies round about me: therefore will I offer in his tabernacle **sacrifices of joy**; I will sing, yea, I will sing praises unto the Lord.* (Psalm 27:6)

*And they shall come from the cities of Judah, and from the places about Jerusalem, and from the land of Benjamin, and from the plain, and from the mountains, and from the south, bringing burnt offerings, and sacrifices, and meat offerings, and incense, and bringing **sacrifices of praise**, unto the house of the Lord.* (Jeremiah 17:26)

*The voice of joy, and the voice of gladness, the voice of the bridegroom, and the voice of the bride, the voice of them that shall say, Praise the Lord of hosts: for the Lord is good; for his mercy endureth for ever: and of them that shall bring the **sacrifice of praise** into the house of the Lord. For I will cause to return the captivity of the land, as at the first, saith the Lord.* (Jeremiah 33:11)

Perhaps it's called a "sacrifice of praise" or a "sacrifice of joy" because sometimes it is a sacrifice to us to worship Him. A sacrifice is something that's painful in exchange for something better . . . whether it's the sacrifice of a goat or a lamb, the sacrifice of Jesus on the cross, the sacrifice of you choosing not to purchase something now so you can do something for someone else.

If we just aren't in the "mood," or we don't "feel like" praising, maybe it is a sacrifice. Then we choose to enter praise and thanksgiving with a willing and intentional heart, not because we feel like it or even want to, but because we've chosen to worship Him.

Connection Space:

Let's just be real with the Lord for a moment:

Lord, I will praise You even when I don't feel like it!

Lord, You are great, and You have created me, and when I am in Your presence, You are exalted!

Lord, how it humbles me to reflect on how Great You are!

You created me, I am nothing without You!

You created me in love . . .

You love me.

You want me to accept Your love.

But You don't force my love.

I am humbled by You, Lord!

I love You, Lord!

I love You, I love You, I love You!

Praise the Lord!

Tell the Lord your honest thoughts . . .

How does it feel to worship such a great and amazing God?

Who also loves and accepts you just as you are!

Let's worship Him some more:

I love You, Lord!

I worship You, Lord!

You are my God and my King,

My Rock and My Salvation!

You are King of Kings, Lord of Lords!

My King, My Lord!

I love You, Lord!

In Jesus name,

Amen

Humility in Praise

Praise creates in us a posture of humility and a sense of how great God is.

There is a humility that comes from the recognition of how great and wonderful He is. When we spend time in praise and worship, we submit to His greatness and Kingship.

We are affirming His worth, His worthiness, His greatness, and His power.

Thine, O LORD, is the greatness, and the power, and the glory, and the victory, and the majesty: for all that is in the heaven and in the earth is thine; thine is the kingdom, O LORD, and thou art exalted as head above all. (I Chronicles 29:11)

For by him were all things created, that are in heaven, and that are in earth, visible and invisible, whether they be thrones, or dominions, or principalities, or powers: all things were created by him, and for him: (Colossians 1:16)

The Lord is my rock, and my fortress, and my deliverer; my God, my strength, in whom I will trust; my buckler, and the horn of my salvation, and my high tower. (Psalm 18:2)

God is a very big God, the Creator of all things, He holds all power, and He is very great and mighty.

We're also seated in heavenly places with Christ Jesus Himself:

But God, who is rich in mercy, for his great love wherewith he loved us,

And hath raised us up together, and made us sit together in heavenly places in Christ Jesus: (Ephesians 2:4,6)

All of those riches in Christ, any place He allows us to sit, is in a place ordered by Him, by a Great and Mighty God.

Great is our Lord, and of great power: his understanding is infinite.

The Lord lifteth up the meek: he casteth the wicked down to the ground.

Sing unto the Lord with thanksgiving; sing praise upon the harp unto our God:

Who covereth the heaven with clouds, who prepareth rain for the earth, who maketh grass to grow upon the mountains.

He giveth to the beast his food, and to the young ravens which cry. (Psalm 147:5-9)

But my God shall supply all your needs according to his riches in glory by Christ Jesus. (Philippians 4:19)

When we praise and worship Him, we develop this sense that not only is He great and mighty, He is our great provider, the Source of all our sustenance, but also that He has given us access in Christ to everything!

Even with the implied holiness and righteousness that He's placed in us, we are still humble before Him in His greatness and His omnipotence and His Godness because He is God and we are man.

It gives us a sense of a very big, real God that's big enough to be inside of my heart here, in your heart there, in her heart, in his heart, in all of our hearts; and yet He still inhabits the entire earth, still inhabits all of heaven, and still inhabits all of the universe; and yet He's so close to me that I can be instantly in contact with God if only I will step into it.

Having this posture of praise and thanksgiving and worship allows me to connect with how amazing and big and complete God is.

Connection Space:

Let's take a moment to express our humility:

Father, I worship You, great and mighty God!

You are my Creator, and I'm so very grateful You have made me as You have!

As I worship You, and admit my own created nature, it fills me with humility.

I am not my own god, I am not the author of my own soul, but You are my Creator, my Lord, and my King!

I worship You!

I love You, Lord!

In Jesus name, Amen

The Psalms as a Praise Guide

We can use the Psalms as a guide or even Word for Word in praise.

Speaking to yourselves in psalms and hymns and spiritual songs, singing and making melody in your heart to the Lord; (Ephesians 5:19)

You can mine the Word of God for more you can use during your own Private Praise and Worship. Here are some of my favorites:

It is a good thing to give thanks unto the Lord, and to sing praises unto thy name, O Most High:

To shew forth thy lovingkindness in the morning, and thy faithfulness every night,

Upon an instrument of ten strings, and upon the psaltery; upon the harp with a solemn sound.

For thou, Lord, hast made me glad through thy work: I will triumph in the works of thy hands.

O Lord, how great are thy works! and thy thoughts are very deep. (Psalm 92:1-5)

The righteous shall flourish like the palm tree: he shall grow like a cedar in Lebanon.

Those that be planted in the house of the Lord shall flourish in the courts of our God.

They shall still bring forth fruit in old age; they shall be fat and flourishing;

To shew that the Lord is upright: he is my rock, and there is no unrighteousness in him. (Psalm 92:12-15)

O come, let us sing unto the Lord: let us make a joyful noise to the rock of our salvation.

Let us come before his presence with thanksgiving, and make a joyful noise unto him with psalms.

For the Lord is a great God, and a great King above all gods. (Psalm 95:1-3)

Praise ye the Lord. Praise ye the Lord from the heavens: praise him in the heights.

Praise ye him, all his angels: praise ye him, all his hosts.

Praise ye him, sun and moon: praise him, all ye stars of light.

Praise him, ye heavens of heavens, and ye waters that be above the heavens.

Let them praise the name of the Lord: for he commanded, and they were created.

He hath also stablished them for ever and ever: he hath made a decree which shall not pass.

Praise the Lord from the earth, ye dragons, and all deeps:

Fire, and hail; snow, and vapours; stormy wind fulfilling his word:

Mountains, and all hills; fruitful trees, and all cedars:

Beasts, and all cattle; creeping things, and flying fowl:

Kings of the earth, and all people; princes, and all judges of the earth:

Both young men, and maidens; old men, and children:

Let them praise the name of the Lord: for his name alone is excellent; his glory is above the earth and heaven.

He also exalteth the horn of his people, the praise of all his saints; even of the children of Israel, a people near unto him. Praise ye the Lord. (Psalm 148)

I can do this privately. I can say these Psalms, I can read these Psalms, I can sing these Psalms. I can walk and sing, and I can sit and read or pray them.

O sing unto the Lord a new song: sing unto the Lord, all the earth. (Psalm 96:1)

Serve the Lord with gladness: come before his presence with singing. (Psalm 100:2)

Singing and praying these praises has been a deeply formative experience for me.

If I'm down,

If I'm prideful,

If I'm stressed,

I can simply pray through a Psalm and connect with His presence, and my down or depressed spirit goes up, my pride goes down, my stress melts away.

My circumstance doesn't change, but my connection with Him changes. My perspective changes, my locus of control changes, and I yield to His power and His Godness in my life.

Here's another powerful passage:

I will praise thee, O Lord, with my whole heart; I will shew forth all thy marvellous works.

I will be glad and rejoice in thee: I will sing praise to thy name, O thou most High. (Psalm 9:1-2)

When we praise and worship, we magnify Him. We acknowledge His greatness.

Counterintuitively, this actually builds ourselves up, not down, when we submit before His greatness. You see, He made us. We are created beings, so we have no worth simply of ourselves, but we have huge worth that was imparted to us by the Creator. When we connect and submit to the Creator, we can experience the full value and weight of the worth He created in us.

Here are a few more Psalms we can praise with:

I will extol thee, my God, O king; and I will bless thy name for ever and ever.

Every day will I bless thee; and I will praise thy name for ever and ever.

Great is the Lord, and greatly to be praised; and his greatness is unsearchable.

One generation shall praise thy works to another, and shall declare thy mighty acts.

I will speak of the glorious honour of thy majesty, and of thy wondrous works. (Psalm 145:1-5)

Praise ye the Lord. Praise God in his sanctuary: praise him in the firmament of his power.

Praise him for his mighty acts: praise him according to his excellent greatness.

Praise him with the sound of the trumpet: praise him with the psaltery and harp.

Praise him with the timbrel and dance: praise him with stringed instruments and organs.

Praise him upon the loud cymbals: praise him upon the high sounding cymbals.

Let every thing that hath breath praise the Lord. Praise ye the Lord. (Psalm 150)

We can continually use His word, recorded praise and worship, and even our own imagination and thoughts to come up with the words to praise Him.

Connection Space:

For this break, just choose one of the Psalms in this chapter and read it aloud . . .

Add your own thoughts to it as you read:

Thank You Lord!

I worship You Lord!

You are my God and my King!

Lord of Lords, and King of Kings!

You are worthy, You are worthy!

You are worthy of my praise, You are worthy of it all!

I love You, Lord!

You are majestic and awesome, I love You!

I bless Your name, You are King of Kings and Lord of Lords!

Thank You Lord!

You can make each Psalm your own prayer . . .

And you know it's praying out the Word of God in your life!

Thankfulness

One of the most powerful things we can do is to be thankful, and express thanksgiving to God.

Enter into his gates with thanksgiving, and into his courts with praise: be thankful unto him, and bless his name. (Psalm 100:4)

I will praise the name of God with a song, and will magnify him with thanksgiving. (Psalm 69:30)

And let the peace of God rule in your hearts, to the which also ye are called in one body; and be ye thankful. (Colossians 3:15)

Let us come before his presence with thanksgiving, and make a joyful noise unto him with psalms. (Psalm 95:2)

I will offer to thee the sacrifice of thanksgiving, and will call upon the name of the Lord. (Psalm 116:17)

Be careful for nothing; but in every thing by prayer and supplication with thanksgiving let your requests be made known unto God. (Philippians 4:6)

Rooted and built up in him, and stablished in the faith, as ye have been taught, abounding therein with thanksgiving. (Colossians 2:7)

We don't have to thank Him for imaginary things, or fake it till we make it ... but thank Him for real-life things that are in your life right now. No matter how rough it is, you can find something to be thankful for.

Start there.

You can also thank Him in advance for something you are expecting from Him.

Here's an example of a thankfulness prayer:

I am thankful.

I am thankful that I'm able to take this time with You. I'm thankful for some of the things that have gone right in my day, in my week, in my life. I may thank him for some of the things that he's fixing in my life.

I might even thank him for a challenge that I've been through because of the fruit that it's produced. Father, I am so grateful.

I'm so grateful that I have this opportunity to spend this time with You. I'm so grateful for what You've birthed in me through the trial. I'm so grateful for how You're using me in Your kingdom right now.

I'm so grateful that You have showered Your love on me. I'm so grateful that You have given me a fresh understanding of Your blood and forgiveness. I'm just so grateful right now to be in Your presence.

When we express gratitude it simply reminds us of who we are in Him. It may not make the circumstance any better, but sometimes our circumstance isn't as bad as we see it to be. Sometimes we take one aspect of our circumstance that's bad and we put all of our focus on that one thing, but we don't see everything else that's actually still pretty good in our life. Gratitude and thanksgiving reminds us of all the things that are good in our life and our circumstances. And it reminds us of how good God is, even in the midst of our circumstance.

Connection Space:

Let's take this time for thanksgiving.

Think of just five things you are thankful for in your own life, and thank God for these things!

Thank You God for . . .

Thank You God for . . .

I am so grateful Lord for . . .

I am thankful for . . .

Thank You God for . . .

Sometimes if I am thanking the Lord but I don't especially feel grateful, or my mind goes blank, I might think big picture down to little picture, like this:

Father, thank You that I live in a place where I'm free to worship You and write books like this . . .

And Father thank You that You have allowed me to go through troubles in my life so that I can share solutions that only could have been gained through the troubles . . .

Father, thank You for providing for me all these years, and providing for those around me . . .

Father, thank You for the humans You've placed around me lately to encourage me . . . thank You for the woman and man that walked up to me earlier as I was taking a break from writing, and offered to pray for me . . . and prayed exactly what I needed for today!

Father, thank You for giving me those three words today that had so much meaning, and helped me stay inspired to stick to this writing today: urgency, waterfall, and focus.

Father, thank You!

In Jesus name,

Amen!

An exercise like this . . . taking 5 minutes during the day to be thankful, can literally change the course of the rest of your day.

Perhaps over time it becomes a habit that anytime you are not talking with someone else or working on something, you are quietly talking with the Lord.

Paul instructs us:

Speaking to yourselves in psalms and hymns and spiritual songs, singing and making melody in your heart to the Lord;

Giving thanks always for all things unto God and the Father in the name of our Lord Jesus Christ; (Ephesians 5:19-20)

That's how we should be living our daily lives. Speaking to ourselves in psalms and hymns and spiritual songs. Making melody in our hearts to the Lord.

Connection Space:

Consider what it would look like to make melody in your heart to the Lord.

Perhaps hum lightly a familiar song.

Perhaps sing along with a worship song on the radio or on an app.

Perhaps make a set of playlists you can refer to when you want to make melody in your heart to the Lord!

Hum that to yourself . . . making melody in your heart.

Give thanks.

Maybe not for something huge, some miracle.

What about thanking Him right now for something today:

Your health

Your mind

The weather

> *The time you have to read this now*
>
> *His presence*
>
> *How you are growing closer to Him*
>
> Perhaps now, you've sung a song, you've made melody in your heart, you've thanked Him for a few mundane things . . .
>
> Perhaps now tell Him what You think of Him:
>
> Lord, You are worthy of this break
>
> Lord, You are good, You are so good to me
>
> Lord, I love You . . . I want more of Your Presence

Local Praise and Worship

Local praise and worship has been a critical component of my own growth, as it creates an environment where I can fully lean into His presence without distraction.

Many times in the context of a praise and worship church service, or even listening to praise and worship online, our experience may be deeply driven by the environment and the leading of the worship team. That can provide a complete framework and experience for your worship time, and/or it can provide an atmosphere in which it's easier to praise than it might be privately, especially when you are first learning to praise and worship. But over time you can develop the freedom to worship the Lord with different words or meaning than the service itself is leading, of course within respectful limits if others can hear you!

When I am worshiping in a corporate setting, I make a specific effort to worship God, not just sing along with the songs and enjoy the tune. I am literally making the songs and the words into my own worship.

I think of myself as worshiping God directly. The music and the team leading may be giving me a framework for worship and I might lean into that, or I might consider their worship as a backdrop and an atmosphere for my own praise and worship.

I may also pray or sing in tongues during the worship. I may lift my arms, or I might sing with my hands held open in a receiving position. I might imagine I'm giving to God even as I am worshiping. I'm laying it all down for Him, even as I'm involved in a worship service with others. It's powerful time with the Lord.

I will also incorporate some of the same worship and praises, the same words I use with the Lord privately, and praying or singing in tongues, in my own praise during a corporate worship service.

If you are blessed to live in a place with good local praise and worship, I encourage you to take advantage of it.

I would encourage you to be willing to worship with other Christians who don't necessarily hold all the same denominational beliefs you do. As long as we are following Jesus, we look to the same Lord and Savior, but it's easy to allow our differences to divide. But if a group of believers are worshiping together, we can love each other and worship together, even if we don't agree on the exact interpretation of some of the finer points in Scripture!

Of course, private praise and worship can be experienced any time of the day or night, in the comfort of your own home, walking in a local park, or even in a quiet empty sanctuary or chapel. You'll likely need to exercise more attentional discipline because you don't have the leadership of a worship leader, but you have the freedom of being able to engage as much and whenever you desire.

The Impact of Praise and Worship for Me

Praise and worship, both corporately and privately, has had a huge impact on my progress in growing closer to Him. It's created a depth of humility combined with the ability to focus on Him for extended periods of time.

It's as if worship has laid the groundwork and opened the atmosphere for me to experience the other elements of growing close to Him.

It's beautiful because I enjoy worship, and not only do I feel close to Him, but it's easy to stay focused on Him when I'm worshiping.

I encourage you to spend time with Him each day in praise and worship. I believe you will find not only great joy in it, but a closer relationship with Him, and a deeper sense of your own completeness in Him.

11

Reading the Bible

One of the very best ways to not only grow close to God, but also to understand what His Voice sounds like and what it says, is to spend time reading and studying the Bible.

The Bible is God's original Word to us. If we want to know what God sounds like, we can read the Word. Many times His personal word to us will quote the printed Word. But if we haven't read it, we aren't familiar with the words, and our mind won't be able to process it as His printed Word.

Imagine studying the Word with the intent of finding solutions to our life problems. Expect that a solution is in the Word. Study and find an account or story that matches or resembles your situation. Study it from multiple perspectives. Did this person handle things correctly, and this is an example of WHAT to do? Or did this person handle things incorrectly, and this is an example of what NOT to do?

You can take a Psalm like Psalm 91 and apply it line by line to your life. If you are going through a battle, you can study the battles in the Word. If you are going through relational issues, you can study those out. Be willing to go deep, asking questions, even reading Christian books about the topic.

Studying for Direct Instructions

Seek out all the verses in the Bible that address the situation you are going through. Pray over the study of those verses. If you find 20 verses that all line up in a certain direction about your situation, you might gain powerful clarity!

Or you might find that in different scenarios, the Word seems to offer a contradicting view on what's best. Study that out; ask yourself and pray about why these instructions seem to contradict? What light does that shine on my current situation?

Find examples in the Word that mirror what you're going through. There are so many Bible accounts of situations where people are faced with decisions, and they've made good decisions and bad decisions. We can learn from both the good decisions, and the bad ones.

For example, we often focus on Solomon's wisdom, riches and blessing. But what we sometimes miss is that he strayed from his faith in a pretty serious way for a significant part of his life. He aligned with Egypt by marrying a princess there (1 Kings 3:1), he took on as many as 1000 concubines and wives combined (1 Kings 11:3), and experimented with wine (Ecclesiastes 2:3). The wisdom revealed in Ecclesiastes is likely not just the pure wisdom Solomon received by God giving him a wise and understanding heart (I Kings 3:11-12), but also wisdom gained through mistakes and failure.

Samson was a judge for 20 years (Judges 15:20), and then he went to a neighboring town to find an alluring woman (Judges 16:4-31). He meets Delilah, plays games with her and with his gifting from God, and loses the power that God had given him (Judges 16).

Jacob was a cheat and a liar, and if you read the entire journey of his time with his Uncle Laban, you see that the cheat was cheated. He eventually wanted to turn his life around, leaving Laban and making good with his brother Esau. During that time he received the vision of the ladder where the angels were ascending and descending. (Genesis 25-33)

Esther was placed in a precarious position. She had access to the King when she learned of a plot to kill all the Jews. She decided to risk her life and ask for attendance with the King, and ultimately the Jews were saved. (Esther 1-8)

What Biblical character went through something similar to what you are going through, and what can you learn from their story, either from their failure, or their success?

This process of study can give life to your Bible Study, and also give hope, ideas, and the revelation of God's timeless promises and consequences that are applicable to our real-world situations.

Connection Space:

Tell the Lord how you feel about reading the Bible:

Have you felt confused or bored in the past?

Did you not know where to study or what to study?

Did you feel like you were reading a lifeless book?

Does it feel like it doesn't relate to your situation?

Be honest with God, He can handle it (He knows your heart anyhow!)

I've gone through periods of time when I thought, I already have read these words, God, I need more than just re-reading these words.

So for a time I didn't give His Word as much attention.

But He's drawn me back into His Word.

I have realized that the more that I know the Word, the more He can speak to me using His words from the Bible.

And when He can use exact words from the Bible and you are familiar with them, those words can confirm themselves!

God wants us to communicate with His Spirit, but He gave us His Word as well, so we might as well use it!

Perhaps ask the Lord for a renewed hunger to read or study His Word.

Or ask Him where He would have you to read, or where you can find a good study guide.

Then keep your eyes open for a few days . . . you might see the answer in plain sight!

Example of Applicational Bible Study

To model what this applicational Bible Study looks like I've chosen a passage I often use in my own prayer time.

Although I'll just share a few sentences (or less) for each verse, sometimes I might spend 15 minutes with the Lord on one verse or one concept. I might cross reference or look up other verses that contain some of the same words or meaning. But this will give you the general concept and make it real.

Let's get started in Psalm 91:

1 He that dwelleth in the secret place of the most High shall abide under the shadow of the Almighty.

I consider how mighty is the Almighty. My own consideration might be that He is more mighty than anyone else, than any other "god," than any other person in my life, in the world, in the universe. His shadow is huge. I might see that shadow as being like the shadow of a giant angel, or the shadow of a huge cave that He has me in.

I can see dwelling, living, in that secret place, under His wing, in the cave, hidden by Him. And when I am hidden in that way, I'm under His shadow, I'm under His protection as well.

2 I will say of the Lord, He is my refuge and my fortress: my God; in him will I trust.

I consider that if He is my refuge, what does that mean? A refuge is a place I might go to hide, hideout, get away from trouble in my life, so He is my refuge.

He is also my fortress. I'll consider what a fortress is. In my mind's eye, it's a castle, it's the strongest part of the castle, or it's the walls around the castle. I am thinking of 13th century stone walls, impenetrable by any enemy, and He is my fortress!

And now I will say of Him, He is my refuge, He is my fortress.

I'm not just reading it, I'm saying it. I'm saying it out loud.

Now, when I read, "in him will I trust," I consider that to "will" is a decision. That I must will with my intention - I set an intention to trust Him. So I am willing to trust Him.

3 Surely he shall deliver thee from the snare of the fowler, and from the noisome pestilence.

I'm considering that because I dwell in the secret place - under the shadow of His wing, in the fortress, hidden behind the walls of the castle - and because I am willing to place my trust in Him - the promises can be fulfilled.

His promise is to deliver me from the snare of the fowler. What is the snare of the fowler? I might have to look up the word fowler! And see that a fowler is someone who catches or traps wild birds. So the fowler is using a snare to trap wild birds.

In life, I encounter situations that feel like I am being snared, I am being trapped, and this verse - right in the morning, during my quiet time - reminds me that He shall deliver me. Wow! I can meditate on that.

You are reading this quickly, I am writing it concisely so it fits into this book easily - but in reality, I might meditate and consider that for quite awhile. Seriously, He shall deliver me from the snare of the fowler ... the snares, the traps the enemy sets for me.

I also consider that in this passage there's no elaborate begging prayer - or even a prayer at all - to receive His protection.

Instead, I'm simply positioned with Him. I'm positioned in a place of protection, because I dwell under His shadow. And he does all of this for me!

Next, it says He'll deliver me from the noisome pestilence. What is a noisome pestilence? Maybe at that time it was a noisy band of locusts that would come through and eat the crops, making noise, being bothersome - and impossible to stop. Consider trying to wave off an acre of locusts!

Well, my own troubles are sometimes like a noisome pestilence! They are coming through my life and I'm waving my hands at them, but with an acre of locusts in my life, I can barely touch them - but His Word tells me He will deliver me!

Again, not because I'm begging or praying fervently - but because I'm resting under His wing, in the shadow of His Presence.

4 He shall cover thee with his feathers, and under his wings shalt thou trust: his truth shall be thy shield and buckler.

Now I consider the visual of being covered by His feathers as protection. He is like a large eagle to me; He is big enough to cover me. When the world is rough, I am covered by His feathers. The enemy can't get to me, and under His wings shall I trust ... because I know He's trustworthy, because I know the enemy cannot get to me under His wings!

He tells me that His truth is my shield and buckler. Not only am I protected by His presence and His wings, but by His truth itself - and that truth I can live by is my shield and buckler! I can live with His protection as I live out His truth!

5 Thou shalt not be afraid for the terror by night; nor for the arrow that flieth by day;

Wow! This strikes me, particularly if I've been worried and waking afraid, worried about things that terrify me - but with all of these promises, I can see that I don't need to be afraid, because He has my back. He is protecting me, He is protecting me so much that I don't need to be afraid of anything I might worry about at night. In fact, if there is a real terror - not just something I'm worried about - but something that is trying to attack me in the night - He is right there, protecting me.

Not only is He protecting me during the night, He is protecting me during the day. This is no ordinary protection; He is protecting me against the arrows that fly during the day. You see, arrows are particularly dangerous, because they can fit through the spaces in the walls around us. They can penetrate armor and chain mail, they can slice through and poison. But He says He'll protect me from the arrows too!

Can you feel this? Can you sense the power that I am gaining as I meditate and read this passage in the morning?

6 Nor for the pestilence that walketh in darkness; nor for the destruction that wasteth at noonday.

I am reading that if my current situation isn't already covered by a previous verse, this pretty much completes my protection. If there is a pestilence at night while I am sleeping, He has me covered. If there is any kind of destruction during the day, He has me covered. I'll stay short and sweet here for the sake of this book, but if this is my morning contemplation and I'm going through something - I might camp out here for a while!

7 A thousand shall fall at thy side, and ten thousand at thy right hand; but it shall not come nigh thee.

This is particularly powerful. Not only is He going to protect me from the fowler, or the pestilence, or the locusts, or anything else, He is saying that even if the thing that attacks me takes out everyone around me - a thousand people around me are taken out by any one of these disasters or attacks - the devastation won't come near me. In fact, ten thousand might be affected - but I am protected!

8 Only with thine eyes shalt thou behold and see the reward of the wicked.

I don't spend long here, but I acknowledge He's saying that I will see the reward (or the retribution or the effects) of what the wicked has done.

9 Because thou hast made the Lord, which is my refuge, even the most High, thy habitation;

This verse sets up another conditional situation - because I have made the Lord my refuge, I have made Him my habitation, my dwelling - then the things in the next few verses will also be true:

10 There shall no evil befall thee, neither shall any plague come nigh thy dwelling.

I won't be overcome with evil in my life. It won't overtake me. This gives me great comfort, especially if I am under attack, or if I am worrying about being under attack. I can be content that any plague (or sickness or dreadful disease) will not come near me.

11 For he shall give his angels charge over thee, to keep thee in all thy ways.

I think of the word "For" here as having the meaning of our word "Because." I feel He is saying to me that I don't have to fear these things "because" he shall give His angels charge over me.

Yes, He said angels, not angel. The hebrew word translated "charge" is "tsawah" which means to make firm, establish, or appoint over something, with a context of an order or a direction from God. So His angels - plural - are going to take charge over me, perhaps even carrying out an order from God regarding me or my circumstances - e.g., the attack against me, the mess I've made, etc. And they will keep me in all my ways. I consider that means they will keep an eye on me; keep me from stumbling and making things worse.

12 They shall bear thee up in their hands, lest thou dash thy foot against a stone.

Now it tells me that these angels will do even more than take control of the situation and keep me out of trouble, but they will also bear me up in their hands - angel hands. In case I might fall and break my foot, in case I might fumble and mess things up AGAIN - the angels are there not just to watch over me, but to actively intervene and protect me with their own angel hands!

13 Thou shalt tread upon the lion and adder: the young lion and the dragon shalt thou trample under feet.

This verse takes it to another whole level. So far much of this passage has been about His protection against things that are coming against me, or situations in my life. I am protected, resting under His wing.

But this verse says that I will tread on the lion and the adder (snake), and I will trample the dragon as well.

Assuming the lion and adder and dragon were known enemies back in the day of the Psalms, I'm guessing that since we don't have lions and adders and dragons to worry about now, this means He'll give me the power to trample on other things that might come against me.

A business problem, a personal problem, an attack against me, gossip against me, any plots against me. Not just that I have protection from them, but that I have the ability to trample them down myself (with His power).

14 Because he hath set his love upon me, therefore will I deliver him: I will set him on high, because he hath known my name.

Now the person of the speaker changes. It's now coming from the voice of the Lord: because I have set my love on Him. It's my delighting in Him. I love Him. I love the time I spend with Him.

Now, because I have set my love on Him, because I am delighting in Him, He will deliver me.

Not only will he deliver me - which would be cool and powerful all by itself - but He will also set me on high.

He'll do this because I have set my love on Him, and because I have known His name.

I believe that "known" is a deep level of know - not just to know "of" His name, but to deeply "know" Him - to understand Him in a way that couldn't come without time and attention.

15 He shall call upon me, and I will answer him: I will be with him in trouble; I will deliver him, and honour him.

It doesn't stop there! It gives me yet another promise - I can call upon Him - I shall call upon Him - and when I do, He will answer me. He will hear my voice and reply!

He will be with me in trouble. He will deliver me. Not only will He deliver me, He'll honour me.

Wow! Honour me! What does that even mean, to honour me? Something else to contemplate!

16 With long life will I satisfy him, and shew him my salvation.

He promises to give me a long life, and give me salvation!

Connection Space:

How does it feel to study the Word in that way?

You don't need special education or study tools to do it. Simply contemplate each verse and what it might mean to you personally.

That can be flavored by considering what it might have meant originally, to the original audience.

You can cross reference other verses that speak on the same issue.

If you want to go deeper, you can study the original Greek, Hebrew, or Aramaic words and their meaning as well.

Also note, you don't have to know the meaning of every verse to just move to the next verse.

Allow Him to lead you, to guide you, as you read and study His Word!

What I've demonstrated can be done for many, many passages in the Word, and there are so many that apply to so many different situations. If you dig deep, as I demonstrated, you can get solid guidance from the Word. That solid guidance, over time, helps inform your mind as you process what you are hearing from God, and it helps you sort what's from God and what's from your own mind, or even the enemy.

His Word is a message of love and hope, and normally your communication with Him will reflect that; sometimes it might give chastening or re-direction, and sometimes it might give you wise advice for navigating a tough situation. But the more you understand the Word and the meaning and context from it, the easier you'll be able to hear and discern His Voice.

I find that the more I've studied the Word, the more I can proactively apply His ways to my situation. The Word informs some of my conversation with Him, and I can talk with Him about His Word and what it means.

12

Prayer

Prayer includes praise, worship, conversation, making petitions, interceding for others, and thanksgiving. In one sense, many of the activities shared in this book are prayer. We also use the word "prayer" to indicate specific times when we petition Him for ourselves, for others, or when we engage in short bursts of praise or thanksgiving. Those are the types of prayers we'll consider in this chapter.

The Bible is perhaps the best source of models of prayer. And yet our ideal prayer life wouldn't be composed of just reciting those prayers. Surely we can pray long detailed prayers if we want and it makes the most sense, and yet Jesus was critical of the Pharisees who would say lengthy repetitive prayers. (Matthew 23:14)

I used to pray lengthy, extensive prayers. God answered many of those prayers, some with a solution, a miracle, an answer, or the exact result I prayed for. God answered some of those prayers with a wait, a wait and see what happens, a silence that turned into a realization that the thing asked for wasn't in my (or His) best interest, or a different answer than I asked for. And God didn't answer some of those prayers.

Now, I generally take my requests to Him in a much more concise manner, focusing much more on praise and thanksgiving than on the petitions, and trust Him as a good Father to respond as He wills. He continues to answer my prayers.

Perhaps my own journey had to be one of less dependence on the "right words" and the "right faith," because I had become too dependent on my own striving effort in prayer. For some folks reading this book, the opposite may be true: perhaps you've under-relied on prayer and so your lesson about prayer is to gain more structure and have more active faith! Maybe this is the perfect example of how God works in each of us to bring about His perfect will, and that journey of sanctification is different for each of us.

> **Connection Space:**
>
> Consider how you naturally pray:
>
> Do you have memorized prayers?
>
> Do you have prayer outlines?
>
> Do you struggle to come up with the words?
>
> Do you feel like your prayers are too unstructured?
>
> Do you feel like your prayers are too structured?
>
> Take a few minutes to consider your prayer style or habits and ask yourself, what would you change if you could?

Ask Him, what would He have you change, if anything?

Lord, we want to honor You with our prayers.

We want to pray as You want us to pray.

Not too much.

Not too little.

Your way.

Show us the way to pray.

Show us how to talk with You.

Grow us in communication with You!

We love You, Lord!

One realization this year in my own life is from Psalm 37:4:

Delight thyself also in the Lord: and he shall give thee the desires of thine heart.

That is a promise and a statement.

When I am praising and worshiping, I am delighting myself in the Lord. He knows the desires of my heart. I tell Him the desires of my heart. And sometimes maybe He conforms the desires of my heart to want what He is going to give me.

I rely on Him, have deep communication with Him, praise Him, and worship Him. He has met needs I haven't asked for, He has answered prayers I didn't pray, and He has provided answers to things I didn't ask for or even know I needed.

Recalling Psalm 91 where the Word talks about protecting us as a function of having trusted in Him:

Because thou hast made the Lord, which is my refuge, even the most High, thy habitation;

There shall no evil befall thee, neither shall any plague come nigh thy dwelling.

For he shall give his angels charge over thee, to keep thee in all thy ways.

They shall bear thee up in their hands, lest thou dash thy foot against a stone.

Thou shalt tread upon the lion and adder: the young lion and the dragon shalt thou trample under feet.

Because he hath set his love upon me, therefore will I deliver him: I will set him on high, because he hath known my name. (Psalm 91:9-14)

The condition in these verses is making Him my habitation. No asking implied. No other conditions mentioned.

He asks us to pray (which includes much more than intercession), but He is also a good Father who wants to bless us and protect us.

When we are delighting in Him, making Him our habitation and our resting place, placing our eyes on Him, focusing our attention on

Him, and are "praying without ceasing" through all the ways in this book (and others that are not); He is providing for us miraculously, in abundance, and to His hearts' content.

The Lord's Prayer

The Lord gave us a model of prayer:

After this manner therefore pray ye: Our Father which art in heaven, Hallowed be thy name.

Thy kingdom come, Thy will be done in earth, as it is in heaven.

Give us this day our daily bread.

And forgive us our debts, as we forgive our debtors.

And lead us not into temptation, but deliver us from evil:

For thine is the kingdom, and the power, and the glory, for ever. Amen. (Matthew 6:9-13)

We can use this as a model for our prayers.

We open our prayer with praise and adoration for the Father.

Next, we ask for His ways to be done on earth. That could be in our own lives, our situations, those situations on earth that we pray for.

When we are in perfect harmony with Him, we are living out His will on earth. If we have a situation that needs praying for, the first thing we want in that situation is His will and His way.

Next we might pray for our providence. Daily bread of course is symbolic of our needs. We can bring our needs before Him.

We ask Him to forgive us where we have gone wrong. And embedded in His prayer is the statement that we've forgiven those who have wronged us. It's not an ask, it's a given!

Next, we are asking for His protection. Protection from falling for our temptations, protection from the work of the evil one.

And finally this prayer ends with *For thine is the kingdom, and the power, and the glory, for ever. Amen.*

It's as if everything in that prayer comes under the submission of God's power and glory. The kingdom belongs to Him, and everything is under His sovereignty.

Wind, Be Still

This is when the disciples were crossing to the other side of the sea, and Jesus was sleeping in the boat. Here's the account in Mark:

And there arose a great storm of wind, and the waves beat into the ship, so that it was now full.

And he was in the hinder part of the ship, asleep on a pillow: and they awake him, and say unto him, Master, carest thou not that we perish?

And he arose, and rebuked the wind, and said unto the sea, Peace, be still. And the wind ceased, and there was a great calm.

And he said unto them, Why are ye so fearful? how is it that ye have no faith?

And they feared exceedingly, and said one to another, What manner of man is this, that even the wind and the sea obey him? (Mark 4:37-41)

Jesus was not concerned about the storm that was raging. But the disciples asked Him to help . . . actually they asked Jesus, "do You not care about us, allowing this storm to rage?"

Jesus speaks directly to the storm and tells it to be still, and the storm stops.

We can look at two prayer lessons within this passage. One is that Jesus answered a prayer that was barely a prayer:

Master, carest thou not that we perish?

He responds by taking action and speaking to the storm.

But notice also the brevity of His prayer. It was more of a statement to the storm. We don't need long and elaborate prayers in order to have faith.

The fervent effectual prayer of a righteous man availeth much, even as Elijah prayed for it not to rain and for 3 ½ years it didn't. Then he asked for rain, and quickly there was rain. (James 5:16-18)

James tells us that was fervent effectual prayer. But when we look at the actual words recorded, they aren't wordy:

As the Lord God of Israel liveth, before whom I stand, there shall not be dew nor rain these years, but according to my word. (I Kings 17:1b)

Elijah had absolute faith that God would do the thing. And it rained when he asked for rain after 3 ½ years had passed. (I Kings 18:41-45)

I recall the Hebrew boys who said, God is able to deliver us from this ... but if He does not, we will not bow to your statue, O king:

If it be so, our God whom we serve is able to deliver us from the burning fiery furnace, and he will deliver us out of thine hand, O king.

But if not, be it known unto thee, O king, that we will not serve thy gods, nor worship the golden image which thou hast set up. (Daniel 3:17-18)

I believe there is an element of paradox - which we don't fully understand - about Jesus' insistence that we can simply ask mountains to move, have faith and they will move - and the real world reality that even Paul asked God three times to remove an apparently very pesky problem and for some reason God didn't remove it. (Mark 11:23, II Corinthians 12:7-10)

We don't know if He removed it later in life, or even as soon as the letter was finished. We do know Paul had faith, he had a deep, deep faith in Jesus, and yet the thorn in his flesh was not taken away.

But Paul didn't stress out over it; he shared it, it made it into the Word of God for a reason, and he accepted that God didn't remove the thorn in his flesh.

Oh! That I would have extreme faith like Jesus, and yet also have complete reliance and submission to Him like Shadrach, Meshach, and Abednego, Paul, and even Elijah after the still, small voice!

My Own Pattern of Prayer

When I pray for someone, or I pray for a need in my own life, I generally follow a loose pattern.

This pattern is similar to that of Jehoshaphat's prayer in II Chronicles 20:6-12, David's prayer during the time of the building of the temple (I Chronicles 29:10-19), and even the Lord's prayer (Matthew 6:9-13).

I will typically open with praise and/or thanksgiving, acknowledging God for Who He is, what He's done, and some attribute of His.

I will tell Him of my concern, and state why I believe it's important.

I will then ask for the thing to be done.

I will thank Him in advance for solving the problem, for giving peace, and for making a way.

I will typically close with praise and worship of some kind, and/or additional thanksgiving, appreciating Him.

Here is an example when I prayed for someone with a migraine:

Father, I come before You so grateful to be in Your presence today. I thank You for [my friend], who has had a rough couple of days, and is walking in Your footsteps even today, to be here in this room right now.

I thank You for Your providence and how You take care of us.

I lift up to You [my friend], I lift up to You this migraine and I ask that You will take it away, that You will relieve [my friend] of the migraine.

I ask that it will quickly dissipate, and that he will have the energy and clarity he needs to do Your will today.

I'm thankful to You in advance for healing [my friend], and I'm thankful for Your work in his life.

In Jesus' mighty name, Amen.

I prayed that out of care for [my friend] and out of respect for the God who asks me to pray for people sometimes, but I wasn't expecting an instantaneous healing miracle. I was expecting that over the course of the day the migraine would disappear.

There's nothing special about that prayer. It loosely follows the pattern I shared, but there's nothing demanding about that prayer, there's nothing that makes it match some perfect formula in the Word.

[My friend] went on to participate in leading a service, and about an hour later, I asked him how his head was doing.

He looked at me quizzically, as if he didn't know what I was talking about.

I said, your migraine ... does it feel any better?

He immediately smiled and said, oh! It went away right when you were praying!

God answered my prayer according to His will, in His time (which happened to be instantaneously), and He did it for His children, who were delighting in Him and making Him their habitation.

Your relationship with God is unique to you. The Bible teaches us extensively about prayer, and yet there's no place where there's one specific structure for every kind of prayer. He has given us models and samples and guidelines, but just as you wouldn't want your child memorizing the "right words" to approach you with, I don't believe God wants us memorizing the "right words" to approach Him with. He wants our honest communication, sharing and talking with Him personally and from our heart.

Connection Space:

Lord, we thank You for knowing our needs.

We thank You for giving us grace as we grow in prayer and praise and communication with You.

We thank You for being right here on the journey with us.

Lord, show us how to pray the way You would have us pray.

13

Hearing His Voice

You Can Hear His Voice

Jesus said that we can hear His voice:

My sheep hear my voice, and I know them, and they follow me: (John 10:27)

He didn't say, work up to something and you will hear My voice. He didn't say, do this, or do that, and you will hear My voice.

He said, *"My sheep hear My voice."*

If you are His sheep, the expectation is that you will hear His voice. Knowing that we can hear His voice, then He must be able to talk with us and get through to us.

Perhaps the first place to start is to expect that you will hear His voice.

Trust that He will find a way to get His voice through to you. It might not be what you expect; possibly as with Elijah, the voice wasn't in the earthquake, and the voice wasn't in the fire, but the voice was a still, small voice. (I Kings 9:11-12)

Sometimes the voice might be through other people. The voice might be through a book like this. The voice might be in a conversation with a local Christian brother or sister. The voice might be a still, small voice in the middle of the night. The voice might be a still, small voice in the middle of the afternoon.

Keep in mind, in order to hear a still, small voice, you may need to be deeply focused on Jesus. You may need quiet. You may need to get away from other noises. You may need to put your phone away. You may need time away from texting or scrolling. You may need to get away from people. You may need to get away from the rush and scurry and flurry of the day. Get away with Jesus.

Connection Space:

Do you feel like you can hear His voice at will, or when He speaks to you?

Have you felt like you've heard His Voice in the past?

Do you want to hear His Voice more?

Let's pray into this:

Lord, we want to hear You clearly.

We don't want You to speak more than You want,

> But we don't want to miss anything You have for us.
>
> Help me to hear Your Voice better!
>
> Help me to know when it's You, and when it's my mind.
>
> Help me to hear You better!
>
> I love You Lord!
>
> In Jesus name,
>
> Amen!

Tuning in to Hear Him

I think He is always - or frequently - speaking to all of us, but if we aren't tuned to hear, we don't. I think of a radio dial. If the station you want to listen to is, say 101.7, but your dial is on 90.1 or 97.8, you aren't going to hear anything on 101.7.

If He is always speaking something, and we are never tuned in, we never hear 101.7.

But once we somehow get a glimpse of 101.7, we are praying or listening or just possibly even feeling a nudge, and we take action on it, we hang out for a moment, we ask, is there more? We do what we think we hear, and then maybe it becomes easier for us to find 101.7 on the radio dial.

I think back over 20 years ago when I distinctly remember hearing what I thought was Him, but I also had some level of OCD or compulsive thoughts, and I would mix up what I thought was Him with whatever compulsion there was, and I would tie my mind up in knots trying to do everything, and sort through it all. And although I didn't turn my back on Him, I disappointedly recall saying, "God, I can't handle it anymore, if that's really You trying to get through, I'm going to risk not hearing You because it's just so hard." I was desperately trying to turn the dial down on my own internal thoughts, but the more I reflect on it, I turned His voice down too.

Now, loving Father that He is, He never went away . . . but I was so tuned out I didn't hear Him at that depth for years. He was there all along, listening, providing, nurturing, but I missed out on years of direct instruction.

So about a year before writing this when I started making a deep effort to try to hear what He might be saying, I was concerned that His Voice would still be mixed with my own thoughts, like the time ~20 years prior. I did a thought experiment to see if I could sort through it.

I imagined a grandfather who asked his grandson to do 5 tasks, and I imagined that the little boy heard 10 things. 5 were from the grandfather, and 5 were from his own mind, and he only did one of the 5 things from his grandfather, because it was the only thing out of the 10 that he felt sure was from his grandfather.

Then I imagined that the same grandson chose instead to do all 10 things that he heard, 5 that were from his own thoughts, and 5 from his grandfather, not knowing which were his grandfathers' requests and which were not.

So the grandson in this case did 10 things: 5 that he was asked to do, and 5 more.

Which of the two choices produced the most work for the grandfather, or responded best to his grandfather's requests?

The choice that resulted in doing all 5 requests, plus the 5 more.

Now, there wouldn't be any difference in his heart in either case; each was an effort to do his best to listen and perform. The former choice was to only do what he is certain his grandfather says to do, and he misses some things, and the latter choice is doing everything possible to make sure he does everything, even if he isn't certain.

I look back at much of my life, and it's been like the first option for the grandson, only doing what I absolutely knew was from God. (But of course doing many other things in life that were not from God, or they were from my own mind.)

Once I had this realization, I started doing much more that I heard in my mind, obviously weighing it against the Bible and good sense, and then evaluating afterwards, do I think that came from the Lord or not?

Nearly immediately after I shifted my approach, I began to hear more and more what felt like it was coming from Him (even though I'm sure I did a few things that were NOT from Him in the process of learning to hear His voice better).

There is a process of discovery, of learning what He sounds like, of actively listening, and it takes time to lean into all of it.

Just as children fall when they are learning to walk, the Bible says:

For a just man falleth seven times, and riseth up again: but the wicked shall fall into mischief. (Proverbs 24:16)

There is an expectation that we will stumble and fall at nearly anything we learn to do.

Just as in conversation with other humans, when we meet someone new who perhaps has an accent, or a different flavor of humor, or a unique lens through which they view the world; we have to learn to understand their "dialect." Learning to converse with God, and especially to hear from Him, is much the same.

You might learn a new language; or you might learn a new way of thinking if you meet someone from another culture, and there's some fine tuning to understanding them. When you first start having conversations with God, there's some fine tuning and adjustment to make to understand and hear Him best.

Only when I became immersed in Him for hours each day did I begin to feel confident that I was hearing from Him. I was also making an extra effort to discern His voice and test what I was hearing, during that time. I believe that the increased time in His presence, combined with an active effort at discernment and evaluation, has made it so much easier to sense His Voice.

It's so much easier to sense, to know, to have peace and calm about something, when I'm in the Presence of the Lord. I can directly choose to get into the Presence of the Lord (because He's in me, it's really just a matter of intentionality and connecting), and then it seems easier to hear His Voice.

At times it's like I was seeking His Voice as these perfect English sentences with clarity and direction, but He chose instead to give me His Voice through downloads and impressions. Sometimes I'm basking in His presence, and I don't hear anything, but I get a thought that makes the entire situation immediately clear in a flash.

Connection Space:

Even as you are reading this Connection Space, can you sense that He is here?

If you cannot sense that He is here, do you have an awareness - even just a knowing - that He is here?

How can you make an intention to acknowledge or notice His presence more often?

Let's pray:

Lord thank You for Your Presence!

Thank You for always being here with me, even when I'm not aware.

Thank You that I can reach out - or in - anytime, and You are right here, waiting for me!

Thank You for Your Presence!

I love You, Lord!

Differentiating Between the Voice of God and the Voice of the Enemy

You want to hear the voice of God, but you have your own thoughts in your mind, and you know the enemy is sending ideas and thoughts as well.

I've personally struggled in the past with being obsessed with compulsions and repetitive repentance that's rooted in condemnation and earning my way into God's ear.

Many people historically have led others astray claiming to hear the voice of God, and maybe they believed it for themselves.

I have heard and even journaled things in the last year that I wasn't sure was from God.

But over time and through intensely spending quality time with God, I believe I've developed a discernment that differentiates between God's voice and the voice of the enemy, and I believe you can too.

The Word tells us that as we exercise (practice) our senses, we can learn to discern between good and evil:

But strong meat belongeth to them that are of full age, even those who by reason of use have their senses exercised to discern both good and evil. (Hebrews 5:14)

One way to begin to discern between God's voice and the enemy's voice is to learn the qualities of God's voice and the enemy's voice.

Here are a few differences:

The voice of God says "You can." The voice of the enemy says, "You can't."

I can do all things through Christ which strengtheneth me. (Philippians 4:13)

The voice of the enemy wants to hold you back, stop you from getting help, stop you from spending time with Him, break up relationships, serve as a wedge.

The enemy comes to kill, steal, and destroy. The enemy is out to destroy you, to fill you with evil thoughts, thoughts to harm others, to harm yourself.

The thief cometh not, but for to steal, and to kill, and to destroy: I am come that they might have life, and that they might have it more abundantly. (John 10:10)

The enemy speaks condemnation to you, the enemy pushes you to doubt yourself and the calling God placed in you.

The voice of God carries no condemnation whatsoever. The voice of God is full of love and forgiveness and future and hope.

There is therefore now no condemnation to them which are in Christ Jesus, who walk not after the flesh, but after the Spirit. (Romans 8:1)

The voice of God wants to give you freedom, push you to success and improvement, draw you close to Him, nurture right relationships, empower the wisdom to separate from ungodly unions, and bring you peace and calm.

Each time you hear something and you aren't sure, you can ask yourself, does this push me towards fear and condemnation and doubt and hurt?

Or does this pull me to peace and calm and joy and freedom and change for good, and the love of Christ?

If you are spending only ten minutes a day with Him, it's likely going to be much more difficult to separate the voices than if you are immersed in His Presence for several hours a day.

If you are praising or praying in tongues throughout the day, it's going to be more normal and natural to hear the Voice of God, and the voice of the enemy is going to be more easily revealed and dismissed.

> **Connection Space:**
>
> Let's pray:
>
> Father, we ask that You will show us Your voice, and that Your voice will be clearer than the enemy's voice.
>
> Show us when we are hearing the enemy, and help us to discern.
>
> We want to hear You and hear You clearly!
>
> Thank You for Your voice in my life!

Thank You for speaking to me directly.

Thank You for giving me wisdom to hear from You clearly!

Thank You Father, Thank You Jesus!

Amen

Do What He Tells You

So many times we ask God to give us direction or tell us what to do in a certain situation, but we haven't done what He asked us last to do.

If you ask someone in the natural to do something for you, and they don't do it, do you continue to ask them to do more things?

If someone continually asks you for advice, but you notice they are persistently not taking your advice, will you continue to give advice?

I believe it's similar with God - if we don't listen, if we don't take action, if we don't take His "advice," I believe He may hold back future advice.

Ask Him what He's asked you to do that's undone, and if He still wants you to do it. (Sometimes He may ask you to do something, but if you don't do it, the season changes, and He wants you to do something else). You may know off the top of your head what it is. Do it!

You will likely find that if you get unfinished business taken care of, you will hear more new instructions from Him.

Connection Space:

Ask the Lord, is there something You've asked me to do, but I haven't done it?

I want to finish the work You have given me, if that's Your will today.

I want to let go of it if the season has passed.

Please give me wisdom and discernment to complete the past directions, or move on from the past instructions and become ready for new direction.

What do I need to let go of from past instructions?

What would You have me do this next season?

Do You want me to finish what You've given me in the past?

Do You want me to do it differently than You gave it to me, or should I run with what You gave me?

What would You have me do next?

Thank You Lord!

Amen

Guided by the Holy Spirit

Sometimes you will feel a nudge in your spirit, or even just a sense that pops into your mind, to "don't do that," "don't say that," "do that thing," or "help that person."

I can't say it's always the Lord, but I find that most of the time when I override that nudge, I look back and think, I should have listened.

Here's what I suggest:

1) Listen to the Spirit, the nudge in you that says, "don't do it," or that says, "take that action."
2) Checked by the Bible, do or don't do that thing.
3) When you mess up, clean it up; don't defend, be peaceful.

Obviously, the size of the impact will create a natural condition where wisdom must come into play. If it's something simple, like helping someone right now, or saying something/not saying something in conversation, the impact is low if you are wrong.

On the other hand, if it's a big life decision, the Word is clear that "in many counselors is wisdom," and we would be wise to take less risk as to what is Him and what is not.

I believe we can learn to better discern His Voice through small things initially, then as our hearing improves, our discernment is sharper, and our confidence is stronger, we can more quickly move on to the bigger things.

Obviously, once you know that you know that something is from Him, take action!

How do we learn these things if we don't go through them, and test them out?

The answer: We don't.

We can read in a book 1000 times to listen to the Spirit. But until we listen to His Spirit and do what He says, again and again, and until we ignore the Spirit possibly many times and learn from ignoring, we aren't going to actually learn to trust the voice.

You can test it over time. It's wise to test and learn. If you feel led to do something, and you do it, when you reflect on it, were you hearing Him or your own voice? If you feel led not to do something, and you do it anyway, reflect back on it and ask yourself, would it have been better if I didn't? That may not give you a conclusive answer about whether it was Him or not, but I do believe that over time the reflection helps hone your awareness of His voice.

> **Connection Space:**
>
> Can you remember a time recently when you felt a nudge and you weren't sure it was the Lord . . .
>
> But then later in the day, the thing occurred, or you see that it was a warning.
>
> How did that nudge feel?
>
> Can you become attuned to the next time you feel a nudge, so that you acknowledge it mentally as feeling a nudge?

You don't have to act on it, but register it so that later you can evaluate it.

Should I have listened to the nudge?

Does it feel like something in life confirmed that nudge?

Looking back, can you get a sense for how it felt well enough to recognize it in the future?

Simply become sensitive to what's possible.

Don't pressure yourself to "get it right fast,"

And you don't need to make rash decisions to test it . . .

Start small.

When you feel a nudge to help someone . . . if it feels right, help them.

Evaluate what happens.

If you feel a nudge, a holding back, when you are talking, to not say something . . . try not saying it.

Or note when you ignore the nudge not to say something and you do anyhow, what happens?

Do you realize after you spoke that you shouldn't have?

Can you begin to sense when a nudge is from the Lord?

Confirming Words

Several times I've been talking with God about something, and I'm not sure it's Him, I'm not sure I am getting it, I'm not sure I'm hearing His voice. Then He's sent me someone - often out of the blue and totally not predictable - that confirms what I was talking with Him about. I'll share with you a few examples.

I had been experiencing "fear of man" and frustration with myself for not approaching folks and sharing when I had the opportunity.

I happened on an outdoor worship service and spent some time worshiping. After some time, I leave.

I walk about 100 steps away and I feel a tap on my shoulder and simultaneously this lady appears in front of me. She had run from behind me after I left, to catch up with me. She says to me, "do you believe in prophetic prayer?" I say yes.

She asks if she can put hands on me - maybe my shoulders or arms. Yes.

She begins to pray in the Spirit.

And pray in the Spirit.

And pray in the Spirit.

And finally she says, "God, bring fire into this man, give him the fire to say what he needs to, give him the fire to overcome the fear of man, it's time to step out and leave the fear of man behind."

I'm blown away. I've just been processing this with the Lord. And I think someone had prayed something similar earlier that day.

She asks me, "So does that resonate?"

I told her, "Yes, not only does it resonate - it's exactly what I needed to hear today. Like, I'm blown away."

She says, "Yeah, that was tough . . ." She says, "I just kept praying in the Spirit and it finally came to me . . ."

So I asked her, "So you didn't just get that as a word for me and you came to tell me?"

She said, "No, I felt a nudge to go pray for you, and when you left, I knew that if I didn't, I would regret it all day, it would nag at me, so I ran over to you . . . but I had no idea what to say.

"So I just prayed in the Spirit until He gave me the words."

That was exactly what I needed right then - and even the lesson in just praying in the Spirit until she had the answer.

She offered me the advice to step out more and pray in the Spirit until I hear more, and her momentary meeting and spiritual advice has been part of my learning journey this year.

Another time I'm working on this book, and I feel woefully behind, and it's Saturday morning and normally I go to a prayer meeting, and I'm thinking, if I do that, it's another two hours before I can write, and I won't be fresh . . . . And I was also feeling that if I went to that prayer meeting, I would be just looking for a word, and I make an effort not to seek a word. But then I was also wrestling with, am I not willing to receive prayer?

I talked with the Lord and felt His confirming voice, don't go. Write. It's all good. I'll show you.

So I sit down to write. A few minutes later a lady and a gent approach me and ask if they can pray for me. I don't know them, I've never seen them before. It feels like they are out looking for people to pray for. Her prayer was along these lines: "Give him peace in this life situation, that He'll know you are in control." I felt such a confirmation in that moment!

Another time I was praying or considering something and I'm walking at the park. This young girl and an older lady walk up to me randomly and ask if they can pray for me. The young girl asks, "is it okay if my mom prays for you in Spanish?"

Her mom prays out in Spanish specifically what I was needing/dealing with that day. There is no way she could have known. She doesn't even speak my language!

These are just a few of these occurrences. Many more have occurred in church settings; usually the person praying didn't know my personal situation to pray into, and yet I have received multiple prayers that spoke directly to my need.

Another time, I was in a meeting and folks were praying for someone. I was praying in the Spirit, and felt led to say something very specific. But I was very cautious, afraid to get it wrong, afraid to impose my own message, so I held back. I deeply sensed it was Him, but I wasn't 100% sure, and I had some fear.

As the prayer went on, I stopped fighting it so much, and accepted that I had either missed the opportunity, or I was just wrong. But then as several others began to offer short words, most of them specifically would have confirmed the exact words that were in my mind. I went through this mental process of thinking, yes, Lord, that was You - I wish I had spoken up.

Prayer continues. There was one part of what I had in my mind, that others had not mentioned. So I finally mustered up the boldness to step over and speak to him. I recall it being very well received - as if it was "just what he needed to hear."

After the meeting, I happened to be the last to leave, other than the leaders. One of the leaders says to me, "You just really need to start speaking what you hear. I saw you had something, and I was just pushing and pushing for you to speak, but you didn't. You hear the Lord, stop doubting it, step out and say what He gives you."

I was not only so humbled, but it was one more confirmation for me that God has been teaching me to hear Him and hear Him clearly.

If you want to hear Him, and you have His Spirit, you can. I want this to be a deep, humble encouragement to lean in to Him and use what I've shared in this chapter to help you hear Him. He wants to speak to you.

Friend, I don't know your exact situation of course. But I do believe that as you draw near to Him, He will find a way to get His message to you. This book might be part of the answer; I might be writing this with you in His mind, knowing you are going to read this, and He knows what you need. Or maybe it's a random person who prays for you. Or it's another book, or a message you hear online, or anything else He chooses to use to get His message through to you!

14

Conversations With Jesus

Talking With Jesus

As my prayers shifted during the course of the trial and my intense journey with Him, I began to converse more naturally with Jesus, sharing with Him my problems, thoughts, desires, and dreams.

For most of my life, I loved Jesus, I prayed most days, and I was quite intent and disciplined about prayer. But it was mostly one way prayers along the lines of asking for help, asking for things, asking for other people's needs, asking for healing, and so on. I learned to praise, worship, and offer thanksgiving mostly in the context of "preparing my heart" for the rest of the prayer - which was mostly asking Him for things.

However, currently in my own day-to-day walk with Jesus, communing with Him and the Holy Spirit, I ask for things as a very small part of my prayer time now. I'll make my needs and desires known, but for the most part I'm simply delighting in Him. The Word tells me He'll give me the desires of my heart if I delight in Him (Psalm 37:4). I've discovered that in the last year or so of mostly praise, worship, thanksgiving, and praying in the Spirit, He has been meeting my desires, answering even my shortest prayers, and accelerating my understanding and my relationships to a level I've never experienced before.

I suspect that this type of conversation is also what God intended when He began communicating with us in the Garden.

Think about talking with Jesus as just having a normal conversation with another human.

I enjoy talking with Him and I get value out of it. He gives me balance, He gives me direction, He gives me ideas, and He protects me. He created me and He gave me the mind I have that works in a unique way, He gave me my personality, He was there when I was wounded or hurt by others or my reaction to them. He has been there with me through every trial, He knows when I'm tired, He knows how my mind has been affected by my last year, and so on. He knows me intimately, and He can give me direction better than anyone else on earth or in Heaven!

Asking Jesus Questions

I am constantly sharing things with Him, telling Him my thoughts, yes, my worries, my concerns, and talking through nearly everything with Him.

But He usually isn't talking while I am!

I have to stop, wait, listen.

Sometimes the clarity simply comes to me as I share with Him.

Sometimes it comes later, perhaps while I'm praying in tongues, or even as I'm sleeping or when I wake up, or when I'm in conversation.

Whether I'm in active conversation with the Lord, or I'm just coming to Him with a single question, I may ask something like this:

Lord, what do You want me to know about this?

Or

Lord, what do You want me to know today?

Or

Lord, what do You want me to focus on today?

I'm in a posture of listening, of waiting, of expectation.

When I am looking for a Word from God, and I want to ask a question and get an answer from Him, I focus on Him.

Sometimes that happens naturally. I'm in prayer or worship, and my focus is on Him; then I ask a question and I get a flow of thoughts and I believe it's from Him.

Or I may simply quiet my mind and ask Him a question and wait for an answer.

If I am specifically in conversation with Him, I might take the time to worship Him, to visualize Him, to speak directly to Him. I might laser focus specifically on Jesus.

Then I am totally focused on Him, and I ask a question,

Lord, what do You want me to know about this?

I sense an answer from Him.

The answers over time help inform me of the accuracy of His voice. If I ask Him the same thing ten days in a row, and it's calmly the same thing each day, I grow in confidence that's Him.

If it's important, I'm praying into it, and I'm likely receiving confirmation from other sources or other time I spend with Him.

I've had people randomly come up to me and pray into my situation - without me telling them what it is - specifically along the lines of how I've been talking with Him!

Words will jump out at me from the Word that support my discussion with Him.

I do believe that learning to discern His voice is highly sensed and felt, and must be developed over time.

But strong meat belongeth to them that are of full age, even those who by reason of use have their senses exercised to discern both good and evil. (Hebrews 5:14)

In your relationship with Him you'll lean into Him and you'll learn to hear His voice.

Connection Space:

Take something to the Lord . . . .

A challenge or a problem in your life.

Just close your eyes and say this:

Lord, I am struggling with _____ .

Pause. Listen. Wait.

Lord, what do You want me to know about this?

Pause. Listen. Wait.

Lord, what do You want me to do with this?

Pause. Listen. Wait.

Is there another question?

Ask it.

Do you feel you have what you need?

Thank Him!

In Jesus name,

Amen

Questions:

Consider what it is you specifically want to know more about, and ask Him a question, perhaps one of these:

Lord, what do You want me to know about this?

Lord, what do You want me to do about this?

Lord, what is my next step?

Lord, what insight do You want me to have?

Lord, how should I handle this?

Lord, how would You handle this?

Lord, _____

You can ask Him anything!

Lord, I am feeling ____ about _____. What do You want me to know about this?

Let Him speak. Question Him, ask for clarification if you don't understand.

Lord, what do You want me to do about this?

Let Him speak. Or feel it in your mind, or your stomach, or your bones.

Lord, what else do You want to say to me?

Let Him speak.

Let Him love you.

Let Him surround you.

Feel the peace.

Don't be stressed if you don't hear something or sense something. The answer might come later. You may not receive an answer. That's okay too.

When I have one of these conversations, I feel so much peace afterwards.

If He asks me to do something scary, like call someone or have a tough conversation I might say:

Ok, Lord, I'll do that . . . I need your strength. I need Your words.

Sean, I'll give you the words. I'll make it easy for you. Just do it.

Lord, please give me peace about this.

Sean, you have my peace. Now pick up the phone and make that call!

I also think one roadblock to hearing Him is rushing and not truly listening.

When I feel I get the most direction, I am asking one question at a time, and waiting for a response.

If I am asking multiple questions at a time, I often feel overwhelmed, or I don't feel clarity from Him.

There is no prescription for the perfect conversation with God. You might find yourself asking Him the same questions day after day. He may give you the same answers, or He may lead you through sequential revelation.

When you are curious, ask Him. When you want more detail, ask Him. When you want more clarity, ask Him. When you want to know what to do next, ask Him.

Connection Space:

How would it feel to talk with Him once or twice a day like this?

Do you feel it would get easier to discern what He's saying to you?

What's scary about this?

Can you take that fear to the Lord?

Lord, I want to ask You questions and hear You clearly . . . but I'm scared . . .

I'm scared I won't hear You.

I'm scared I'll mistake a voice in my own mind for Your Voice.

I'm scared You won't talk to me . . .

I'm scared I won't say the right words . . .

Now listen to Him . . .

Maybe it won't be words

Maybe it's just in your spirit

What is He saying to you?

Perhaps He's giving you calm . . .

As if there's nothing to be scared of . . .

Your own admission of being scared . . .

For example, being scared of "getting it wrong" is evidence of your desire and your humility . . .

And He's a loving God -

He'll work with that

And He'll guide you to hear Him

Especially if you keep your heart focused on hearing Him

And you come to hear Him frequently so you can learn His voice.

> Go ahead . . .
>
> Ask Him another question . . .
>
> And close your eyes and just listen . . .
>
> Then ask Him a follow up question
>
> Thank Him for talking with you.

More Conversations

Let's make this practical. Imagine a fear you have in your life today.

Ask Jesus,

What do You want me to know about that fear?

Be silent, let Him speak. What do you hear? Maybe you just sense something.

That's okay. Just be aware.

Then ask Jesus,

What do You want me to know about myself?

Be silent, let Him speak.

Now ask Jesus,

What do You say about me?

Be silent. Wait. Listen. Sense. Perceive.

Now ask Jesus,

What do You want me to do?

Listen.

Jesus, how do You want me to do it?

Jesus, is there anything else I need to know about this?

Jesus, I love You.

Jesus, thank You.

Now let's reflect on that experience:

What happened?

What did you sense?

Write it down.

You can take any need, any fear, any situation, anything to Him at any time in this way.

Trust Him to get through to You.

He has promised to speak; He promises we can hear His voice. So if you can't hear it, just trust Him that He'll get through some way.

He gives you direction and you go do it.

It's just that simple.

Example of Conversation:

You: Good morning, Lord

God: Good morning, _____

You: I love You Lord. This is a bit scary for me.

God: I love you, son (or daughter). Don't be afraid, just relax.

You: ok, Lord... Lord, what do You want me to know today?

God: I want you to know I have your situation under control. I was there when it started, I was there through it - and I'm right there in it now.

You: Thank You! How do I know that's You?

God: Son, don't worry about it. Just focus on Me. The words aren't important. Our time is.

You: Ok... so Lord, I am feeling (anxious, scared, worried, etc.) about this situation. What do YOU want me to know about it?

God: *Like I said, I have your situation under control. Give Me your fear. Just hand it over. You don't need to carry it anymore.*

You: *Ok, that's scary, but here's my fear. What's next?*

God: *Let's leave it there. Let ME keep your fear. No fear today. Each time you feel fearful, just recall this conversation. I'll take care of the scary stuff.*

You: *Thank YOU Lord. Thank You! Wow!!*

An Example of Time With Him

God, I worship You.

I worship You.

I bring this time to You.

I bring these challenges to You.

I bring this day to You.

I lay it all down before You.

I submit it to You.

I only want You today.

Lead me in Your way, Your will.

My note: so many of our prayers end right there. That's our morning prayer, and it's a fine prayer, it sets our heart right.

But sometimes He's like, wait, wait . . . you haven't heard My Voice.

So in this time with Him, I did have challenges, and unknowns, and stress. I was apprehensive even this morning as I was writing in this book, knowing He wants me to release this quickly, and yet having things in the natural world that seem looming. They *are* looming! So my stance in praying that was that I lay it all down, I submit, and I just want Him today.

So then I asked:

Lord, what do You say?

And here's what I sensed:

Sean, stay calm. Sleep in the boat calm. Finish the book. Go through today with peace and calm. Make decisions slowly. I will keep you.

My note now as I am writing: I recall I was in great unrest, not peaceful and calm.

I was wrestling with a strong decision, and spent some time on it, and ultimately felt He wanted me to table it for now, and just work on this book. So here I am writing. And as I read those words "make decisions slowly" I realize that's what He was referring to. And yet, had I not written it down, had I not referred to it now, I wouldn't have recalled it.

I simply stand in faith on that one now and I don't see the result of that yet.

My response to Him during my time with Him:

Thank You, Lord.

Give me strength.

It feels so overwhelming and daunting - like a huge mountain before me.

Then I felt Him say:

Sean, recall Zerubbabel: Ye shall say to this great mountain, be thou removed....and it shall move...

Stop and say to the mountain, move, in Jesus name.

I spoke these words aloud: Mountain and overwhelm and daunting, I command you to leave, in Jesus name.

Sean, now believe it moved.

Go walk this day out. I'm with you every step today. Just believe.

Thank You, Lord.

End conversation.

Friend, every conversation is different.

Even as I am going through this day, I can see Him working in the way He said during that time.

There's no formula to having the kind of conversation I had with Him, except perhaps a deep leaning in, a slowness, a calmness, a leaning in to hear Him. Asking Him, *Lord, what do You say?*

Waiting to see what I heard or sensed or felt.

Writing it out.

Reflecting back on it later.

Ideally, I would have referred to it during my decision making time. If He gave it to me as guidance for the day, why wouldn't I refer to it during the day?

Often I do refer to what He gives me, but often I don't. And when I re-read it later in the day or a few days later, I think, I should have leaned on that more heavily during the day.

He doesn't give us words just to be speaking . . . if He is giving guidance we might as well lean in as much as possible and USE the words He gives us.

I've also discovered that when I take action on what I hear, it's as if I hear more easily next time. But if I hesitate and don't take action on something I hear, then it's harder to hear the next time.

I believe part of the process of learning to hear His voice clearly is taking action on it, and testing what we have heard.

As you go through this process, in faith, you are able to hear more clearly!

Connection Space:

Sit.

Think.

Imagine.

He's here.

Right now. Not tomorrow.

He's here right now.

Not after you do all the things.

Or after you do some of the things.

But if you are born again, He's right here, right now with you.

You are in His Presence, and He is in you.

You are connecting.

When He is there, when you are connected, you are:

Calm, peaceful, joyful, not easily provoked, not angered.

It's a state of being, not a state of doing.

Talking With Him During the Day

What does it look like for me to stay in peace, get back in peace, and really draw close to the Lord, throughout the day? What else would I do right now, to draw even closer to the Lord if there was something that had distracted me or pulled me away from Him during the day?

I might go for another walk with the Lord, I might pray in tongues, I might praise Him, and I might ask Him if there's anything He wants to say to me.

That's it.

I wouldn't probably have a long conversation.

I wouldn't probably pray in any sort of formulaic way.

I wouldn't have certain words.

It would be more about just spending time with Him. Listening. Soaking in His presence. Praising some but not much because I'm tired. I would pray in tongues if only so I don't have to think up the right words, I could just let Him determine the meaning of my prayer. I would be away from the hustle and bustle of the people and the demands and the work.

I would draw closer to Him. I would feel closer to Him. I would be in peace. I'm in peace, even as I write about it, knowing that He is right here, with me. He's in me, He's beside me, He's watching me write these words. He's checking them for me.

Going to the Lord When I Need Direction During the Day

When I need direction during the day, I might just ask Him in the moment, or in a quick prayer. But if I sense I need more than that, that I need to be in a position to listen, perhaps to talk it out, or to hear carefully, I'll separate and spend some time with the Lord.

I will typically open with praise, worship, and thanksgiving:

I worship You, I'm glad You are here with me. (Pray in the Spirit for a minute or two). Thank You for being here.

At this point I'm already feeling calm and peace. Within seconds I begin to feel a measure of peace, but after 3-4 minutes with the Lord, there's a deep sense of peace. He is here. He is for me.

Then I will ask the Lord questions, one at a time, waiting for His response before I ask another question:

"Lord, what do I need to know about this?"

"Lord, what am I missing about this?"

"Lord, what do I need to do?"

I sense something in my spirit - usually not huge but something small: go do this little thing, make this call, let me handle it, etc.

Then I thank the Lord. Praise for a minute or two.

Connection Space:

What do you need direction from the Lord in?

Take it to the Lord:

Father, I need help with _____.

I am struggling with _____.

What do I need to know about this?

What am I missing about this?

Listen.

The answer might not be right away.

It might appear as if spontaneously later in the day.

Accept His answer.

Don't rush it.

He knows your needs and your problems.

He wants you in perfect peace with Him.

In fact, as you draw closer to Him regularly, some things that feel like looming problems today may shrink in the future, or they may simply not seem as big.

God wants to give you direction!

Consider Proverbs 3:5-6:

Trust in the Lord with all thine heart; and lean not unto thine own understanding.

In all thy ways acknowledge him, and he shall direct thy paths.

He makes it simple - trust in the Lord with all your heart, don't rely on your own understanding, and acknowledge Him in everything . . . and He will direct your path!

Lord, I bring my path to You!

I need direction, I need to know Your will

I need You, I need You to show the way, and to light the way for me

I know You can, and I know You will

And I'm asking You to help me keep my eyes stayed on You, and help me acknowledge You in everything . . .

And reveal to me the path You want me to take.

Thank You Lord for Your direction!

15

Journaling

Journaling What You Hear From God

When you talk with God verbally, you get revelation, you get peace, you get answers, and you get companionship.

But often, in a few months, you don't remember the details, if you don't write it down. If you have a question about what you heard, you don't remember.

With journaling, you can look back at what He said. You can evaluate it in hindsight.

When you encounter fear or doubt about something that you know God has shared with you about, you can open your journal and read through it.

I look at what's in my journal, I look at the prayers and His words to me, and continue to remember that so much - nearly everything - in the rest of the journal either fits or has been confirmed.

You can read through the journal entries like a book.

The ones from you, and not from God, will stand out like a sore thumb.

God's very specific words to you will shine out like a bright shining beacon on a hill.

I can't explain it in words.

But if you do it, you'll understand it too.

When you are having these conversations with the Lord, they are wonderful, and give you great clarity and comfort.

If you write down what He gives you, it makes it easier to remember, keep track of, and see if you have done what He's given you.

Journaling Conversations

There's another way you can communicate with Him in conversation and that's having an actual journaling conversation.

The conversation is not spoken, but it's written in your journal. The conversation occurs as you are writing in your journal.

This is similar to an out-loud conversation like those modeled earlier. But instead of silently "listening," I'm ready to write, and I write what I sense, feel, or hear.

With the journaling, sometimes when I was seeking guidance, and felt like I wasn't hearing something new, or I wasn't clearly hearing

Him, I would open up my journal for the last month or 3 months, and re-read what He shared with me in the journal entries.

In doing that, I would often see themes. He would say the same thing several times. And some things would go in waves.

It was especially interesting because several times a particularly unique situation would come up in life, and I would refer to the journal, and several times, 2-3 days before the event or the crisis, I would notice a very specific phrase or instruction that had no meaning at the time, but a few days later when the real live event occurred the phrase made perfect sense, and it contained actual advice or a warning.

The phrase or verse or warning had no special meaning to me at all when written.

If I had not written it down, it was so out-of-context that I would not have recalled it when the event occurred.

Is everything in the journal from God?

Probably not.

It could be. But likely it's not.

Anything we write or even say, we are filtering it through our own minds and even our writing.

So it may not all be inspired.

You may ask, well how do you know what is inspired?

You don't at first, but over time you grow in understanding.

I can read through my journal notes, and I can sense what is inspired and what was my own thoughts.

You will get to where you can tell when it's Him speaking to you and you writing that down, and your own thoughts and emotions speaking through.

How to Journal

At it's simplest level, it's identical to having conversations with the Lord, except that you are writing what you hear immediately. Sometimes in the process of writing, especially when you are first learning to hear from God, you can "hear" more effectively when you are writing.

Many times I will open my journal immediately after praise and worship or during my quiet time, and simply expect that God will give me words. I might also open my journal as the opening moment of my time with Him, and just listen. Or I might ask Him something (there's no formula for this, but you'll likely see a pattern):

Lord, what would You say to me today?

I simply write what I feel or hear in the moment.

Lord, what do You want me to know today?

Wait. Listen. What do you feel? What are the thoughts that immediately come to your mind?

Lord, what do You have to say today?

With each question, write down the first thoughts you hear/think/have.

We tend to hear from whom we are focused on.

If you are focused on Jesus, you are more likely to hear Him, and when you are focused on Him, the thoughts you have are more likely to be from Him.

Lord, what would you say to me?

Then just wait.

Be quiet.

Listen.

Write what you feel.

Lord, what do You want me to know about this?

Wait, listen, write.

Lord, what do You want me to do?

Wait, listen, write.

Don't worry about whether it's God or not.

Just write.

Write in flow.

Write what you feel, what you hear.

Don't force anything.

Just write.

And when you no longer feel you are hearing anything . . . just stop.

It might be 3 sentences.

Some days it might be 3 pages.

Just stop. Then read it. Don't judge it too much. You may be surprised that some of it came from your own hand.

My best advice would be to not attempt to overly evaluate it, is this from God or not? Just come back tomorrow. And then the next day. Be consistent. Over time you will be able to sense what's Him and what's you.

Start journaling with the Lord. Evaluate. Talk with Him about it. Make changes if necessary.

As with talking with Jesus, you can ask anything in your journaling with the Lord.

I do find that with journaling questions, I don't tend to write (ask) the same things over again as much. I seem to get more clarity from Him at one time, and don't find myself asking as many questions, but your experience might be different, so go with the flow.

Connection Space:

Let's take this time to start a journal.

Maybe it's just a notebook at home.

A simple composition book is fine to get started.

Perhaps start with a daily habit of a few minutes or even just a few lines of journaling each morning.

I will often open my journal after my initial praise and worship, or even some time of just sitting quietly, and I immediately sense He is telling me something.

Or you can ask Him a question, for example:

Lord, what do You want to say to me today?

At first, it may feel uncomfortable or you don't feel like you are hearing anything. It has been that way for me at times; I will simply advise to stick with it for 30 - 60 days before you evaluate or give up!

The sooner you start, the sooner you'll be communicating with Him in this way!

The more frequently you journal, the easier it becomes!

Just start!

16

Praying in the Spirit

Communicating with the Spirit

We've talked about hearing the voice of God, where we likely hear Him in our spirits or we sense His answer; or we may notice confirmations in the Word, in the world around us, or from people. But we haven't talked about specifically praying in the Spirit, connecting with His Spirit more experientially from our spirit.

Paul encouraged us to pray in the Spirit:

Praying always with all prayer and supplication in the Spirit, and watching thereunto with all perseverance and supplication for all saints; (Ephesians 6:18)

What is praying? It's communicating! It's talking with God, it's talking with Jesus.

You see, in our modern vocabulary we usually think of the word "to pray" as to "ask for things from God," but in the context that Jesus used it in the Lord's prayer, when the disciples asked Him how to pray, prayer included worship, praise, forgiveness, thanksgiving, protection, intercession, and praying for His blessing.

When Jesus prayed to the Father in John 17 it was like a conversation; He told the Father what He had accomplished, and that He had done what the Father asked. He then asked protection and blessing for the disciples, and not just for them but for those who would come after (us). And He prayed that He would be in them (us), and the Father in Him, and that we would be one (in unity) in the Father and the Son.

When I contemplate the breadth of prayer, as Jesus, my model and example, used it, prayer wasn't a one way stream of talking to God. Prayer was immersive, it was like conversation, and it carried a deep width of richness.

Jude exhorts us:

But ye, beloved, building up yourselves on your most holy faith, praying in the Holy Ghost, (Jude 20)

(The original word in Greek is the same for Spirit and for Ghost: "pneuma." It's commonly translated as "Spirit" but in this case was translated "Ghost." It's the same Person).

My personal belief is that praying in the Spirit is one key way we communicate and pray through which we have access to the deep things of the Holy Spirit!

Jude specifically precedes his admonition to pray in the Holy Ghost with the directive to build up yourselves in the most holy faith. He doesn't say, build yourself up in the most holy faith by any other means, he specifically states praying in the Holy Ghost. The Holy Ghost Who has the mind of Christ, the Holy Ghost Who has access to the deep things of God, which He freely gives to those who love Him.

Imagine praying in the Spirit realm (as in a place, another level of existence, the Spirit dimension that overlaps the physical dimension of our world and is present in us as He dwells in us), and be so completely linked to His Presence and His mind that when you pray it is like the Spirit is praying.

Imagine if you pray in a deep awareness of His Spirit hearing you and being with you. In that awareness of His Presence, His Spirit is in you and you are in Him. Imagine you would be praying in the Spirit if you are praying while in that level of awareness of His Spirit.

Imagine you are praying for something, for wisdom perhaps; maybe you see someone who might need a word of encouragement, and you pray in tongues for a moment, if only to be a physical tangible awareness to you of His Presence but certainly having meaning and weight nevertheless. Then in your spirit, or with words but emanating from your spirit, you ask, what do You want me to do, Lord? And then you sense a nudge, go say this, do nothing, etc. You continue to talk with the Lord.

You are in the Spirit, praying in tongues, aware of His Presence, He is in you, and you are in Him; you are in the Spirit. So when you are praying at that moment, in that space, you are praying in the Spirit.

As you spend time with Jesus in this way, you'll grow closer to Him.

This is just like building an earthly relationship; you grow closer over time and experience together.

Connection Space:

Let's use this time to enter into a time of deep communication with the Lord and the Holy Spirit.

Allow yourself to be completely aware of His Presence within you, through you, and actually wrapping His arms around you.

Lord, we enter this time, so aware of Your Presence!

Thank you for being so approachable, for being a very personal God and Savior.

Thank You that I can enjoy You and You can enjoy me.

I simply rest in Your Presence now.

(Perhaps allow yourself to rest in His Presence for a moment. Just accept His Presence. Be aware of His Presence. He is there with you, He is communing with you.)

Tell the Lord how much you love Him:

Lord, I love You so.

I'm so grateful for Your Presence in my life.

I'm so glad You found me, and You've brought me into Your Kingdom, even right here on earth.

Thank You for making me Your Son or Daughter, with all the rights, with all the love, with all the position, with all the freedom and closeness to You.

Thank Him for how He has rescued or changed or transformed you:

Father, Thank You for rescuing me from a life of insecurity, fear of judgment, and fear of not being loved.

Thank You for staying with me all the way through, every time I strayed, every time I went somewhere beside You for satisfaction, every time I took my eyes off of You.

Thank You for rescuing me and healing me and giving me freedom, not just spiritually, but emotionally and relationally.

Thank You for giving me new, fresh life in You.

Thank You for loving me!

Thank You for allowing me to experience Your Presence in this way!

You can continue to spend time with the Lord . . .

Thank Him in your own words.

Appreciate His Presence in your own words.

Rest in Him.

Perhaps you are sensing some level of closeness or true awareness of His Presence right now in a way that perhaps you haven't in the past.

You can have that more often. You can have that for longer. And it can become a deeper awareness and closeness.

He is always there. As we spend more intentional time with Him, we draw closer to Him who is always there.

There is no end to the closeness we can have with the Lord if we follow Him, follow His ways, walk in the Spirit, spend private time with Him, and keep our eyes on Him in all things.

Experiential Example

If you've been leaning into a depth of communication with Jesus in the Connection Spaces and your own private time with Him, I suspect you have become aware of His Presence.

That is just a taste of what you can experience when you truly draw close to the Spirit of Christ and build a deep, solid relationship with Him!

A beautiful thing happens when you spend enough time with Him so that you deeply know Him personally, and not just intellectually.

You find yourself having times with Him that are very very special. Some people call them "experiences." I've heard some call them "encounters," or some might just see them as "wow! The Lord really showed up in my prayer time today!" Regardless of how we might call this sweet, deep time with the Lord, when you grow close to Him, you can have "experiences" like that.

These experiences are not completely describable when they occur, and each is different. Just as when you spend time with a close human in your life, the deepest times with them, the times you share a pain together, or you share a joy together, or you just enjoy each others' company, no two of those times are exactly alike.

Next, I'll share with you what this time feels like to me. I believe anyone can experience this level of depth with Jesus, simply by taking the time to truly appreciate Him for Who He is, make a point to be present and aware of Him always, especially during your prayer and worship time, and give Him focus and attention and love that grows over time.

Praying in the Spirit, for me, is a place where the sense and the transmission of thoughts from me to heaven, and from heaven to me, transcends words.

There is a felt sense of being in His Presence. Him in me, and me in Him. Together. Like One. It's not explainable in words.

This to me is being in the Spirit.

I think thoughts and know He knows them instantly. I sense His calm and yet His joy at the same time. It's like all the fruit of the Spirit all at one time. Completely consumed by His Presence. In His Presence and Him in me, all at the same time.

I can just rest in this place. I may be praying, I may be praising, I may be praying in tongues, I may be singing in tongues, I may be deeply emotive, in tongues, almost like a wailing. I can't explain this in words, there is nearly a sense of being lost in the experience. In fact, sometimes I feel like I lose awareness of time, I lose awareness of those around me if it's a corporate setting. I am lost in His Presence.

Oh! How experiential this is. If it sounds weird to you, that's okay; it still sometimes sounds weird to me. Remember I followed Him, much of the time quite closely, for 40+ years, and if you had told me that you experienced this I would possibly not have believed you. So I totally get that this may feel weird to you right now.

I can sit in silence, or I can walk in conversation with Him, or I can pray or praise and know that I am in His Presence. I can know that He is in me. I can know that I am in His Presence - out there - and at the very same time, He is in me; He is in my presence. I am in Him and He is in me.

And in that state, in that place of oneness, I can think a thought and know it's a prayer. And I can receive a thought and believe it is from Him. It's more like an impression than a thought. Almost a felt thing, but no feeling like any I've experienced on earth.

There is a closeness that is not explainable. I can say that coming to this level of closeness hasn't happened overnight. I notice that incrementally over time, I can enter this place of His Presence faster and faster, with more depth, and with less awareness of what's going on outside my spirit. Just this morning during worship I experienced this closeness at one of the deepest levels ever. And in fact as I am writing these words I sense that He is activated in me, in a felt and sensed way, and that I am tapping into the spiritual world even as I write this.

An overwhelming sense of His Presence within me, and not just in me, but it's like I am in a cloud, His Presence fully throughout me, but it doesn't just end at my skin, when my skin meets the air, instead, I am engulfed in His Presence.

Even though I have a physical body that restrains my movement to this current place on earth, my thoughts and my intentions feel as though they are connected with Him, and I feel that I am closely connected with the Spirit.

In this moment. I exist right now in this moment. Nothing outside the bubble of this moment matters. I am lost in this moment, enjoying the Presence of the Lord.

Growing Close to Jesus

When I first started leaning into His Presence, and being aware of Him there, I had no idea I could experience everything I've written in that last section. I couldn't have fathomed it, had you told me. Perhaps that's where you are. I want to encourage that if you want it, I believe you can have it.

For me, this level of sensed Presence has not only taken time to get to, but it's grown over time.

And yes, He can be one in you and you in Him, immediately, right now even as you think it. But experientially for me, this awareness of being one in Him, and spending significant time in that place, has grown over the last year. In addition, the ability to think thoughts as prayers and think/sense His voice did not occur immediately, and has grown deeper over time.

I believe that for most if not all people, this is something that He gives you over time, as you spend time in praise and prayer and worship and possibly praying in tongues.

It is certainly worth the time and the effort (which is enjoying His Presence anyhow) to be able to speak to, and hear from, the Holy Spirit at this depth.

For me, there are two components that I believe greatly accelerated my growth in relationship with Him in this way: 1) praying in tongues and 2) a deep trust in Him in every situation.

When I spend time talking, praying, or even singing in tongues, I find myself much more open to His nudges, His voice, and the sensation that He is very close. I have found that the more time I spend with Him in the spirit language, the easier it is for me to simply think thoughts that are prayers, or hear thoughts that I believe are His voice.

The deep trust has been partly cultivated through trials over the years, and especially the trial of the 18 months. Having no idea what to do, feeling powerless to do anything effective, and having no control over an outcome; and simply having to rest and trust Him that He would provide, that He would come through with a solution, or if He didn't, that He would be right there with me all the way through; has significantly increased my sense of a deep trust in Him.

I experience this desire that I just want to be right there, and I have this thought, I am aware that You are right here, in me, and I in You, and then I am there.

Sometimes it's just a decision that I want to sit with Him, and I will step into it. I'll have an awareness that He's here. I create that awareness with my mind and my attention. It doesn't just happen to me. I will ponder it, I will think on it, considering how close He is. And while I am pondering how close He is, I begin to sense, He's right here. And then I think, I am in His Presence. I am in the Presence of the mighty God. Like Moses in the presence of a mighty God at the burning bush. Perhaps even Moses when the glory of God went by him on the mount.

I am still, my mind is still, I am quietly observing His presence as a thing. It's not something I see, it's something I just know. And in that moment I sense an incredible level of peace. Like nothing out there matters. I am in Him and He is in me, and all is well.

As I write that, I think, "peace that passes all understanding."

But we don't seek it as peace. When we receive His Presence, it is peace. It is peaceful. And it passes all understanding. But I am not seeking peace, I am not seeking calm. The peace and calm are part of the fruit, the result. But I am seeking His Presence, I am aware of His Presence, and the peace and calm are a side-effect.

I am resting in His Presence. Just here. No thought of later. No thought of tomorrow. No thought of the challenges and troubles and demands of the world. They will be there later. He is here with me now. Of course He will be with me later. And my time deeply in His Presence now will strongly inform how I act and respond during that time.

Coupled with the awareness of His Presence in me, and me in Him, is a deep, accompanying trust in Him. A rest in Him. A knowing that He has the storm in His hands. Like when the disciples cried out, "Master, carest not that we perish?" So stressed. And yet Jesus just said, "oh ye of little faith. Peace, be still."

Experientially, when I first started having this deep awareness of being in His Presence, it was generally after deep time in prayer or praise or tongues. I made a great effort to "shut out the world" and to "ignore distractions." There's been a progression from a lot of labor and thought to get to this place to now I can just think I am in His Presence and I instantly know that I am.

I can think of His Presence in me, and immediately I'm aware of His Presence filling and engulfing me.

Of course I know that I am always in His Presence. This is a deep awareness of it, a deep knowing that it is so, and it's accompanied by a sense of peace. I'm not seeking the peace. The peace is a sign. It's just a result, the inevitable next step to leaning completely into His Presence and in His care, because if I am completely engulfed by Him as if by a cloud or a big hug blanket, then there is no fear that can touch me. So I rest in peace.

I'd also like to distinguish that this is not the same as some calm or peace you might experience if you sit still and do breathing exercises or breath work, or even if you sit and meditate and "watch your thoughts." Yes, I've experienced a certain amount of calm engaging in those kinds of calmness exercises in the past.

But this felt sense of calmness accompanying my awareness of His Presence completely eclipses that feeling of calm from a breathing exercise or a meditation time. I can't even put a number on it. I could say this is 10x calmer, and that wouldn't feel sufficient.

This Presence, this calm and peace that accompanies this awareness of His Presence, comes on me nearly immediately once I am aware of His Presence. I don't have to work up to it, or breathe 10 times, or have my eyes closed for 5 minutes. It's nearly instantaneous. It's almost as if it's coming from somewhere else, like He is giving it to me, like He is infusing me with it.

This is experiential. Over time, over the last probably less than a year, as I have had more of these experiences, and spend more time in many of them than initially, there is a heightened sense of His Presence over time.

Meaning that although it's instantaneous, and I don't do any work (unless you consider just having the thought of awareness and being aware, work) to get to this. I don't enforce or create any level of peace by trying to be calm or by breathing slow or anything. It's like the peace just comes on me.

I don't have to work up to it at all, I don't have to work at being calm; in fact, I don't focus on calm or peace at all, I simply focus on His Presence. And in His Presence I experience that calm and peace.

This can be possible for you as well. Perhaps you begin to experience this in the next Connection Space. Or perhaps as you continue to do the exercises through the book and learn new ways to communicate with Him, you'll begin to experience what I've described.

I would also caution that we aren't seeking an "experience," we are seeking the Presence of Jesus, we are seeking intimacy and closeness with Him. The felt peace is simply a result of that time with Him and fully acknowledging His Presence.

Paul summed it up in this prayer:

Now the God of hope fill you with all joy and peace in believing, that ye may abound in hope, through the power of the Holy Ghost. (Romans 15:13)

The peace and joy is real and results in hope, and it's through the power of the Holy Ghost (the Holy Spirit, the Spirit of Jesus).

Let's take this next Connection Space to step into the mentality that He is right here with you now, and that you can simply rest into that awareness:

Connection Space:

Let's do that now.

Simply think, He is here with me right now.

Just let that sit.

He is here with me right now.

Consider that He dwells in you.

He is in you, and you are in Him.

He is here with you.

His presence is within you.

His presence is filling you.

As you are sensing His Presence filling you, talk with Him.

Tell Him how this feels to you.

Tell Him if it feels odd or different.

Share with Him if you want more of this.

Share with Him if you want to grow so much closer to Him.

Just enjoy His Presence for a few more moments!

My Journey to Get Close to Jesus

When I look back over not only 40+ years of walking with Jesus, and especially over the 18 months or so during which I grew most recently with Jesus, I can see there were a few things that have been critical to my experience and journey.

One is the depth of desire I had to understand certain things. I would be dealing with shame or guilt, and I would dig so deeply with the Lord, either in mourning or lamenting, or in discovering how I could be right with Him. I would be dealing with disappointment or sadness and I would be desperately seeking His comfort. I would be facing a decision, or a challenge, or a roadblock and I would desperately need His intervention or direction. And tying it all together was this basic desire to please Him, and to understand how or why I wasn't completely in line with His heart, or why we weren't closer.

Another is the significant amount of time I initially spent in prayer and praise and praying in tongues. For months I spent 4-5 hours a day with the Lord, combining corporate time with personal time. It's certainly not that level of dedicated time today. At that time I didn't have the same awareness of His constant hour by hour and minute by minute presence, and I needed that level of time with Him to be fully connected. Now, I have a much deeper awareness and connection hour to hour, whether I'm in dedicated prayer or not.

We tend to experience things more deeply if we spend more time on them. This isn't just spiritual things. If you spend two hours on social media looking at people's worldly feeds, you are likely to experience some level of envy, disgust, or insecurity. That's an effect of that negative time in your day.

When you spend time in the Presence by praying in your understanding, or praying in tongues, you are spending very positive time, and it's time that's linked to Heaven. So it's natural that you would experience something positive from that time in the Presence. Although at any moment you can step into the awareness of His Presence, it certainly gets easier and feels deeper when you've done it more frequently, for longer!

For months I would pray, "God make me a thin space in this world." The concept being that a thin space is a place where God's Presence comes down from heaven and touches earth. I would pray for God to make me a thin space.

As I prayed for Him to make me a thin space, I would begin to melt mentally into an awareness that I was in His Presence. I now know experientially that He is within me, that there is no need for me to become a thin space. I am a thin space, simply by having Christ in my heart. But of course without awareness, we are not likely to walk it out, to connect with the Holy Spirit within us, or allow the Holy Spirit within us to flow out and touch other lives.

Chronologically this was before I had this great, deep sensation I have written about in these last few pages. You could say this was the formative stages of what I experience now! And I suggest that as you grow into your own understanding and awareness of what this all means to you, experientially, you may go through some phases where you picture it one way now, and that changes over time!

As I sensed His Presence around me, connecting with me as a thin space, I would sense it filling me. I would then sometimes pray, "God let Your Presence overflow to those around me. Make this thin space 3-6 feet around me." I would pray for those around me, I would imagine the thin space encompassed them as well.

This time praying for His Presence to be in me, to connect me with Heaven, and to surround me, however incorrect theologically that is, likely grew my understanding of His Presence and helped me become more aware of His Presence in me. So I don't share that with you to suggest that His Presence flows any deeper in a "thin space" than anywhere else, but to highlight part of the process of awareness that I've gone through in the last year or so before writing this.

But that was the genesis of my own conceptual understanding that His Presence was fully within me, not just symbolically living in my heart, or as if His Spirit had a physical location in my body. After a few months of conceptualizing this "thin space," I developed the awareness that He is just always here, and I don't need to "become a thin space," I can simply be aware that He is completely in me and completely around me, and I am filled with the Spirit.

The time I spend with Him is a joy because I'm not working for or striving to please a far away God, but instead my acts of praise or prayers or speaking in tongues is practically an activity with the Holy Spirit, since He's right here with me.

Not only do I spend time with Him in quiet time, or worship, or time I've set aside to praise or pray, but when I notice my peace has gone, or is going, I'm conscious that I need to spend more time with Him. Not because I am seeking the peace, but because the receding peace is symptomatic of not being completely connected with Him. Because when I am totally connected with Him, I have peace.

Reflections on my Experiences in His Presence

I've just written deeply about my sensed awareness of being in the Spirit, in His Presence, and Him in my presence.

But I think that is still only one way we might experience being "in the Spirit," and that you or others might experience it differently.

I see God as being like the facets of a diamond in His uniqueness, and that we are created uniquely as well, so different people might have different experiences of being "in the Spirit."

I don't know if what I experience is what Paul experienced (II Corinthians 12:1-4). Others have visions or dreams in the Spirit. I don't. Or perhaps I should say, don't yet! There may be other manifestations of being in the Spirit that I'm not aware of or haven't experienced. I'll be the last to say this is "the" way to be "in the Spirit." It's my own sensed and felt experience!

I can spend time with the Spirit. It might be a time of that sensed awareness I wrote of earlier, or it might be just spending time with the Spirit, intentionally knowing that we are doing something together. I might even be enjoying a hobby or with a person, and yet I am with the Spirit. Now, the Word instructs me to pray without ceasing. I can pray in out-loud words, or I can pray silently with words in my mind, and I can even pray by thinking thoughts that are prayers.

You can see this is highly nuanced, and perhaps that's very intentional on the Lord's part, because different people might pray in the Spirit a little differently, based on how they interact with Him. Our different personalities or communication styles might come into play.

For example I typically pray in words, either out loud or sometimes in my mind. And when it's in my mind, I am typically seeing the words in my mind. So if I can pray in words, either out loud or seeing the words in my mind, but you cannot see the words in your mind like I can, but you can think in visions and pictures, and perhaps you pray in visions and pictures, which I don't do, then my praying in the Spirit might be mostly out loud or seeing the words in my mind, and your praying in the Spirit might sometimes include praying in pictures!

So much as I wanted to share with you my own experience because it's amazing to me, and I am so grateful He's given it to me, I don't want it to constrain you from whatever way through which He wants to connect deeply with you.

We each have such different personalities and connection and communication styles, and God in His infiniteness connects with each of us uniquely.

Use what I've shared here as a motivation or a guide to growing closer to Jesus, but know that because you are connecting with the Spirit, He'll direct you uniquely, and according to His perfect will and knowledge of your needs!

17

Praying in Tongues

Praying in Tongues

Praying in the Spirit realm, or praying from your spirit, can include praying in tongues, which is the gift of praying in a spiritual and angelic language.

I have prayed in tongues for years, but in the last year I have gone from praying in tongues occasionally and usually very privately, to praying in tongues nearly every day during my prayer time, sometimes for hours, and often many times during the day; and praying in tongues in corporate environments, and with other believers. I believe that the time spent praying in tongues has been a crucial component of drawing closer to hearing things at the Spirit level, and has helped me have a deeper awareness of His Presence.

But I believe everything I have written about praying in the Spirit, and everything I have written about in terms of becoming aware of His Presence, His Presence in me, and me in Him, can be attained without the gift of tongues, although I would assume it would take longer to become tuned in to Him at the deepest levels.

I believe praying in tongues has rapidly accelerated my ability to connect deeply with the Spirit of God in me. But there are many times when I connect with the Spirit and I'm not praying in tongues.

Paul himself said:

For if I pray in an unknown tongue, my spirit prayeth, but my understanding is unfruitful. (I Corinthians 14:14)

Many Christians believe that tongues are not for today, and they were only an initial sign in the early church. You might feel that way. My role and purpose here is not to attempt to persuade you that tongues are for today. That's between you and the Lord! I would simply encourage you to read for yourself all of the verses in the Word about praying in tongues, talk with the Lord about it, and decide for yourself.

If you don't pray in tongues, or if you don't believe tongues are for today, as some do, that's okay. You can pray in the Spirit and not pray in tongues!

I completely believe that you can access all the spiritual treasures in the Spirit without speaking or praying in tongues. But because I speak in tongues, and it's been a vibrant part of my experience and my journey, I'll be sharing here the depth of what it's meant for me, and what I believe praying in tongues can do for you, and how it can accelerate your progress in connecting with the Spirit.

If you are interested in the gift of praying in tongues, this chapter is for you. If praying in tongues is not for you, just skip this chapter and everything else in this book is still available to you! (Of course, because God is an unlimited, awesome God!!)

Let's get started:

When we pray in tongues, in the Spirit language, we relinquish control over the content of our prayers. We don't understand it unless we are given an interpretation. We are praying in a language that only God understands. He can make those words mean anything He wants. If we need something, and we don't know what to pray, we can pray in the Spirit and He converts those words - those nonsense sounding words - into words that have meaning in His kingdom. That allows the perfect prayer.

Then He can take that prayer, and activate solutions or angels on your behalf.

We are a spirit being first, even though most of the time we think of ourselves as flesh and bone and mind. When we talk in our natural language, we can give it structure and realization of what we are praying. If He had given us a "language of angels" that we observe as a new language, as if we learned Spanish or Rwandan, then we could study a book and learn the new angel language. But then, even though it was the language of angels, we would still exercise a level of control over our words - because we would be saying words out of our own understanding. But because we don't understand the words in the Spirit language, we must relinquish control over the words, the intent, the prayers, and the results.

Because we are spirit beings, when we are communicating in the Spirit language, we can communicate - and exist - at the Spirit level. One of the keys to being able to connect with God more closely is being able to tune out the world's noise and focus on Him.

Sometimes we don't have that focus. Stray thoughts, worried thoughts, and planning thoughts enter our mind and it's much harder to control them. If we are praying intently in tongues and in the Spirit it becomes easier to stay focused on Him and stay in the Spirit world.

I encourage you to spend more time in the Spirit, even when it doesn't make sense, and even when it's not praying in tongues! Wait for His leading. Give Him plenty of time in the Spirit and let His prayers develop for you.

When I am praying in tongues, it's part of praying in the Spirit. My mind is on Him. I may even go silent but my mind is still praying, silently. I might switch back and forth between tongues or English or silence, just a knowing He is there and He knows my thoughts. Tongues for me is part of the experience of praying in the Spirit, although sometimes I may pray only in tongues.

I have discovered that when I pray in the Spirit, and especially when I release my understanding by praying in tongues, I personally get great benefit. If I'm stressed, I become calmer. If I am chaotic or confused, I get more clarity and calm.

Sometimes God will give me answers to problems during or after praying in the Spirit and in tongues.

Sometimes God will guide me to pray in the Spirit and in tongues towards a problem or a challenge.

I believe that praying in the Spirit and in tongues adds another dimension to our prayers, and can possibly contribute to angelic warfare on our behalf. (Psalm 91:11-12)

The Spirit makes intercession for us according to the will of God (even when we don't know what to pray for).

Likewise the Spirit also helpeth our infirmities: for we know not what we should pray for as we ought: but the Spirit itself maketh intercession for us with groanings which cannot be uttered.

And he that searcheth the hearts knoweth what is the mind of the Spirit, because he maketh intercession for the saints according to the will of God. (Romans 8:26-27)

How many times do you not know what to pray for?

For me, it's often.

When I'm in trouble and it's a nightmare and a disaster, as it was for 18 months, I would try to pray for things . . . but I didn't know the source of the problems, or the right solution . . . I didn't know what to pray for.

I didn't know His will as a resolution. I didn't know what to pray for. But I was able to stand on the Spirit Himself making intercession (prayers) for me with groanings that cannot be uttered.

I believe that not only does He pray in groanings for us when we don't know what to pray and we are not praying in tongues, but that also when we are praying in tongues and we don't know what we are praying, He is praying for us with groanings that cannot be uttered!

Now, in the understanding it's hard to pray about something when we have no idea what words to form - so we may only pray a few minutes.

But in the Spirit, praying in our hearts, praying in our spirits, or praying in tongues - we aren't forming words we understand, so we're not making an effort to form words and thoughts - so it's not as hard.

I can pray for 30 minutes or an hour in tongues and I'm not tired like I would be from forming the "right" prayers in the body - when I don't even know what those "right" prayers are!

This means I can pray for longer in the Spirit than I can in the understanding - and He is praying prayers for me with groanings that cannot be uttered!

I don't have to know what I am praying, I don't have to know what He is praying, I don't have to know what His groanings are as they cannot be uttered anyhow!

I trust that His groanings are the right prayers at the right time and that they are effective just like we are promised about our own prayers:

The effectual fervent prayer of a righteous man availeth much. (James 5:16b)

The Spirit knows what we actually need, because He knows the mind of Christ, and inside the mind of Christ is the will of God.

For what man knoweth the things of a man, save the spirit of man which is in him? even so the things of God knoweth no man, but the Spirit of God.

For who hath known the mind of the Lord, that he may instruct him? but we have the mind of Christ. (I Corinthians 2:11,16)

As we are praying in the Spirit, we may be able to tap into the will of God for us in certain situations, and we may not even realize it. It might be spoken in groanings, it might be revealed as a mystery, it might be revealed over time, it might be downloaded to us as an idea, but at its deepest core it's the will of God!

But as it is written, Eye hath not seen, nor ear heard, neither have entered into the heart of man, the things which God hath prepared for them that love him.

But God hath revealed them unto us by his Spirit: for the Spirit searcheth all things, yea, the deep things of God.

For what man knoweth the things of a man, save the spirit of man which is in him? even so the things of God knoweth no man, but the Spirit of God.

Now we have received, not the spirit of the world, but the spirit which is of God; that we might know the things that are freely given to us of God.

Which things also we speak, not in the words which man's wisdom teacheth, but which the Holy Ghost teacheth; comparing spiritual things with spiritual. (I Corinthians 2:9-13)

Eye has not seen and ear has not heard or entered into our hearts, the things which God has prepared for us who love Him. He reveals them to us by His Spirit. We can know those things that are freely given to us by God.

Consider with me that even as you are progressing in the Spirit, you are discovering new things. I am discovering new things. We never get to the place where He has given us the very last new thing we could ever know. More is revealed to us as we spend more time with the Spirit!

The more time we spend with Him, and the more depth we lean into with Him, the more of these treasures we will be able to access.

Now, of course we aren't seeking these treasures only because we are curious and want to know more, even though that's exciting, but these treasures are designed to edify us and edify others.

We have the Holy Spirit so we can know the things of the Spirit.

And we have a heavenly language in which we can communicate.

In Corinthians, Paul says:

For if I pray in an unknown tongue, my spirit prayeth, but my understanding is unfruitful. (I Corinthians 14:14)

He's saying his spirit is praying, but he doesn't understand what he's praying.

He then goes on to say:

What is it then? I will pray with the spirit, and I will pray with the understanding also: I will sing with the spirit, and I will sing with the understanding also. (I Corinthians 14:15)

Paul is saying, I will pray with the Spirit, in tongues, or even in thought or in groanings (Romans 8:26) (which I don't understand) and I will pray with the understanding also!

When we don't know what to pray, we can pray with the Spirit.

When we are tired, when we are frustrated, when we are out of words, we can pray with the Spirit and in tongues.

This just fires me up, this gives me life!

I can pray in the Spirit and in tongues and He prays what's best for me!

I can pray in the Spirit and in tongues as much as I want, as much as I can.

If I spend more time praying in the Spirit, and He has treasures of knowledge that He reveals to His own, and He is willing to give them to me, how much am I edified when I pray in tongues!!!

> **Connection Space:**
>
> Imagine you have the mind of Christ (you do!)
>
> Pray in the Spirit if you can . . .
>
> Pray in the natural if you want . . .
>
> Lord, give me Your mind
>
> Lord, I accept Your mind
>
> You know what I'm dealing with
>
> I want Your answers, not mine
>
> I rest in Your peace
>
> I rest in Your presence

> And I'm simply expecting that because I have the mind of Christ
>
> I will get inspired ideas to help solve the situation
>
> Inspired ideas to move forward on the calling You have placed in me
>
> Thank You for the mind of Christ!
>
> In Jesus name,
>
> Amen

How to Speak in Tongues

If you've never heard praying in tongues, it's hard to explain. It's literally like another language. But everyone gets their own words in this other language. So I can't just give you a vocabulary! You must lean into and submit to the idea that you are saying things you don't understand.

Praying in tongues is best modeled and taught live, locally, with someone whom you can hear and have confidence with. But since we are meeting together in the pages of this book, I'll do my level best (Lord, help me here!) to share with you my own understanding and personal interaction with the Lord using the gift of the language of the Spirit.

It's a gift, along with other manifestations of the Spirit. Since it's a gift . . . it's given to you. You can't force it, and you can't take it by force. It's a gift. (I Corinthians 12:7-11)

Though it's a gift we are an active participant. We have to listen, we have to open our lips and allow sound to come out, and we have to use the gift for it to grow and for us to become more comfortable.

However, just as with other gifts, you have to accept it. You have to receive it. You have to open your lips to speak. At first it's not comfortable. The more you actually practice praying in the Spirit, it gets easier. You become more comfortable and open to the leading of the Lord.

Many pastors will help folks receive the gift of the Spirit language by helping them form words they don't understand. I don't recall my own initial first experience with tongues; it's been with me for years. Over the last couple years I've gotten much more comfortable praying in tongues, especially in the presence of others, but I think that has as much to do with simply praying more, and losing some of my fear of man, than about becoming "better" at praying in tongues.

1) Ask God for the gift of speaking in the Spirit. It's a gift, He gives good gifts to His children, so just ask. I'm hesitant to give you some elaborate scripted prayer . . . just ask Him!

2) Once you've asked Him, become open. Listen. Be aware when you hear others praying in the Spirit. If perhaps you are desiring it, and feeling something bubbling up inside you . . . . lean into the idea of possibly just opening your lips, and speaking what you think you feel . . . even if it's nonsense. Even if it's not. Be open to God speaking THROUGH your lips!

Keep in mind, God gives you the gift, but since it's coming through your lips you have to make sounds with your lips for the Spirit language to emerge. At first it might feel fake, it might even be fake, but your faith will trust that God will convert it to useful language. Over time, as you become more comfortable and less worried about "getting it right," I believe you will simply let the Spirit give you the words, and you participate by saying them out.

But God isn't going to force you to speak. You are the operator, you are His hands and feet on earth. And just as He isn't going to force your body to drive to the grocery store and buy food for a starving person, instead He will nudge you to do it, He isn't going to force you to speak.

Remember this, you have the Spirit of God within you. He gives you the strength to minister to others; the fruit of His Spirit produces love, joy, peace, patience, etc. But just as He won't force you to be loving, and He won't force you to be peaceful, He won't force you to say words you don't understand and simply allow Him to place meaning on those words.

My own experience has been that even today I'm not always sure I'm praying exactly what He has in mind. But when I get lost in the Spirit language, He does amazing things, and I know it's from Him.

We know that the Spirit prays for us with groanings that cannot be uttered, and that when we pray in tongues, we don't understand what we are saying:

For if I pray in an unknown tongue, my spirit prayeth, but my understanding is unfruitful. (I Corinthians 14:14)

So the Spirit prays when we pray in the understanding.

And the Spirit prays when we pray in tongues that are guided by Him.

So what if we speak gibberish, not knowing if it's the gift or it's our own silliness . . .

If He prays for us when we speak in the understanding . . .

And He prays for us when we speak in tongues . . .

(and we have His Spirit within us and He is a good God and He loves us, and He sees our heart)

Why would He not pray for us when we speak in gibberish as we are attempting to learn?

What Father tells his child he'll never walk because he falls the first 75 times he tries to stand up on legs that never walked, only crawled?

What Mother tells her child she'll never pass 7th grade English because at 12 months she only has 4 words and they are only discernible to her Mother; no one else has a clue what she is saying?

Personally, I believe that God is such a loving God that if we want to do something for Him, and we try and we strive (even though we don't need to strive!) and we have a heart, and we have His Spirit - He will receive our offering of an effort, and He will instruct and grow us!

Allow yourself the grace to fail at first, the faith to believe He will speak through you, and the tenacity to pray more in the Spirit until it becomes natural.

Also, you can pray in the understanding, and you can pray in the Spirit, and you can move back and forth from praying in the Spirit and praying in your words and understanding.

> **Connection Space:**
>
> If you pray in the Spirit, take something to the Lord, and pray in the Spirit.
>
> Just trust Him with the words, just trust Him with the outcome.
>
> Take something you don't know what to pray for, and pray something like this:
>
> Lord, I don't know how to pray for this.
>
> I know You can help me, but I don't know the words.
>
> Will You give me the words?
>
> Or will You simply pray it for me?
>
> Then be silent . . .
>
> Just wait . . .
>
> What do you sense?

Is it possible He's listening, and He's praying for you?

Is it possible you could ask Him, Lord, I'm going to just thank You for the next 5 minutes . . .

And while I'm thanking You will You turn these words into Your own groanings, Your own prayers for my situation?

Thank You, Lord

Thank You, Lord

Oh! Lord, I thank You for this clarity . . .

I thank You in advance for the solution

Thank You for hearing me

Thank You for praying for me

My note: I can sense my own spirit bubbling up to pray in tongues . . .

Ala sha ma ka

Ba maka la mala ka

Oh! Lord, ala ma la

I love You Lord!

This so uncomfortable to me!

But I ask that even these syllables would be converted to the reader's prayers . . .

Oh! Lord, I worship You!

Give the reader what they need . . .

Their next step

Their next revelation

Their next step in the Spirit,

I love You Lord,

Ala ma ka va neku

Asha ba ka lama

Ka ra ka lapeku to go tu

Oh! Lord . . . I love You Lord!

May Your Spirit continue the work You are doing here . . .

I sense Your Spirit groaning even as I struggle to type out the right syllables . . .

I'm not used to cognitively thinking like this when praying in the Spirit and yet I feel so compelled to allow it to bubble up . . .

Go ahead, Son . . .

Ava ka le mu

Ah ka lo re mu

may ka la ro ki mu li va

Gra la ma ka ve nu mi

Oh! Lord my God -

May Your Spirit breathe life on these syllables

Even each time a reader perceives them . . .

That there's life and interpretation in these syllables to the reader

I love You Lord!

When Speaking in Tongues Doesn't Come Easily

To all who have begged God for the gift of tongues, perhaps you have sat in His presence for hours waiting for Him to speak through you, I suggest:

Simply start talking.

Speak gibberish if you need to at first.

Have faith that just like a 12 month old with words no one can understand and a 15 month old that falls 75 times to take his first step, if you speak gibberish for a few hours or a few days or even a few months, over time God will speak THROUGH you.

My suspicion is you will actually have the Spirit of God speaking through you in the first few minutes.

Let Him lead.

In faith.

Have faith.

But don't just be silent and expect Him to force your lips to move.

He doesn't force you to pray certain words in the natural, why would He force certain words in tongues!

The other spiritual gifts don't work without our participation, either. For others to be healed, we have to pray and lay hands on them. For people to be saved we must speak. For foreign nations to have the first Bible in their language, missionaries had to learn the language and write out the translation.

For us to speak in tongues, we have to participate and speak!

I encourage you to have faith and step out and start speaking in tongues. Say words you don't understand and trust that you are in participation with the God of the Universe and the Spirit of God within you to produce prayers you don't understand that availeth much. Trust that He is praying for you with groanings you don't understand.

The Bible tells us that without faith it is impossible to please God (Hebrews 11:6).

Contrapositive to that statement is that we please God with faith.

Just like a small child drawing a picture of a tree that looks more like a scarecrow than a tree, but that child pleases us with their drawing so much we want to cry, we please God when we have faith; we please God when we try to do something we don't understand, just to please Him.

Take a few minutes now and talk with Him.

Ask Him to empower you.

Ask Him to give you words.

And just start talking!

Connection Space:

Just take that time now!

No guidance from me . . .

Just take 5 with the Lord!

Let Him lead your voice!

Extensive Private Praying in the Spirit

I have discovered that when I spend more time praying in the Spirit, I get more clarity, I experience a deeper level of calm, and it's easier to communicate with Him in the understanding.

Jude tells us:

But ye, beloved, building up yourselves on your most holy faith, praying in the Holy Ghost, (Jude 20)

We are built up and edified when we pray in the Holy Spirit.

Earlier in my journey, praying in the Spirit language, in tongues, felt like an effort, as if it were work. I had to work hard to remain focused and intentional. I felt as though I were striving to do some "work" or to speak with intent and authority.

But over time, praying in the Spirit has become much more natural and calm. If I am fighting a battle, I may pray in tongues and I can feel as though my prayers - even though I don't understand them - are being converted to prayers that are used on tasks of His choosing!

There are times when I will pray in the Spirit for 30 minutes or an hour, and even times when I have felt Him ask me to pray in the Spirit for an extended period of time, with the specific intent of praying into something He is doing in the Spirit world.

Many times if I pray in the Spirit long enough, I will no longer see the problem as a problem, or I realize that He's got it covered, I don't worry about it, and a few days later the problem has been resolved. Praying in the Spirit is so very very powerful, and it's worth the effort to get comfortable with it!

I've also felt led to pray in the Spirit several times with an intent to pray on a specific topic, but allowing the Lord to convert my prayers into the exact prayers needed. I simply pray in the Spirit, and trust Him that He is converting my prayers into the words He chooses to activate His will.

> **Connection Space:**
>
> Set aside time soon to just pray in tongues.
>
> This might only be 5 or 10 minutes at first; that's okay.
>
> Just spend time praying in tongues.
>
> Accept that you don't know what you are saying.
>
> Accept that it might not all be right.
>
> Accept that you are uncomfortable.
>
> Accept . . . anything.
>
> Just spend that time with Jesus, praying in tongues!
>
> You don't understand . . . that's part of the point!
>
> Spend time with Jesus!

PART 4: WALKING WITH JESUS

18

Time With Jesus

We've covered a lot so far, essentially the primary practices I've engaged in to draw radically closer to Him. I know from experience that each of those components don't happen overnight, and you grow into each of them. There's time and ongoing engagement that simply has to occur! And without intentionally implementing that engagement with Him daily and over the long term, you are unlikely to grow as close to Him as you want.

Plan Time With Him

Decide on some times daily when you will spend with Him, and you can spend more time as you wish.

That might be in the morning, lunchtime and evening. Or it might be a more robust session in the morning or the evening. Try it out and test out what works for you. If you are not a morning person, trying to get focused before your normal waking time likely won't work long term! And if you are not a night person, you will likely fall asleep during an evening quiet time!

Meaningful Quiet Time

Let's design a meaningful quiet time. Considering these practices:

Praise and Worship

Thankfulness

Prayer

Bible Study

Talking With Him

Journaling

Praying in the Spirit

We can engage in any of these activities at any time; they don't need to be organized as a quiet time, or one unit.

I'll share what I typically do in a quiet time, time I've set aside to fully engage with Him.

But there are many other times during the day when I will simply pray for 30 minutes, or I am singing with praise music while driving, or I am praying in the Spirit for some time, or I am even talking with Him between appointments, recording sessions, or classes. Or I just go for a walk with Him and talk. Or even just soak in His Presence. And for those things, there is no formula!

SAMPLE QUIET TIME:

Praise and worship 10-15 minutes

Bible Study 10-15 minutes

Prayer for myself 5 minutes

Prayer for others 5 minutes

Talking or Journaling 10-15 minutes

Praying in the Spirit 15 minutes

How hard it is to put time frames in there. It's not a formula. It's different every day. Sometimes I praise for 45 minutes and read the Word for 5 minutes. Sometimes I praise for 5 minutes and I'm so engrossed in a Bible passage that I spend 45 minutes there. Sometimes I don't pray for myself. Some days I pray more. Some days I don't pray for anyone else. Some days someone is on my heart and I pray more.

Each day is different.

And there's no set amount of time.

Sure, I might set aside 30 minutes or an hour, and I might not spend that much time with Him.

Or I might spend more.

Some days I might just walk and talk with Him in the morning over my first cup of coffee or two.

I'll likely spend an hour walking with Him today.

And some time praising in the car.

Each day is different.

Each quiet time is different.

> **Connection Space:**
>
> Reflect on this with the Lord:
>
> Imagine spending enough time with the Lord, throughout the day, that you feel constantly "plugged in" to Him and His Presence.
>
> How does it feel to consider being constantly "plugged in" to the Lord?
>
> Is it scary, exciting, perhaps unknown?
>
> Have you experienced having a quiet time in the morning, and feeling like you are "filled up" for the day?
>
> Have you ever experienced coming to a time in your day when it felt like your "filling up" had run out?
>
> Have you yearned to spend more time with Him . . . but life was in the way, there was noise and chaos around you?

How does it feel to consider that possibly you can live that constant presence - all day long - even in the presence of people and noise and chaos?

Take this to the Lord, in your own words . . . .

Tell Him how you feel about being so close.

Ask Him anything . . .

The strength to lean into it . . .

The desire . . .

If you have fear . . . ask Him to help you with it.

If you are excited . . . thank Him for it.

Tell Him your heart . . .

Ask Him how you can spend more time with Him during the day.

Ask Him how you can be more aware of Him throughout your day, and even in breaks between activities.

He wants to be closer to you!

Lord, we love You, and we are so grateful You are drawing us closer!

Thank You!

Sample Devotional Time

Sometimes perhaps you want to spend time with Him but you are tired or it's late or it's too early, and you just don't know where to start.

I've written a sample devotional or quiet time guide:

Opening Prayer:

Lord, I come to You joyful and hesitant to start this journey. I invite You into my thoughts, my mind, and my heart.

Thank You for being here for me, thank You for Your love, thank You for Your availability.

Guide me in this time with You, lead me to think Your thoughts, to hear from You, and to enjoy my time with You.

In Jesus name, Amen!

Worship the Lord:

You are Worthy, Lord, I love You Jesus,

I'm thankful for Your presence, I'm thankful for this time.

You are the Source of all my thought, of all my supply, meeter of all my needs.

You are my Provider, my ever present help in time of need!

You are always here, waiting for me, praying for me, loving me.

Thank You for being here with me and for me!

You are worthy, Lord, You are worthy.

Thank You Lord for all You are and all You do!

I love You, Lord!

Bible Reading

Choose a passage from the Word. Some great places to start when you don't have a theme in mind are:

The Psalms

The Gospels (Matthew, Mark, Luke, John)

The short epistles (Galatians, Ephesians, Colossians, Philippians, James)

The Proverbs

The longer epistles (I & II Corinthians, I & II Thessalonians, I & II Timothy)

If you read through all of those books, you'll have quite a bit of exposure to core themes in the Word and practical advice.

You can read a chapter a day, and contemplate the meaning of the passage for yourself.

Talk With the Lord:

Lord, I am feeling _____ about _____. What do You want me to know about that?

What do You want me to do?

What's my next step?

Talk with Him

Talk with Him openly and conversationally. Be thankful. Possibly praise more. Spend time praying in tongues if you can. Lean into Him and His presence.

Spend time in prayer:

Tell Him your needs and concerns.

Thank Him for His solutions and providence.

Talk with Him about your love for Him.

Talk with Him about what's going on in your life.

Intercede for others in your life who need help and need Him.

Pray blessing over those in your life, even those who have hurt you.

Pray for your own strength and ongoing focus on Him.

Anything you are focusing on where you need strength from Him, ask for it!

You can share your deepest needs with Him!

His desire is to give you the desires of your heart!

Pray in the Spirit as you are able.

I have found that praying in the Spirit is so very empowering, and adds a strong level of closeness in my walk with Jesus!

There is no limit to how you can pray and just talk with the Lord!

Close with Reflection and Thanksgiving, in your words

Thank You Lord for hearing my prayers, for being here with me!

Thank You for advising me, and giving me ideas!

Thank You for being here even as I'm searching new ways to hear and understand You!

I love You, Lord!

Of course you can add or subtract anything from this sample devotional guide. It's really given to give you a starting point should you desire one. However, it's very similar to the pattern I typically use during a quiet time or devotional.

How Much Structured Time With Jesus?

How much structured time do you need to spend with the Lord? On the one hand we can think, I want to spend as much time as I can. But on the other hand, in reality, sometimes you get bored or tired of whatever the activity is you are engaging in with Him, and there are real-world limitations on how much time you have in your day.

Our human nature, distractions, people around us, and our own emotional and mental noise, can make it hard to take the time we need.

At first you may need to spend more time with Him. Later it might not be as much, or the activities change. Maybe you go through a time in the future where you want or need more time. Although time doesn't make you closer, time is the container in which you worship and praise and talk with Him.

Some people like to meet with Him first thing in the morning for 20 minutes, 30 minutes, an hour. Others prefer to spend the last hour of the day with Him.

You might find that 15 minutes in the morning, 15 minutes at lunch time, and 15 minutes in the evening is better for you.

That's the structured time you set aside. You might also have pockets of time during the day when you find yourself scrolling or otherwise wasting time that could be converted into time with Him. (Is it okay if I suggest that mindlessly scrolling, or worse yet, seeing other people's vanity feeds that make you feel insecure, is wasting time?)

What if you were to convert some of those pockets of time into time with Him? Could you add some additional 10 - 15 minute segments of time with Him at various intervals during the day? Perhaps there's a walk you can take during the day that can be directed to time with Him.

In a family situation that has shared values about spending time with Him, some of that time could be shared time. You worship together, you pray together, you pray in tongues together.

It truly varies from person to person, lifestyle to lifestyle, and family situation to family situation. And it may also morph over time.

Connection Space:

Consider when you can best spend time with Jesus.

Ask yourself, what would work best for you?

How can you fit in quiet time with Him in your current schedule?

Is there something you can remove - even temporarily - so you can spend more time with Him?

Write it out if you need to.

Let's pray:

Lord, show us when to spend more time with You.

Help me in the process of determining what's best now, and long term.

> Where can I spend more time with You?
>
> Are there small moments when I can add in small segments of prayer or worship?
>
> Lord, we love You and want to spend more time with You!
>
> Amen.

Intentional Focus on Jesus In the Morning

Sometimes when we wake up, our mind immediately goes to our problems or our challenges.

What would happen if you thought about something different than that, first thing in the morning?

Imagine you had a morning declaration that contained some level of resolve to focus on Him exclusively for some period of time and you would say that over yourself, or to God, each morning?

When you do that, you immediately are directing your mind to Jesus rather than allowing it to go whereever it chooses.

Here are a few examples:

I look to You, Jesus, the Author and Finisher of my faith, and I know You will take me all the way through this day.

I set my eyes on Jesus today, and I will keep You first in everything.

Good morning, Lord! Help me keep You first today! I'll focus on You this first hour of the day to set the pace.

Jesus, I look to You for wisdom and guidance today, and I'll wait for Your leading before I begin my day.

What could yours be?

When you start the day with a statement of intention like this, it immediately refocuses your mind on the fact that you want to keep your eyes on Him all day. Your eyes are now on Him. You choose to spend more intentional time with Him.

Walks With the Lord

Sometimes I find it difficult to just sit and talk with Him. I enjoy walking, I enjoy talking with people while walking, so why not walk with God?

I go on walks - some very long walks - with the Lord. Through parks, greenbelts, even neighborhoods. I've walked with Him in the mountains, around parks. We enjoy our time together!

On these walks I might engage in any or all of the activities in this book: praise and worship, conversing with Him, praying in the Spirit, or just talking out loud and knowing He's there.

When you walk with the Lord, keep your eyes on Him, and give yourself the space and time to truly engage with Him in the same type of worship or conversation you would have in your special chair or prayer closet. Those walks can be mighty special, and yield great fruit.

Spending Personal Time With Him

I remember one time in the heat of the battle I felt like I should just spend the evening doing not much of anything. Wandering.

I was thinking, God, this feels so unproductive. No conversation with You. No Bible Study. No journaling. Just wasted time.

I heard His voice in my spirit:

Sean, if you could spend the next 3 hours with another human...

Just hanging out.

And you enjoyed your time with them.

And you did nothing.

Or nothing of consequence.

But you enjoyed the time, you enjoyed their presence, would it be wasted time?

No, Lord, it would not be wasted.

It would have been valuable.

Why?

Because we simply enjoyed the time, we enjoyed each others' company.

We grew closer.

The Lord said,

And that's how it is with me.

Come, walk with Me. Wander with Me. Enjoy Me and I'll enjoy you.

Friends, that was an amazing evening, just walking and wandering, with the Lord.

Connection Space:

Consider an activity or a time you can spend with the Lord with no expectation.

Just you and He.

No expectation.

Talk if you want.

Listen if He speaks.

Just enjoy time with Him.

What would it mean for you to have a few hours or even a day or two to just spend time with the Lord with no expectation, no formula?

If you need to, start small. Ask Him when He wants to spend "wasted time" with you!

19

Community

People in Your Growth With Jesus

So much of this book has focused on your own individual steps in your journey to closeness with Jesus. Your walk with Jesus is personal, and so much of it can only be lived out with Him.

However, Jesus designed the church so that we can help each other and support each other in our pain.

Wherefore comfort yourselves together, and edify one another, even as also ye do. (I Thessalonians 5:11)

Even extracting from one of the core passages in this book:

And the glory which thou gavest me I have given them; that they may be one, even as we are one: (John 17:22)

His original design is for us to grow together, to be one together, to grow with Him together. We are designed to love each other and support each other and be there for each other.

In my own journey, I spent significant time alone, growing close to Him. Then I would spend time with others and would receive words and encouragement. I would take that back to my private time with Him and receive new insights. And then come back to group time!

Jesus did the same thing! He spent 40 days in the wilderness alone. Then He spent significant time with His disciples as a group. He spent significant time ministering to people in small groups, in their homes, bonding with them, and guiding them. Then He would get away to the mountains or the "other side of the lake." He would refresh His Spirit privately, allow His natural body and soul the break it needed, then He came back together in a group.

We are designed to have a vertical relationship with Him that's very private, plus a holistic group relationship with Him that's not so private, and yet it's still deep! But we also don't grow closer to Jesus just by absorbing someone else's relationship with Him.

However, some of the things that hinder us from closeness with Jesus, like emotions or pain or unforgiveness, are things that can be worked out in the presence of others.

During my own trial, I learned to be vulnerable and share with others my deep pain. And yes, before you ask, I was hurt some by doing that. Some people didn't keep some things to themselves and I was hurt by it. Some people said things to me months later that were hurtful. Some people I hadn't seen in months and their first question felt unthoughtful, condemning, or as if they were more concerned with some detail than about me personally.

And I was hurt.

Did they mean to hurt me? Very unlikely! Is it possible they were sometimes unthoughtful or not considerate of the private feelings shared with them? Possibly. Maybe in my own pain I was over-sensitive.

The bottom line is, I was hurt, and I worked with the assumption they didn't mean it to be hurtful.

So I accept that I was hurt, but I love them and move on.

But I also know that I wouldn't have experienced all the healing I received if I hadn't been vulnerable in some small groups where I didn't know and trust everyone. But I shared anyway.

And I cried. And people saw my pain deeply.

And I was hurt some.

But it was worth it.

So I encourage you to reframe not being willing to share vulnerably because you might get hurt.

You probably will get hurt.

But it's probably better to release things, cry, and be hurt a little by others, than to hold onto it all for the rest of your life. That's the perspective that's helped me the most.

I needed the release of the vulnerability of sharing, and the benefit was far greater than the occasional pain from people saying hurtful things later (or even at the time!).

I don't believe there's a one size fits all solution to this. I went to some groups for one session. I realized that group wasn't a good fit for me. So I didn't go back. I went to some groups for 3 months, while I was benefiting. But once I received my healing on that issue, the group was no longer helping, so I stopped going. And there are some circles I'm still involved in a year later.

There's likely to be trial and error for you as well, finding the right group of people to help support you during your trial or growth. And that group might not be the right group for months or years; it might serve a purpose now but that changes over time.

As you process life with others you can gain insight from their own faith walk and their own walk with Jesus!

Growing With People's Words

Although most of what's written in this book is rooted in the Word, much of it I discovered through other people.

In discussion with fellow brothers and sisters.

Being exhorted by fellow brothers and sisters.

Discussing a thorny issue, and being given a fresh perspective from someone who was a step (or many) ahead of me in that area.

God uses His community, and the people within it, to live out His purpose in our lives as well. He may answer prayers through people. He may give direction or correction or encouragement through people.

I recall that when I was going through the first 10-12 months of my own recent trial, so many people came to me and prayed over me and offered words of encouragement, words that were often likely words of knowledge. I wrote most of those words down in a journal.

When I was talking with the Lord about direction, or to recall His participation and guidance, I would read through those words. In retrospect, I can see a thread of progression in those seemingly random words. Initially, they were words and pictures of deep pain, phrases like "I see God reconstructing your life all the way down to the roots," "There will be fruit from this trial, much greater than you can imagine," and even the encouragement to allow His consuming fire to burn away the wood, hay, straw, and stubble I resultantly prayed out.

Over time the messages became messages of endurance, keep your eyes on Jesus and He'll take you all the way through, that God is working a new thing, that there is a hope in the future, that what He is orchestrating is bigger and better than anything in the past. As the active part of that trial came to a close, shortly before the beginning of this book, I heard words of encouragement. Afterwards words indicating rest, and confirmations that I am hearing His Voice. And since then I've received fewer words of knowledge, direction, or confirmation. As my own internal closeness and dialogue with Him has grown much deeper, I have been receiving fewer encouraging words from others; instead I'm hearing more from Him.

It's very interesting, but as that shift occurred, I have found myself saying things to folks, not necessarily feeling inspired by God, but sometimes so, and those folks telling me that they were just asking God about that a few days ago, or that what I was sharing was confirmation to them about something in their lives.

Looking back, I see that I went through a progression of seasons in what I received and in receiving His voice through others, and that over time I began to enter a progression of seasons where I have been speaking to others. It's awe-inspiring for me to consider it, because it renews my personal, internal sense of how carefully He shepherds us with exactly what we need at the time, through others, and how He shepherds others with exactly what they need, through me and others.

And the most recent example of His use of His church, His children, and His community is in the confirmation to write these pages about community!

The book was nearly finished, but I was feeling there were a few small topics that were not addressed: this material on community, confession and recovery after backsliding or a sinful slip-up, the impact of confession and vulnerability, and how to bring emotions like fear, anxiety, and worry to the Lord.

I was having a conversation with the Lord, telling Him (yes, the audacity!) the pros and cons of adding still more material. Feeling doubt that I was still following His guidance in finishing the book. Even doubting that I had put in too much depth. Lord, are these topics necessary and relevant under the umbrella of "Growing Close to Jesus"?

I head to a coffee shop to do the work, my natural intention to write these out and then somehow make the decision to add or not add the new content, continuing to wrestle with the decision. As soon as my coffee was delivered, I looked up and two brothers were meeting with no agenda except they had said let's meet up and see where the Lord leads us. Within minutes we are 30 seconds apart in a coffee shop, having never seen each other there in the past. After a time of sharing between us, they asked about the topics. I shared with them the topics, my concern that they were extraneous material, one jokingly suggested another book, and then finally laid out the following argument:

> Deal with fear and anxiety because they block us from growing closer to Christ.
>
> Deal with community because He has given us community to grow us closer to Him.
>
> Confession and vulnerability are vital to drawing closer to Jesus.

Although that's a paraphrase from memory a few minutes ago, you can see how that language aligns so deeply with my own words (hopefully inspired/directed by God) in this book . . . and they haven't read it, nor even excerpts.

I immediately began to feel a deep sense of His awesome, expansive, and yet personal presence. An incredible sense of calm came over me, identical to what I experience when in personal communion with Him, or deep in a worship set. But right here, in a coffee shop, people all around, and two brothers looking me in the eyes. I felt such an amazing confirmation that He had just given me His answer not in a silent prayer, not as a nudge in my heart, but in the words spoken by my brothers in Christ.

I sensed such an amazing confirmation that He uses people to answer many of our prayers, He uses community to draw us closer to Him.

I encourage you to spend time with fellow Christian brothers or sisters, without expectation, but open to His leading, growing deep together.

God is such a loving, loving God, and His model for growing close to Him includes people, whether we think of it as "church," "fellowship," "community," or "that they may be one in us."

So many of the words, encouragements, and confirmations have occurred in seemingly random occurrences that were led by God, but they occurred in proximity with fellow believers (or even in random places, but God sent the believers to me).

Spend time with Christian brothers and sisters, share vulnerably, take the risk of being hurt, and be open to Him speaking to you through them.

A Model for Vulnerable Sharing

Entire books have likely been written about how to share vulnerably, and yet I've seen modeled a very simple yet scalable framework.

I've been a part of this with as few as 3 people, and in as large a group as 27, personally.

In a larger group, it might be explained that this will be a time of sharing, holding space, and listening to what's going on in each others' lives. Sometimes "groundrules" are announced: no teaching, preaching, or giving advice. We're simply listening and caring.

In a smaller setting, one person might open with a question to one of the others, such as, how are you really doing? or, what is painful right now?

The person responds honestly and vulnerably with the good, the weak, what they may be struggling with. Others in the group might ask a few clarifying questions, but it's not an interrogation. Advice is not given unless specifically asked for. Someone might ask, can we pray for you?

There is no judgment or correction. No agenda except to create space. Then it's someone else's turn.

In some theoretical sense, each person might share for 5 - 7 minutes. But in reality some take longer and others need less. Ideally it's spirit - led but we are humans and not everyone in a group may have the same depth of connection with Him - some more, some less.

In a larger group, there may need to be a moderator, someone who can pull things back if one person needs significantly more time or emotional support and it's taking away from the group.

Of course this is a great way to see those needs, so someone can step in and offer deeper interaction in a separate setting in the future!

In a very small group, as was honestly modeled by my two brothers in the example of confirmation from God about the inclusion of this material, these brothers naturally asked these questions of each other, they shared vulnerably, and I believe each received something from the Lord much as I received the confirmation from Him through them!

The Impact of Community on My Own Journey

Prior to this most recent experience and God's moving in my life, I had been quite involved in many church communities in the past, as a participant, as a teacher, or as a leader, but I always felt as though I just performed a perfunctory role instead of feeling as if I were a vital part of a community. My role might have been to listen and participate, or my role was to teach, or my role was to lead. But I didn't feel like I was part of a community, nor did those experiences necessarily draw me closer to Him. My growth with Him was normally, for decades, during personal prayer and time with Him.

I had also experienced "church hurt," times when people in church did things I perceived as hurtful, I felt ignored and my opinion unvaluable, and I felt like an unappreciated "worker" at times.

But during the 18 months preceding this book, the Lord showed me, through so many individual humans, His amazing love and grace.

The greeter at one church who would offer me a few words of encouragement week in, week out.

The woman who told me she perceived I was worshiping the Lord by striving and trying to prove something to Him, and that I didn't need to strive to worship and please Him; that radically impacted my worship and my relationship with Him.

A short term worship community in which I met someone who modeled worshiping the Lord with abandon; being focused only on Him and not others' judgment. Worshiping alongside her was transformative for me, and that experience was a formational part of my journey. That short term worship community no longer meets in that way, and yet the seed of growth in me was orchestrated by God through a godly Christian sister who was so humble and non-assuming, as she danced with the Lord.

The advice I received from a dear brother in the Lord about hearing the voice of God . . . the confirmations I've shared elsewhere in this book, the people who have told me that my boldness in worship inspires them . . . the man who showed up (randomly?) at the same restaurant as I was meeting another brother to give advice . . . and his wife gave me critical advice to be used during my meeting, without which I would have been rudderless and possibly hurt more than I helped.

I could go on and on.

For all the personal activities in this book that grow us closer to Jesus individually, so much of those would not have occurred without the community of saints around me - many of whom I've shared were one-time "chance?" meetings in parks, plazas, or worship services.

Of course there's one thing that's necessary for any of this to be possible: to engage in community in this way requires getting out of your house, out of your comfort zone, and not just "going to church," but participating, being in groups, open to talk with people, spending time in public.

None of these occurrences happened with someone stepping through a wall into my private closet! They have all occurred in public, in gatherings, with other Christians, or in coffee shops or parks.

20

Walk in the Spirit

Walking in the Spirit is accompanying, setting our affections on, and being led by the Holy Spirit in our day-to-day lives, such that we exhibit the nature and characteristics of the Holy Spirit in our daily lives (the fruit of the Spirit):

But the fruit of the Spirit is love, joy, peace, longsuffering, gentleness, goodness, faith,

Meekness, temperance: against such there is no law. (Galatians 5:22-23)

Walking in the Spirit is living and walking out the life of Christ inside us.

It is accompanying and keeping in step with the Spirit as we live out our daily lives.

It's minding the things of the Spirit instead of the things of the flesh:

For they that are after the flesh do mind the things of the flesh; but they that are after the Spirit the things of the Spirit. (Romans 8:5)

It's being led by the Spirit:

For as many as are led by the Spirit of God, they are the sons of God. (Romans 8:14)

Walking in the Spirit is doing the life we have inside:

If we live in the Spirit, let us also walk in the Spirit. (Galatians 5:25)

When we are led by the Spirit, we walk out the fruit of the Spirit, and we live in peace and joy. We live empowered, and content, and generously. We are given insights and wisdom from the Lord.

Paul clearly defined walking in the Spirit as being free from the law of sin and death, operating in the Spirit instead of the flesh, and ultimately the righteousness of the law is fulfilled in us:

For the law of the Spirit of life in Christ Jesus hath made me free from the law of sin and death. (Romans 8:2)

That the righteousness of the law might be fulfilled in us, who walk not after the flesh, but after the Spirit. (Romans 8:4)

He even concludes, as Jesus said in Matthew 22:37-40, that the law is fulfilled in loving each other:

For all the law is fulfilled in one word, even in this; Thou shalt love thy neighbour as thyself. (Romans 5:14)

Simplistically, we have the fruit of the Spirit (peace, joy, love, gentleness, faith, humility, self-control, patience, and goodness) and the lived - out fulfillment of that is loving our neighbor, our family, and our community. And when we are living it out, we won't commit the sins of the flesh:

This I say then, Walk in the Spirit, and ye shall not fulfil the lust of the flesh. (Galatian 5:14,16)

It's all wrapped up together: freedom from the letter of the law, walk in the Spirit and the righteousness of the law is fulfilled in us, and as we walk in the fruit of the Spirit, we simply won't operate in the sin of the flesh!

But it also is not something that automatically just lives out the life of God in us. I believe that's why it's called a walk: because although He provides the power and the life and even His Spirit, we have to accompany His Spirit, focus on Him, and allow Him to lead us. Paul said his flesh wants to follow the law, but his mind wants to walk in the Spirit:

I thank God through Jesus Christ our Lord. So then with the mind I myself serve the law of God; but with the flesh the law of sin. (Romans 7:25)

We have the Spirit of God dwelling in us. The fruit of the Spirit is evident when we are walking in the Spirit. But we have to walk with Him in order for us to live out the abundant life and freedom he has provided!

If we were to reverse engineer walking in the Spirit by the fruit, we would see that we would be walking in peace, joy, love, gentleness, faith, humility, self-control, patience, and goodness.

When we are immersed in His Presence, we are connected to the Jesus that lives inside us as the Holy Spirit, and we are filled with the Spirit, we live out the fruit of the Spirit.

This isn't something we do as much as something we are, something we become.

When I am in peace - not just an earthly calm - it is such a feeling of contentment that it is like joy. And when I am in peace and joy, and it's overflowing, I'm naturally patient.

And if I'm in peace and joy and patience and love, and fully immersed in those qualities, I'm really everything else as well.

If we walk out the fruit of the Spirit, we live powerful lives, we live out the Spirit of God that lives in us, and we live out the life Jesus was talking about when He said:

I am come that they might have life, and that they might have it more abundantly. (John 10:10b)

Walk in the Spirit, Be Edified, and Help Others

We are directed to walk in the Spirit so we are edified personally, we are helpful and loving towards others, and we leave behind our former life of the lust of the flesh:

If we live in the Spirit, let us also walk in the Spirit. (Galatians 5:25)

Wherefore comfort yourselves together, and edify one another, even as also ye do. (I Thessalonians 5:11)

Let us therefore follow after the things which make for peace, and things wherewith one may edify another. (Romans 14:19)

How is it then, brethren? when ye come together, every one of you hath a psalm, hath a doctrine, hath a tongue, hath a revelation, hath an interpretation. Let all things be done unto edifying. (I Corinthians 14:26)

This I say then, Walk in the Spirit, and ye shall not fulfil the lust of the flesh. (Galatians 5:16)

When we walk in the Spirit and actively produce the fruit of the Spirit, the result will be that we do good works, both for those who are fellow believers, and for those who are not believers! We will naturally live a life of giving to others, helping others, and being hospitable; and by actively walking in the Spirit and producing fruit, we will naturally stamp out (replace) our old sinful desires.

Here are just a few passages that indicate how we can walk out the Spirit-filled life:

Let him that is taught in the word communicate unto him that teacheth in all good things.

And let us not be weary in well doing: for in due season we shall reap, if we faint not.

As we have therefore opportunity, let us do good unto all men, especially unto them who are of the household of faith. (Galatian 6:6,9-10)

I believe this passage is one of the best single-source descriptions of how to daily live the Christian life:

Be kindly affectioned one to another with brotherly love; in honour preferring one another;

Not slothful in business; fervent in spirit; serving the Lord;

Rejoicing in hope; patient in tribulation; continuing instant in prayer;

Distributing to the necessity of saints; given to hospitality.

Bless them which persecute you: bless, and curse not.

Rejoice with them that do rejoice, and weep with them that weep.

Be of the same mind one toward another. Mind not high things, but condescend to men of low estate. Be not wise in your own conceits.

Recompense to no man evil for evil. Provide things honest in the sight of all men.

If it be possible, as much as lieth in you, live peaceably with all men. (Romans 12:10-18)

I think it's important to note, these are not just lists of good things to do, like a New Testament law that replaces the old law!

Instead, these are the things we should naturally be bubbling up inside wanting to do, because of the Holy Spirit inside us urging us to help other saints, and even to help those who are not believers. Here are a couple more short passages that give us additional guidance:

Let brotherly love continue.

Be not forgetful to entertain strangers: for thereby some have entertained angels unawares.

Remember them that are in bonds, as bound with them; and them which suffer adversity, as being yourselves also in the body. (Hebrews 13:1-3)

And above all things have fervent charity among yourselves: for charity shall cover the multitude of sins.

Use hospitality one to another without grudging.

As every man hath received the gift, even so minister the same one to another, as good stewards of the manifold grace of God. (I Peter 4:8-10)

Taken together, those few passages summarize nearly the entire active Christian walk as it pertains to interacting with other people! Notice these admonitions are all about living out the love that Christ has already shown us.

It should be natural and normal for us to be hospitable, to help those who have needs, to visit those in prison (in bonds), and to have fervent charity (love).

This isn't a big list of "what to do," but instead it's in the spirit of "here are ways you can be helpful, hospitable, and loving towards others."

When we walk in the Spirit, we naturally want to be helpful, hospitable, and loving!

Remembering: *If we live in the Spirit, let us also walk in the Spirit.* (Galatians 5:25)

We have been redeemed; we have the Spirit of the living God living right inside us, informing our thoughts, speaking to us, guiding us, and filling us with His calm, His peace, His joy, and His love. The natural and normal response to that should be to help others and be loving, not because of a command, but simply because we are acting out what we are deep on the inside.

Of course sometimes we need reminders to act in a loving way, and to act in accordance with the Spirit inside of us!

You couldn't ask for better timing on this next story I'll tell on myself: I was literally just working on this section about walking in the Spirit. I was working in a quiet room in a library that I had specifically selected because it was quiet and distraction-free.

While I was writing I was interrupted by someone in such a way that my quiet was gone; there was a human distraction rustling papers and crinkling plastic bags, and now she wants to talk with me, ask me what I'm working on, and tell me about her project.

My initial gut-level and emotional response was to feel frustrated and irritated immediately. I wanted to protect my time and space while writing this "important" book (stepping into the ways of the flesh with irritation, pride, and self-importance).

The Word even tells us to be watchful for this very type of situation:

Follow peace with all men, and holiness, without which no man shall see the Lord:

Looking diligently lest any man fail of the grace of God; lest any root of bitterness springing up trouble you, and thereby many be defiled; (Hebrews 12:14-15)

Now, here's the thing, the situation occurred in seconds. Nearly immediately I was irritated, frustrated, and ready to pack up my computer and go somewhere else. In seconds.

I think this is important because it highlights that we usually don't get minutes or hours or days to decide to act Christlike.

Many moments that test us and show our true colors happen quickly, and our responses often happen before we have carefully considered the consequences.

As I write this, I am considering this verse:

Let your speech be always with grace, seasoned with salt, that ye may know how ye ought to answer every man. (Colossians 4:6)

That verse doesn't have an exclusion for when I'm irritated or interrupted, it says "always."

Thankfully, I quickly recognized what I was doing; it was like the Spirit reprimanded me immediately, and I thought, this isn't the right spirit.

Please note, it doesn't always happen that I respond immediately. Part of why I was so quick to reframe is that I have turned several people away in the process of writing this book, and have regretted each time.

Afterwards each time I've contemplated how hypocritical it was of me to turn away someone who might have only needed a few seconds of encouragement, or might have needed life-changing advice that was truly important, but in the moment I judged the "work I am doing" to be more important.

So when this situation occurred, my mental map told me immediately, this is like the times you failed . . . now is your chance to do it right!

So I reframed my mind, I accepted that this could wait a few minutes, and engaged her in conversation that hopefully makes a difference in her life.

Twenty minutes later I'm writing again. But without her interruption of my work, my fall back into the flesh, and the Holy Spirit's intervention, this passage wouldn't exist!

Just because we have His Spirit doesn't mean we will automatically live out the fruit of the Spirit, nor the loving, hospitable things in these lists; and that's why they are spelled out in the Word for us!

But when we are actively aware that His Spirit is within us, and His nature is to be loving and helpful, when we realize we have stepped back into the ways of the flesh, if only for a moment, we can have that cognitive moment, like I just did, and make a different decision - one to walk in the Spirit and not in the flesh.

Experientially, it's so much more rewarding and even enjoyable to walk in the Spirit than to walk in the flesh.

If I had stayed in the flesh, irritated and frustrated, instead of reframing my mind to set it on the "things of the Lord," ultimately I probably would have had a hard time getting back into the "flow" of writing anyhow, and might have been irritated and grumpy the rest of the day.

But because I chose to walk in the Spirit instead, the person was helped, which gave me personal satisfaction, and I was not only able to be honestly somewhat pleased that I had made the shift (because many times I don't, I end up irritated and frustrated for hours), I am now happily writing and continuing to enjoy the peace of the Lord.

The moral of the story, and I believe perhaps the specific reason I was given that "interruption," was so that we can all remember that our goal in walking in the Spirit is to live out the fruit and glorify God and edify others!

We can have private closeness with Jesus all the time, but if that doesn't translate into fruit that flows into others and builds corporate unity and closeness, then we are not complete in our closeness with Him.

Finally, be ye all of one mind, having compassion one of another, love as brethren, be pitiful, be courteous: (I Peter 3:8)

Finally, brethren, farewell. Be perfect, be of good comfort, be of one mind, live in peace; and the God of love and peace shall be with you. (II Corinthians 13:11)

A new commandment I give unto you, That ye love one another; as I have loved you, that ye also love one another.

By this shall all men know that ye are my disciples, if ye have love one to another. (John 13:34-35)

That they all may be one; as thou, Father, art in me, and I in thee, that they also may be one in us: that the world may believe that thou hast sent me.

And the glory which thou gavest me I have given them; that they may be one, even as we are one:

I in them, and thou in me, that they may be made perfect in one; and that the world may know that thou hast sent me, and hast loved them, as thou hast loved me. (John 17:21-23)

Walking in the Spirit is not only having the fruit of the Spirit for our own use and edification, but for the unity and common good of all the saints!

Power of the Holy Spirit

Consider Paul's prayer to the Ephesians:

That the God of our Lord Jesus Christ, the Father of glory, may give unto you the spirit of wisdom and revelation in the knowledge of him:

The eyes of your understanding being enlightened; that ye may know what is the hope of his calling, and what the riches of the glory of his inheritance in the saints,

And what is the exceeding greatness of his power to us-ward who believe, according to the working of his mighty power, (Ephesians 1:17-19)

The power in that passage is unfathomable!

This is freely available to any believer who accesses it and takes hold of it.

Imagine living in a day-to-day, hour-to-hour reality of that depth of the Spirit.

Walking in the Spirit and living out the fruit of the Spirit.

Mysteries . . . deep things of Christ . . . spiritual discernment . . . exceeding greatness of His power!

Consider the life of excellence in the Spirit in which we could live and breathe and have our being if we were to partner with the Holy Spirit, who lives in us already, to fully partake of the full depth of His mysteries, the full mind of Christ, the deep things of God, and the spiritually discerned things of the Spirit of God.

This knowledge from the Spirit, this guidance from the Spirit, this day in - day out - living in the Spirit that I'm personally experiencing and walking in - and sharing with you - is available to you!

He can empower us to live out a full Spirit-led life of victory, service to others, and the fruit of the Spirit.

Consider this prayer of Paul's in his letter to the Ephesians:

That he would grant you, according to the riches of his glory, to be strengthened with might by his Spirit in the inner man;

That Christ may dwell in your hearts by faith; that ye, being rooted and grounded in love,

May be able to comprehend with all saints what is the breadth, and length, and depth, and height;

And to know the love of Christ, which passeth knowledge, that ye might be filled with all the fulness of God. (Ephesians 3:16-19)

He is praying that the Spirit, who lives in us (in the inner man), will strengthen us by His might. And that as we are rooted and grounded in love, and we are strengthened by His might ... we may be filled with all the fullness of God.

We can not only walk in the fruit of the Spirit and do the things that reflect His glory and His presence, but we can literally be filled with all the fullness of God.

Not some of the fullness, but all the fullness of God.

Not some of the fruit, but all of the fruit.

Not some of the power, but all of the power.

You know that His Spirit resides in you if you follow Jesus, you know you have access to His power, you know you have the fruit of the Spirit, you have the fullness of God, you can completely live out His life, His mission, His call, and His calm and peace in your life.

All the fullness of God.

We don't have to work up to anything, or be good enough for anything, or work for anything - He is already enough.

We simply have to accept it and lean into it so that we can live it out.

Right now, if you are stressed, you can simply remember that all the fullness of God is inside you now, including His complete calm.

You can gently lean into that calm, His calm that's already right there inside you, and you will begin to experience His calm. If you'll allow it, you can experience perfect calm.

God's calm is inside you. God's joy is inside you. God's peace is inside you.

If you are unrighteously angry you can remember that God's perfect peace is inside you, and gently lean into His perfect peace.

If you are impatient and you are so irritated that the line won't move faster, or traffic is crazy, you can literally lean back in your seat, remember that He is perfect peace, and lean into His peace.

When you lean into His peace, your irritation at the traffic will flow out of you and be replaced with a true calm. That might not make the traffic move faster, but at least you'll be calm in the middle of it!

No matter what negative emotion has risen up inside you, the presence of the Spirit can completely replace that emotion with the fruit of the Spirit.

When you are walking in the peace of the Holy Spirit, He simply displaces negative emotions and you become calm!

You can have all the fullness of God through the power of the Spirit of Christ within you - the Holy Spirit.

Imagine walking in love, joy, peace, longsuffering (patience), gentleness, goodness, faith, meekness (humility), and temperance all day every day in every situation!

How powerful!

And yet you can!

There is no condition on "Walk in the Spirit."

We don't have to read another book.

Pray another prayer.

Strive.

Work for His love.

Nothing.

No additional conditions.

We have His Spirit within us.

We can talk with His Spirit at any time.

We can walk in His Spirit by connecting with Him, talking with Him, keeping our focus on Him, and putting Him first.

If we simply walk in His Spirit, we will live in peace and joy and happiness and calm!

Connection Space:

Ask Jesus to help you allow the Spirit to guide you more.

Ask Jesus for wisdom to be open to the leading of the Spirit.

Commit to yourself that you will be more attuned, that you will notice when He is leading.

Notice when you are walking in the flesh, and simply make a commitment to spend some time in the Spirit.

Talk with the Lord now, tell Him your weakness.

Ask Him for wisdom, for His leading in that weakness.

Lord Jesus, I love You!

Lord, I want to be led by Your Spirit!

Lord, I want to come to You immediately when I step into the flesh, anger, or gossip, or anything.

Lord Jesus, remind me when I need to press into the Spirit.

Help me to enjoy spending time with the Spirit!

I love You, Jesus!

Amen

21

Rivers of Living Water

As we grow in Him, He calls us to minister to others. We are to become rivers of living water, pouring His Spirit into others as others have into us.

Before we talk about how we can step into that, I feel it's important to talk about getting the space and rest your body needs. Sometimes in Christian circles, especially when we have a performance mentality where we feel we constantly have to do more for Jesus, we can tend to put others' needs too far ahead of our own. Yes, of course we are to value others, be unselfish and loving, but that must be done within the reasonable constraints that God built into us as humans.

He didn't create us with unlimited capacity, physically, mentally, or emotionally.

Getting the Rest and Space Your Body Needs

We shouldn't be fighting our own tiredness in order to be kind.

We have a responsibility to take care of ourselves, our mind, and get the rest we need.

Jesus rested and the disciples made that clear by including it in the gospels. He is our model, not just for the spiritual things, but also for living real life, right here on earth. When He ministered to the crowds, He took time away to be with the Father, and to rest.

When He was walking from one mission to another, He talked and shared and taught, and stopped for others who had needs. And yet He was never stressed or burdened by it all, knowing He was on mission and was properly rested, in communion with the Father, and having a deep sense of the value of simply spending time with people.

But before I share how you can do that, I want to highlight that doesn't mean your physical or emotional self can handle constantly being with people, helping people, or being available to people.

Even Jesus modeled getting away from people to restore His own soul. After hearing of His cousin John the Baptist's death He departed to a desert place:

When Jesus heard of it, he departed thence by ship into a desert place apart: and when the people had heard thereof, they followed him on foot out of the cities. (Matthew 14:13)

He needed time away. But because the people followed Him, He spent at least the next day praying for them and healing them. Then He performed the miracle of feeding five thousand men plus women and children, with 5 loaves of bread and two fish. (Matthew 14:14-21)

Then He left to get away, again:

And straightway Jesus constrained his disciples to get into a ship, and to go before him unto the other side, while he sent the multitudes away.

And when he had sent the multitudes away, he went up into a mountain apart to pray: and when the evening was come, he was there alone. (Matthew 14:22-23)

Even Jesus needed time alone to recharge, so we should follow His example and get time alone to recharge.

Conduits of His Power, His Love, and His Spirit

Now that we have His Holy Spirit, and we are personally walking in the Spirit and we have the fruit of the Spirit, we become conduits of His power, His love, and His Spirit through us.

Jesus said:

He that believeth on me, as the scripture hath said, out of his belly shall flow rivers of living water.

(But this spake he of the Spirit, which they that believe on him should receive: for the Holy Ghost was not yet given; because that Jesus was not yet glorified.) (John 7:38-39)

Jesus was talking about the Holy Spirit, and saying that out of our bellies would flow rivers of living water. Imagine this is not only an infilling of ourselves with His Spirit and supernatural knowledge, this is also referring to how we will pour into others with His Spirit.

But the manifestation of the Spirit is given to every man to profit withal.

For to one is given by the Spirit the word of wisdom; to another the word of knowledge by the same Spirit;

To another faith by the same Spirit; to another the gifts of healing by the same Spirit;

To another the working of miracles; to another prophecy; to another discerning of spirits; to another divers kinds of tongues; to another the interpretation of tongues:

But all these worketh that one and the selfsame Spirit, dividing to every man severally as he will. (I Corinthians 12:7-11)

These are the various different ways the Spirit flows through us to help other people. We are given words of wisdom or knowledge for others, we are given the gift of healing for others, we are given prophecy or tongues, or interpretation of tongues.

This is the manifestation of the rivers of living water.

Wouldn't it make sense that the more closely aligned we are with His Spirit in us - the time we spend, the depth we engage in - that just as we get more from the Spirit personally when we draw deeper with Him, His Spirit will be able to flow through us more easily and be more evident to those around us?

No matter how much His Spirit intends to use us and flow through us, we have to open our mouths to prophecy, we have to say the words of healing, we have to move our lips to speak in tongues, and with time and use and experience we become more adept and able to do just that.

We become a better, more seasoned vessel over time, with more capacity to impact others with His Spirit.

Can we consider that we actually continue to grow closer to God, to Christ, to the Holy Spirit, when we are allowing His Spirit to flow through us like rivers of living water out of our belly?

Does our closeness to Him time out when we are full, or do we continue to grow closer to Him through the ministry to others?

Through my own 18 month trial, the first 12 months were very much about me. I was crying, and leaning on Him, and revisiting the very basics of my faith. And then I was growing closer to Him through the incredible amount and depth of time I spent with Him.

Over time, I began to share some of what had been happening in me, with others who were going through something similar. Over time that began to look more like I was pouring into others - like rivers of living water flowing through me.

This book of course is an element of those rivers of living water. I believe God has guided me to write this because some angle and aspect of the way I've experienced it is unique in the world, and might give others hope or depth or a new perspective on growing close to Him. I don't suspect anything in this book is new, in fact most of it is directly backed up by Scripture, and yet its very presence should draw others closer to Christ.

The same is the case for you. As you become filled with His Spirit, you embrace Him in a new way, perhaps you let some more go from your past, and lean into His deep Spirit in your life, you will begin to overflow in a new way into others. That's part of the very process of you growing closer to God!

The Spirit is unlimited. A friend of mine suggests that God is like an unlimited faceted diamond, and each facet is one of His unique attributes and each of us carries at least one unique facet. Of course that's not specifically scriptural, and yet when we think of God being infinitely unknowable, and yet able to pour into each of us infinitely over time, the earthly illustration may yet still not scratch the surface of His infinity and our uniqueness!

The question I begin to ponder is, depending on where on the arc of your journey you reside currently, and with the pace at which you are growing closer to Him, what's next for you?

Are you allowing some belief about what God can't put behind you to hold you back from some measure of the Spirit He wants to bequeath to you?

Are you possibly allowing the near unbelievability of the incredible measure of His Spirit and the effects of it to hold you back from believing you can actually access it?

The Word tells us His Spirit is available to all of us, but I do believe it's not just poured over us without our will and participation. It would smother and destroy us, especially if we used it incorrectly.

Imagine that each day for the rest of your life you could engage with God in such a way that each one of those days you grew a little closer to Him, you gained one new insight into Him, and you bequeathed one new insight to one other person in your world.

How much closer would you grow to God? How much more deeply could you engage with God and He with you?

How does it change how we live, and think? How does it change how we treat each other? How does it change how we treat the temple we live in?

We are spiritual beings, and when we immerse ourselves in these ideas, and we feel spiritual as well as just be spiritual, I believe it takes us to another level.

Even as I type, I look up and see people walking around and talking, and I have this realization that they are all spirits walking around. Sure, they are in these earth bodies and doing earth things and talking about earth concepts, but indeed they are spirits at their core.

They are spirits, but they inhabit this earthly body, and they have dreams and pains and hurts and betrayals and needs and . . . and . . . and.

I am not so isolated after all!

I may feel alone.

I may feel alone as I'm writing this.

Or when I'm in a room full of people and yet I feel alone.

But indeed I'm one of many many spirits in the room.

And is it possible that in my introverted shyness, fear of man, or embarrassment, I hold others back from experiencing the fullness of the Spirit?

I have this sense, like a living sense right now, that we are in this together.

I have this sense that He is in me, and I am in Him, and we are in each other. And that you are in a different location, even a different time reading this, and yet somehow we are inextricably linked by our spirits, and perhaps even strengthened by our joint act of me writing and you reading at this time.

Perhaps I've only walked this road a few months ahead of you.

You have grown, just like I have grown. But if you keep it locked inside you, it doesn't grow and spread and share.

And if He is in you, and you are in Him . . . what additional benefit would it be if you were to introduce others to some of the thoughts and the Spirit activity you are now engaged in?

Imagine we have rivers of living water pouring out of us that are fueled by His Spirit, and are designed for the sanctification and growth of those around us.

We are conduits for His love and spirit and grace and power.

In that position of being a conduit for His living water, rivers of living water that flow from us, the riverbed is made for the water to flow through it.

In the same way, with His power, we are designed to be riverbeds for His Spirit to flow through us to empower and touch others.

Because we are humans with limited capacity, we do need to take care of ourselves, get the mental and physical rest our human bodies need, and maintain our connection with His Spirit even as we are ministering or we will not be able to fulfill our calling effectively or without burnout.

In addition to our need for rest and restoration, some of the weariness we encounter in allowing His Spirit to flow through us comes from our frustration with others' personalities and behavior. So it can be helpful to consider the root of others' personalities and behavior.

Imagine we can see others as spiritual beings with needs, hurts, pains, hearts, and dreams.

Just as you have deep wounds and pains, hurts you want to avoid dealing with, perhaps pride you know must go, false shame and guilt the enemy uses against you, or any other hurt or pain, the others in your life have pain as well. Some mask it better than others. Some use pride or anger as a smoke screen so they appear controlling or even offensive instead of allowing themselves to feel their pain inside. And others lean so much into their pain that it's obvious.

So even as we are called, as Jesus was, to heal the sick, bind up the brokenhearted, offer strength to the weak, and comfort the hurting, we must manage our own energy and peace, combined with understanding others' pain and their possible reactions, so that we can most effectively be His hands and feet on earth!

I am personally grateful that part of the workmanship that He has created me personally for, is to share the truths He's unearthed in me, through fire and tears and pain and celebration with Him.

Even as I write that, I think about YOU, the reader.

You are His workmanship as well, and He has created you for works that He designed before the creation of the world.

Even as you are reading this book, He is preparing YOU to have an impact on others that has never been assigned to anyone but YOU, because you have a work inside you that He specifically prepared for you and you only.

He is preparing your heart for greater works than these, He is preparing your heart to give to others in a greater measure, He is preparing your heart and mind and soul to step fully into the work He created for you, before the foundation of the world.

Connection Space:

When you read those last few words about what He has created you for, is there something that comes to mind, perhaps a dream you had when you were a child, but it hasn't happened yet?

Perhaps a skill you have, but you haven't developed it?

Is there something you know in your heart of hearts that God has prepared you for, but it's been elusive?

Are you ready to take the next step towards pouring His love and His ministry and healing into others, as He has done for you?

Let's pray:

Father, I come before You now,

I don't know if there's a clear call in this person's heart right now, or not . . .

If there is, I ask that You will give them a reassurance that You are calling them back to fulfillment.

(If that's you, reader, take a moment to just think on that with the Lord, or if you are comfortable, tell the Lord your thoughts or feelings).

If there is not a clear call, Father, I ask that You will begin to reveal real purpose in this reader's heart and mind.

That as they read this book, apply these principles, pray and connect with You, they will begin to see not only the value in relationship with You, but also the call and drawing You have placed on their life!

We love You, Lord, and we're so grateful to have these moments to reflect and contemplate Your love, and Your kindness, and Your path and Your way.

I love You, Lord!

Amen

PART 5: DEFEAT SIN AND ADDICTION

22

Defeat Sin

Walk in the Spirit and Defeat Sin

If we truly want to be the closest with Jesus that we can, we must allow His Spirit to guide and train us to live better, more sanctified lives.

Part of our process of growing close to Jesus is not only living a life worthy of His sacrifice, but living a life that glorifies Him.

Although He loves us just as we are and we are His children if we never do anything else for Him, we also know that He wants us to live good lives, pure lives. Under the old set of rules, living in the flesh without His Holy Spirit, that was impossible (Galatians 2-5).

But with His power, with the indwelling power of the Holy Spirit, we can indeed live good lives, we can live pure lives before Him. So why not?

Sure, it was hard in the past. And yes, it might take some extra effort on our part to meet Him and be the vessel through which His Spirit can work.

But imagine the freedom when that old sin or pattern is gone! That thing you've wrestled with for years, imagine it's gone, no longer a thorn in your side.

Imagine living in freedom, having nothing in your current life to carry around and be guilty about. Yes, He's placed the past behind us. Our guilt and shame from the past is far behind us. And He loves us just as we are. There is no condemnation, and we are righteous in His sight.

But... if you know that your life doesn't match up to His sacrifice, and you know He's called you to a better life, then why not walk in the Spirit and live out a better life now?

He gives us the power, we can have victory through Him, and we can not only live in no condemnation, but we can live confident that we are fully walking in the Spirit the way He designed!

The good news is that when we are walking with Jesus, and we are filled with His Spirit, He can empower us to be free of the sin, selfish desires, idolatry, pride, etc., that has been in our lives.

The closer I get to Jesus and the more time I spend with Him, the less my old nature, my old desires, peek through. They are barely desires. They rarely nag at me and remind me they are there.

Consider with me:

For if ye live after the flesh, ye shall die: but if ye through the Spirit do mortify the deeds of the body, ye shall live.

For as many as are led by the Spirit of God, they are the sons of God. (Romans 8:13-14)

But notice also Galatians 5:16:

This I say then, Walk in the Spirit, and ye shall not fulfil the lust of the flesh.

If we actively walk in the Spirit, we won't fulfill the lust of the flesh.

Paul goes on to write out a long and detailed list of many of the ways we sin when we are not walking in the Spirit; when we are fulfilling the lust of the flesh:

Now the works of the flesh are manifest, which are these; Adultery, fornication, uncleanness, lasciviousness,

Idolatry, witchcraft, hatred, variance, emulations, wrath, strife, seditions, heresies,

Envyings, murders, drunkenness, revellings, and such like: of the which I tell you before, as I have also told you in time past, that they which do such things shall not inherit the kingdom of God. (Galatians 5:19-21)

It's pretty gruesome. But he doesn't say, work hard on overcoming those sins, he doesn't say, you can slay those things over years of sanctification, but he says:

Walk in the Spirit, and ye shall not fulfil the lust of the flesh. (Galatians 5:16)

As we actively walk in the Spirit, the "deeds" of the body are killed off, not solely through hard work and discipline, but through such a focus on Christ, and walking in the Spirit with such attention, that the sins are starved off (mortified).

Walk Out of Sin

Walking in the Spirit is how we walk out of our past nature and our past sin, and step into freedom in Christ and the fruit of the Spirit, but there may be active patterns or temptations to continue the old sinful behavior.

As Christ-followers, it's our aim and our responsibility to not do the deeds of the flesh, and to not willfully sin, so those patterns or temptations must be dealt with proactively if your behavior does not immediately change as a result of walking in the Spirit.

It's almost like it's two walks in one: walking in the Spirit, actively doing the things of the Spirit, and so many of the activities in this book, but it's also actively turning away from the sin.

We can lean into walking in the Spirit as a positive action: so deeply walking in the Spirit that we don't do the sin. If we are spending time in the Spirit so completely that we don't have mental space or time for the sin, it makes it easier to positively walk out of the sin, than to exert a self-control or discipline against doing the sin.

However, if proactively walking out of the sin isn't effective immediately, that doesn't permit any excuse that we sin because we are not walking in the Spirit "enough" or that our flesh is stronger than our experience in the Spirit.

It's not a passive expectation that the Spirit will do it for us. He may, but if He does not, it is our responsibility to walk in the expression of the fruit of the Spirit that is self-control, which is not doing the sin.

We have a responsibility to actively walk in the Spirit, and walk away from the sin.

Paul said:

Know ye not that they which run in a race run all, but one receiveth the prize? So run, that ye may obtain.

And every man that striveth for the mastery is temperate in all things. Now they do it to obtain a corruptible crown; but we an incorruptible.

I therefore so run, not as uncertainly; so fight I, not as one that beateth the air:

But I keep under my body, and bring it into subjection: lest that by any means, when I have preached to others, I myself should be a castaway. (I Corinthians 9:24-27)

In the absence of fully walking in the Spirit such that we walk out of the sin, we have a responsibility to take action and exercise discipline and self-control and not do the sinful behavior. And we can trust that as we do that, we are relying on Him for strength, and we are actively walking in the Spirit.

I want to be very specific and spell out the importance of having discipline, being proactive, and not using any excuses about how it's "so hard" to do the right thing, not sin, etc. I know how hard it is, because I struggled for years, and there are still things I have to guard actively against.

And until we are so fully walking in the Spirit that we aren't fulfilling the lusts of the flesh, I strongly believe we have a responsibility to muscle up, be proactive, and do whatever it takes to not engage in the sinful behavior.

That might mean making a decision to not walk into a bar or a liquor store if that's your vice, to not meet with the opposite sex in private if that's your vice, to not keep potato chips and ice cream in the house, if that's your vice. Those are simplistic examples, but consider your own vice, your own biggest weakness:

What simple guardrails could you put into place which would immediately eliminate 90% of the sin in your life?

I know that sounds overly simplistic, and maybe it is: but maybe in its simplicity it's the best place to start!

Having said all of that, outside of the initial emergency steps to take to cut off the sin, I believe that as we walk in the Spirit it becomes easier and easier to simply not struggle with that sin.

Jesus certainly made it simple.

When He told the Samaritan woman that she had been married 5 times and was now living with a man that was not her husband, we don't even have a record of Him accusing her, or even telling her not to stay in sin. (John 4)

And yet this is what happened:

The woman then left her waterpot, and went her way into the city, and saith to the men,

Come, see a man, which told me all things that ever I did: is not this the Christ?

Then they went out of the city, and came unto him. (John 4:28-30)

And many of the Samaritans of that city believed on him for the saying of the woman, which testified, He told me all that ever I did. (John 4:39)

When Jesus encountered the woman caught in adultery and lovingly told the accusers that any of them which had no sin could cast the first stone, and they all walked away, He concluded His time with these words:

When Jesus had lifted up himself, and saw none but the woman, he said unto her, Woman, where are those thine accusers? hath no man condemned thee?

She said, No man, Lord. And Jesus said unto her, Neither do I condemn thee: go, and sin no more. (John 8:10-11)

Jesus' simple instructions were to go and sin no more.

After He healed the paralytic man at the pool of Bethesda (John 5), He said something similar to him:

Afterward Jesus findeth him in the temple, and said unto him, Behold, thou art made whole: sin no more, lest a worse thing come unto thee. (John 5:14)

He said, go and sin no more.

Jesus didn't make it complicated.

Let's take that into our lives.

Like Jesus, let's not make it complicated!

Just stop!

Go and sin no more!

Self Control as Part of the Fruit of the Holy Spirit

Now that I've been very clear and direct about our responsibility to walk rightly, even initially, and even during the struggle, and even before we are fully walking in the Spirit, I'd like to share a perspective on overcoming sin that has been incredibly freeing for me personally:

As I shared earlier, when we are walking in the Spirit, we are expressing the fruit: peace, joy, love, gentleness, faith, humility, self-control, patience, and goodness. It's not just peace or love or self-control, etc., it's one fruit that has all of those characteristics.

I'm in self-control because with such peace and joy and love I don't need to be out of control in order to be happy and satisfied.

I don't need an extra thrill to be content.

So much of the sin we live with is an escape from not being content.

Too much drink: escaping not being content.

Too much food: escaping not being content.

All the sexual sins: escaping not being content.

Being angry and bitter: they give an external face to our lack of contentment, by pushing the reason on someone else (they did it to me).

Gossiping: I'm not satisfied if everyone else is good, so I talk about their bad.

But if I am content, in peace, in love, truly experiencing joy, I don't need a drink to escape. I don't need an extra bowl of ice cream to escape. I don't need to be angry and bitter. I don't need to talk about others.

Please don't take offense if I've taken your personal struggle lightly. I've struggled with everything on that list to varying degrees. And it hasn't been easy to admit that they were all a response to not being personally content.

But now that I have this enduring peace and joy and love from Jesus, none of those things holds the same allure they used to.

I don't want to escape reality. I don't want to overeat. I don't want to numb out. I don't want to be angry or bitter. I don't want to talk about others.

Because I'm truly satisfied deep inside with His presence and the fruit of the Spirit He's placed in me.

One of the challenges we deal with is the gap between the starting place of uncontentedness which leads to sin and the other side of the gap, the place where we are so content in Him that we don't even want to sin.

Unfortunately, that rarely occurs overnight. Even sometimes when I hear testimonies of people in whom it apparently occurred overnight, I usually notice they have to set things in place in their life to learn new pathways and new ways of enjoying life without drink or food or sinful sex or anger or bitterness or gossiping.

So what do we do in the meantime, between the time we realize we want to walk 100% in the Spirit but our flesh is still rearing its ugly head, and the actual realization of walking in the Spirit most or all of the time?

Let's consider this again: one expression of the fruit of the Spirit is self-control.

So often we think about self-control or discipline as this separate thing we have to "do," and it's hard. It's a thing we do, it's hard, it takes lots of effort, and is unpleasant.

But imagine we consider it as part of the entire array of the expression of the fruit of the Spirit:

Peace, joy, love, gentleness, faith, humility, patience, goodness ... and self-control.

If we are in peace and love and joy and patience ... why would we not naturally be in self-control?

I personally have experienced that as I have grown in peace and love and joy and patience, my internal level of self-control has grown exponentially.

Not completely without my effort or focus; it hasn't simply happened passively, and yet it's mostly there as a desire to be in self-control, not some external hard thing I have to rustle up.

When I contemplate the 18 months or so (and obviously this is a life long journey so that continues to grow) during which I grew most recently and fastest in the fruit of the Spirit, while I was learning that, I had to exercise more intentional self control. I had to exercise more intentional love and peace and joy!

Make the Choice

There were times when I didn't "feel" joyful or calm, but when I walked into a room I chose to put a smile on my face. I chose to bring happiness into the room, even when I didn't feel it inside.

And the craziest thing happened: the people in the room would respond to my smile, and they would smile, and they would ask, why are you so happy or calm in the face of what you are going through, and I would say something like, "It's tough, but I'm trusting Him," or "He's got it even though it's tough, and I'm choosing to walk in happiness."

And they would have their own realization, and they would begin to smile . . . and in a few minutes a room that could have been dour and depressed is experiencing joy and peace.

I believe there is an intentional effort to walk in the Spirit. We don't just automatically live right and act right just because we set our mind on walking in the Spirit.

This is what happens when we walk in the Spirit:

But the fruit of the Spirit is love, joy, peace, longsuffering, gentleness, goodness, faith,

Meekness, temperance: against such there is no law.

And they that are Christ's have crucified the flesh with the affections and lusts.

If we live in the Spirit, let us also walk in the Spirit. (Galatians 5:22-25)

Is it that simple?

Is that true?

If it is true - that it's just as easy as walking in the Spirit and I shall not fulfill the lust of the flesh (not maybe, not hopefully, not "if it's His will," not, "if He gives me strength," but simply "Walk in the Spirit and ye shall not fulfil the lust of the flesh") . . .

Then . . . if I immediately - right now - begin to walk - not just begin - but just walk in the Spirit - right here, right now, I will not fulfill the lust of the flesh.

This is instantaneous.

Test it the next time you have a sinful thought.

Anger, bitterness, lust, even a bad thought.

Immediately just walk in the Spirit.

Think - or say - "I am connecting with You, Spirit of God in me. I worship You. Thank You for being right here in me, right now. Thank You for being here, thank You for abiding in me."

Is it possible for you to continue to be angry at the same time as you are honestly walking in those words?

It's not just saying the words through gritted teeth. That's not walking.

Walking is releasing yourself to the Spirit of God that lives in you and praying those words with sincerity.

When you do:

Your anger will dissipate.

Your lustful thought will be gone.

Your curse word no longer welcome.

It's just not possible for the anger, the lust, the curse words, the bitterness, the pride, any other sin - to co-exist with the Spirit of God.

If you are saved, you have the Spirit of God living in you. And that means you can instantly connect with that Spirit in just the way I've described.

And as soon as you connect, the sin is gone, the flesh is dead.

What If It Just Keeps Coming Back?

You might be thinking, well, I still feel angry.

The lustful thought is gone - but as soon as I finish praying, it comes back.

The bitterness or the pride comes back.

Let's work through this:

First of all, with something like anger, when you are riled up and experiencing anger or bitterness or hatred, or any other thinking pattern that is accompanied in your body by cortisol or neurotransmitters, the cortisol or neurotransmitters are in your blood, and your body has to clear them before the feeling itself goes away.

The anger can be gone, but your heart is still pounding. It's just a physical sensation. The anger is gone, but your body still feels the residue of the anger.

It's just like if someone jumps out from behind a bush and scares you and your heart jumps and starts pounding . . . once you realize it's harmless, it takes some time for your heart to stop pounding.

Are you still scared?

No, you are not still scared.

But your heart might still pound for 10 minutes, because your body released a 10 minute supply of adrenaline so you can fight the bear that your body thought jumped out of the bush!

You are not scared, but your heart is pounding.

The same thing with anger:

God's love and the peace in you replaces that anger.

But your heart is still pounding, your ears are still red.

And yes, if you allow another recitation in your mind about the thing that angered you, then yes, you may re-stimulate the anger.

What's the solution?

Go back to prayer and talking with Him; connect with His Presence inside you.

It's the same thing with the lustful thought or the bitterness or the pride: just pray again, talk with Him, connect with His Presence.

So what if you have to pray for an hour to replace the sin with the Spirit?

Do you want to be free?

If so - pray and talk with Him and connect with His Spirit!

It's this simple act of walking in the Spirit.

I can instantly and immediately walk with the Spirit - Who lives in me - and instantly and immediately all the sins can be displaced by the Spirit.

I can be thinking a sinful thought, or I can be having a sinful expression of emotion (anger, bitterness, pride, etc.), and I can instantly step into the Spirit world, which I connect with inside of me. With my thought I can connect my spirit to His Spirit. Instantly His peace, His love, the fruit of His Spirit fills me and can displace the sinful desire or expression.

Try it the next time you start to feel angry, just start praising God, and worshiping God, and praying in tongues. Are you still feeling angry in five minutes? Likely not, but if you are, sing and praise some more.

Note I'm not suggesting praying out your anger, "God take this anger away, take this anger away, help me not be angry about ___. They did ___ and ___ and ___ so please take my anger away."

If you spend five minutes with that kind of praying, you will still probably be angry! Because although you are asking God to do something, you are still focused on the anger. Instead, focus on the Spirit instead of your anger:

Lord, I am just giving You my anger. They have wronged me, and I feel anger, but I am going to give it to You.

I worship You! You are amazing! You have done so many great things in my life! List out some of the things you are thankful for. Thank You, Father! Thank You, Jesus!

I keep my eyes on You! I love You Lord! If you have the gift of tongues, pray in tongues.

Just reading that, your anger is dissipating! Imagine praying that!

Now, if at the end of praying all of that, you consciously go back to ruminating about the pain, of course it will come back.

There's a one-two dance here: we give it to God, we pray and praise in the Spirit, we walk in the Spirit, but we can't take it back!

If you give it to God, leave it with God!

Pray in the Spirit for an hour if you have to.

My own experience is that the more time I spend in the Spirit, the less my fleshly desires appear. Yes, I have to use restraint and self-control occasionally, and self-control is a fruit of the Spirit, so His power is available to me for that as well!

But when I am walking in the Spirit, loving others as I should, praying in the Spirit, praising, thinking on "these things," I generally don't fight with the worldly temptations.

Step Back Into the Spirit

If you step out of the fruit of the Spirit in any area, you are not walking in the Spirit.

But do not despair. What does it take to start walking again?

About a 2 second reframe. Literally 2 seconds. Or faster.

You are out of love, judgmental.

You notice it.

Simply decide . . . I am now walking in the Spirit.

Maybe that's accompanied by "Lord, help me walk in your Spirit and have grace for this person, this situation."

Immediately as you begin to walk in the Spirit, you step into love.

This is the same for all the fruit.

Out of peace?

Walk in the Spirit.

Out of patience?

Walk in the Spirit.

When you have done all to stand, stand therefore. (Ephesians 6:13)

Be patient, for the deeds of the flesh reap the rewards of the flesh, and the deeds of the Spirit reap the rewards of the Spirit. (Galatians 6:18)

Be patient, persevere.

It's not easy, but it's worth it.

It takes time to make it a consistent habit and pattern to constantly walk in the Spirit.

But when you are walking in the Spirit, totally connected with Him, you won't commit the sins of the flesh, because you are walking in the Spirit. Instead, you will exhibit the fruit of the Spirit:

But the fruit of the Spirit is love, joy, peace, longsuffering, gentleness, goodness, faith,

Meekness, temperance: against such there is no law.

And they that are Christ's have crucified the flesh with the affections and lusts.

If we live in the Spirit, let us also walk in the Spirit. (Galatians 5:22-25)

> **Connection Space:**
>
> Let's get practical here.
>
> You have something on that list, or some sin you know you struggle with. Or even just a habit you want to get rid of.
>
> Take it to the Lord:
>
> Lord, You know I struggle with _____ .
>
> And Your Word tells me I can simply walk in the Spirit and I will not fulfill the lusts of the flesh.
>
> Lord, that feels so hard.

And yet it seems so simple.

Can I really come to You when I am struggling with that thing, just focus on You, walk in the Spirit, and the urge will go away?

Oh! Lord, if only it were that easy . . . .

And yet, Lord, as I've read the words in this book, and I've read the scriptures about it, and now I'm praying them out, I can sense You can really do this in me.

I ask You to double up Your effect in me.

That You will give me an extra effort to walk in Your Spirit.

That Your Spirit will replace in me the urge to do that thing.

Thank You for taking this away from me.

Thank You that as I walk in Your Spirit I won't do that thing.

And that Your power will flow through me, and You will make it easy for me!

Thank You Lord!

In Jesus name,

Amen

Friend, I hope that even as you read that, as you pray it, you realize that His power is real.

Although you might stumble, especially at first, when you continue to come to Him and you continue to trust Him to help you walk in the Spirit, especially in the face of that sin or habit, it will get easier and easier.

You may need to take a picture of the prayer in the last Connection Space and reference it each time you feel tempted!

I would like to reiterate again the importance of standing fast, and keeping on with the goal of eliminating whatever sin or habit you want to be free of.

You may get tired of continually resisting that sin or habit or temptation. But if you quit the process, it won't work. You see, God won't force His ways on you. He will guide you, give you power, give you supernatural Holy Spirit strength, make it easier, and so on, but just as you and I chose to start the habit and do the thing, and then our bodies or our minds became habituated to it, we have to choose to stop the habit and stop doing the thing.

The Lord is powerful, and His ways are higher than our ways, and His Word is sharper than a two-edged sword - BUT we have to want it, we have to activate it, and at first that might be praying every time we have the urge, even if it's 100 times or 1000 times.

Would it be worth praying 1000 times if necessary, to finally have the Spirit completely take over that fleshly urge?

He can, He will if you let Him, if you yield to Him, if you walk in the Spirit instead of walking in the flesh.

23

Addiction

Walking Out of Addiction

In the last section, we tackled the old sin nature and how we can walk in the Spirit to replace the deeds of the flesh with the fruit of the Spirit, and live godly lives. This glorifies God, and removes the sin barrier that might prevent you from being as close to Jesus as possible.

Some sins, when practiced habitually or repeatedly, can develop into a persistent, addictive pattern which can be more difficult for some people to walk out of, even when they are attempting to walk in the Spirit.

On the one hand, I believe we should be careful that we don't use the addictive nature of some behavior (for example, drinking, social scrolling, or lust) as an excuse to not fully "mortify the deeds of the flesh."

But on the other hand, I believe we can compassionately recognize that a habit - good or bad - is harder to break than a one time occurrence.

However, just as any other sin can prevent you from having a closer relationship to Jesus, so can sinful addiction.

I believe that if you want to have the closest possible relationship with Jesus, it's necessary to escape the addiction.

Note: before I share anymore, I don't know the nature of your addiction, if you have one. Some addictions are dangerous physically to disengage from, so I would advise consulting a doctor or a professional if you are cutting back on any addictive substance or alcohol.

With that in mind, I believe that walking in the Spirit can completely reverse addictions, such as substances, over-eating, wasting time scrolling, and other addictive behavior.

But it may take more effort, and more repeated attempts, than some sins that have not become entrenched addictively. I cringe as I write that, because in no way do I want to lessen the power or the ability of the Spirit, and yet experientially I know that addictive habits are not easy to break!

Of course, with any serious addiction, there may be a physical component, neurotransmitters or neural pathways that have become accustomed to the behavior. You may need temporary natural help with the withdrawal phase, whether you are escaping an addiction to alcohol, drugs, food, excessive scrolling, or any other addiction.

Even something as simple as excessive scrolling produces huge levels of dopamine, and when you stop that "harmless" behavior, your brain craves that dopamine.

The good news is, with time away from the behavior, your brain will come back to a normal setpoint, and it becomes easier in the physical. Depending on the nature and the duration of the addiction, it can take longer to return to that normal setpoint, so be prepared to be consistent over time and do not give up.

Just because we have the Spirit, we are walking in the Spirit, and we have His power, it doesn't mean the walk is easy, especially if we are pulling out of destructive behavioral patterns.

However, even as we're not discounting the reality of withdrawal and the natural pull to go back to the addictive behavior, I believe strongly that we have to be careful not to use the physical component as an excuse to not lean into the Spirit and let Him do the heavy lifting and provide victory.

Another difficult thing about reversing addiction or about changing the way we eat or what we do with our time is not the decision, nor is it the desire: but instead, it's that the thing we do which we dislike: drink, eat too much, scroll incessantly; those things tend to occur like clockwork at the same time each day, or like clockwork in response to the same trigger each time.

Many times addictions start as simple coping mechanisms that might not even be bad in and of themselves (of course some are bad, I won't differentiate here).

For example, social scrolling might start as 5 minutes of "down time," but over time becomes a two hour coping and numbing activity that stimulates the dopamine that should instead be reserved for the motivation to do big tasks, live a productive life for God, and walk in His way - but we are using it instead for a very "idle" behavior that happens to be much less idle than it appears!

Drinking too much might start as a benign-seeming coping mechanism, but over time it's an addictive, sinful coping and numbing activity that's not easy to break out of without the Spirit.

If you remove that destructive, addictive thing, the time is now empty, or you are missing a coping mechanism (albeit unhealthy). If you don't replace the time or the coping mechanism with something else, then there is a time vacuum or a coping vacuum.

It reminds me of the story Jesus shared about the evil spirit being cast out of someone, and they sweep out their house - but a week later the spirit comes knocking on the door, he sees the house has been swept out - and he brings with him 6 more spirits. (Matthew 25:43-45)

Yes, the evil spirit was cast out. But if it is not replaced with time with the Lord, there is a vacuum in that person's life.

With any sin or addiction, if something positive doesn't replace the time or space, then it's so easy for that sin to return.

If the behavior started as a coping mechanism, you must replace the coping with something healthy.

That might be learning healthy ways to decompress instead of the addictive behavior.

That might be learning healthy ways to deal with your emotional response to other people's actions, or your feelings of judgment or insecurity.

That might be learning to step into the Spirit every time you would normally step into the coping behavior that has turned addictive.

From a practical perspective - if you change your diet - don't just eliminate the bad, replace it with something good.

If you stop drinking, don't just stop - instead, identify the time of day you normally drink and replace that time with something productive.

That might be prayer, or a Bible Study - or it might be practical like a pickleball class or a pottery class.

If you cut off some bad friendships, you may not be able to replace the friends themselves quickly, but find something to replace the time you would normally spend with them. Again, that might be a community event, a hobby class, a workout class, or a Bible Study.

If you are spending time with Jesus: you won't be honestly praying, deep in the spirit, and be actively sinning at the same time.

If you are deeply praying, you won't be overeating, overdrinking, or thinking lustful thoughts.

Whatever your vice, it cowers at the Voice of Jesus, and not only that, it disappears. It is crowded out just by placing all of your mind on Jesus, on heavenly things.

Connection Space:

Do you have an addiction or a habit that you want to release?

Are you willing to commit to taking it to Jesus?

Ask Him how you can replace that addiction or habit with time with Him.

Ask Him how you can replace that addiction or habit with something healthy.

Ask Him to guide you all the way through the situation.

You have the Holy Spirit for guidance, and His power is incredible!

But you have to step into it.

When you begin to feel the urge to do whatever it is, get into a new habit of taking it to Him.

Thank You Lord Jesus for taking this desire from me.

Thank You Lord Jesus for helping me stay focused on You when I feeling tempted or pulled by the old addiction.

I shared elsewhere how I started asking the Lord to consume with fire any sinful thought when it popped into my mind.

Within about 60 days, those thoughts were down significantly, plus it's now a habit that when certain thoughts come into my mind, they are immediately replaced by a thought of "consuming fire," "washed by the blood," or even something simple like, "no."

Now I can sometimes simply think something like "no," or "not welcome," and the thought is gone. And if it's not, then I ask the Lord to consume it with fire.

What can you say or do that works for you the way this worked for me?

Lord Jesus, give us the strength to get rid of annoying or sinful thoughts.

Lord Jesus, we only want to think the thoughts You would want us to think.

Lord Jesus, we love You!

Jesus, thank You for Your Presence in my life!

24

When You Sin and Fail

What To Do When You Fall Down

We know that we fail and fall from time to time. We can look at our past to see that. The Word makes it clear that we cannot do it on our own. We will fail. We will fall.

This book has been written about what to do. The things to do to grow closer to Jesus. The things to avoid, and not do.

But the ugly reality is that we don't live up to everything in the Bible, and we don't live up to everything in this book, and we generally don't live up to . . . anything . . . for long, extended periods of time.

We can make new promises, and have a change of heart, and so on, and yet we will fail.

The good news is, Jesus makes provision for that. Once you recognize you've fallen; stop, confess, and repent.

If we confess our sins, he is faithful and just to forgive us our sins, and to cleanse us from all unrighteousness. (I John 1:9)

I don't think there's anything more spiritual about festering in shame and guilt for 3 days or 3 weeks, and wringing our hands over falling and failing yet again, than to immediately go to God and say, yep, I did it again . . . thanks that You will forgive me again.

Which would God prefer?

3 weeks of ruminating and festering and being down in the dumps and unable to give Christian love to others because you are so distraught over your sin . . . or immediately put it under the blood, be forgiven, and move on?

I truly believe He would prefer the faster the better.

Now, this doesn't mean, sin, put it under the blood as fast as possible, and then go sin again.

This means, you sin, you mess up, put it under the blood, and honestly make an effort - both in your flesh and in the Spirit - to walk rightly.

Yes, it's this simple.

Let's take a look at a few passages from the Word that support this approach.

John wrote this next passage presumably to Christians.

If we say that we have fellowship with him, and walk in darkness, we lie, and do not the truth:

But if we walk in the light, as he is in the light, we have fellowship one with another, and the blood of Jesus Christ his Son cleanseth us from all sin.

If we say that we have no sin, we deceive ourselves, and the truth is not in us.

If we confess our sins, he is faithful and just to forgive us our sins, and to cleanse us from all unrighteousness.

If we say that we have not sinned, we make him a liar, and his word is not in us. (I John 1:6-10)

John makes it clear that even as Christians, followers of Jesus, we will sin. It says that if we say we have no sin, we deceive ourselves.

But in the next verse it says to confess our sins, and He is faithful and will forgive us, and cleanse us from all unrighteousness.

There's no provision for waiting a certain amount of time, ruminating and feeling sorry for a long time, or groveling in shame and guilt. It simply says, *If we confess our sins, he is faithful and just to forgive us our sins, and to cleanse us from all unrighteousness.*

If we confess . . . He forgives. And not only does He forgive, but He cleanses us from the unrighteousness. That happens as soon as you confess!

Technically speaking, we are still righteous in His sight even before we confess the specific sin incident, if we are His by the act of belief in Him, according to Romans 4:4-5, where it states that our current righteousness in Christ is that our faith is counted as righteousness:

Now to him that worketh is the reward not reckoned of grace, but of debt.

But to him that worketh not, but believeth on him that justifieth the ungodly, his faith is counted for righteousness.

And Philippians 3:9: *And be found in him, not having mine own righteousness, which is of the law, but that which is through the faith of Christ, the righteousness which is of God by faith:*

But let's not be technical here and pick apart the law and His grace! Let His forgiving love abundantly embrace us, let's make an effort to act righteous, but when we fall and fail, let Him pick us up as fast as possible!

Jesus' blood cleanses us from all sins. Just confess your sin as soon as you discover it, and He will forgive and cleanse you.

Then go and sin no more.

If you fall again, come back to Him for more grace.

It's just that simple.

Keep it simple, my friend!

I believe that's how Jesus wanted it to be.

Now, perhaps you are asking, well, "Sean, I know that the Word makes this so simple. But in real life I get so frustrated with myself when I sin, especially when I don't want to. Especially when I've made a fresh commitment not to. What do you do in the real world?"

Friend, I struggle with that just like you do.

And sometimes I ruminate on it for hours or days before I confess it and release it. Or I confess it, but then I hold onto the shame and guilt for hours or days.

But I don't believe waiting honors the Lord. Is it possible that not accepting His atoning blood for our sins is in some way dishonoring to Him?.

I think at some point, we simply have to make the mental admission that He has covered it by His blood, and that although we feel compelled to continue to ruminate on it, we must simply choose to let it go and get back on track, and then take steps to avoid the sin in the future.

Confessing Our Sin to One Another

This passage indicates there's value in confessing our sins not just to Jesus, but to each other:

So confess your sins to one another and pray for one another so that you may be healed. The prayer of a righteous person has great effectiveness. (James 5:16)

Of course we must exercise great wisdom in confessing our sin. We can confess privately to a brother or sister who is trustworthy and is open and humble about the fact that they have fallen, just as you and I have fallen.

If you are having difficulty feeling as though Jesus has completely forgiven you when you confess privately to Him, consider confessing to a person (or a very small trusted group).

I remember one of the key turning points in my own recovery from the acceptance of my part in the demise of my marriage was confessing openly to a group of 27 people. It was so very painful and raw, and I felt as though it might mean I would have to leave the church once everyone knew my fall.

And yet many of the people who heard me there came to me over the following months, and told me that they valued my openness and willingness to share candidly. Not a single person said they held my failure against me, as I had been so afraid of. Not a single person.

And after that confession, and the tears and shame and fear that surrounded it, it became exponentially easier to never commit that sin again. I attribute a huge portion of my freedom from that particular sin, and my freedom from hiding my flaws for fear of judgment, to that specific moment of confession.

Sometimes I think as Christians we try to make this issue harder than it has to be. It's so simple.

Connection Space:

Take this time to ponder:

Do you sometimes hold back on asking for forgiveness because you are so ashamed that you've fallen . . . again?

Do you ruminate and stew in shame and guilt, perhaps feeling as though you are enduring punishment for your sin, before you will take it to Him and release it?

Let's practice taking something to Him quickly.

Consider something in your life that perhaps you have not already specifically asked Him to wash away.

Take it to Him:

Lord Jesus, You know I have fallen ... again ... in this area:

_____

_____

I'm so sorry it's happened again.

I try and try and try and yet ...

I want freedom, and right now I come to You and ask Your forgiveness.

I was wrong, and I want Your help in staying right!

I thank You that I am righteous in Your sight, not because I do good all the time, but because I believe and You have made me righteous.

Thank You!

Help me!

I love You, Lord!

Be Proactive Towards the Future

One way we can break out of the pattern of constantly having to come before Him with the same sin, the same shame and guilt, is to put some simple plans or guardrails in place to protect us going forward. We talked earlier about defeating sin by walking in the Spirit, but let's add some specific, practical advice here:

Keeping your focus on Him, and having your focus on the positive in your life right now, can sometimes make it easier to not sin and put it behind us. When He is flowing through you and you are walking in the fruit of the Spirit, you are content. You are filled with joy and peace and goodness and patience. Focus on that if you need to. You can even remind yourself that you will lose that connection if you take action on that temptation.

Consider the cost of "messing up." Usually there is a known cost to every sin. The sin feels pleasurable or even non-consequential in the moment, and yet each time you sin in the way you are personally weak, there is a known and countable cost. You pay the cost in shame, guilt, or the natural cost of the sin (hangover, weight gain, the consequences of sexual immorality, the people who are hurt by bitterness, resentment, or gossiping).

So think through it before taking the action to sin, even in the weak moment. Remember the consequence, and allow it to be part of the calculus of not doing what you know you should not do.

Keep an eye on rhythms in your life. If you know that there are times when you are weak, be sure to structure your life so those times you are more guarded.

Don't go places you shouldn't go.

Don't look at things on your phone you shouldn't look at.

Don't go shopping hungry!

Don't take a phone call when you are in a bad mood anyway, and then wonder why you were rude to your friend!

But when you fall . . . take it to the Lord quickly and get back to focusing on Him!

Keep Your Awareness On Him

Now that you have fallen down, committed some sin, and have confessed it and recalled the righteousness you are in Him, let's consider how you can now reset your mind on Him.

Imagine there's a constant, intangible awareness in your relationship with Him. You recall your ongoing commitment to Him. You recall your life in Him, His Spirit indwelling you.

Immediately your mind shifts to Him and the remembrance that you want to have your mind on Him. You stop worrying or planning or whatever else your mind is focused on, and think of Him. Any competing thought you have, replace it with thoughts of Him.

It's a constant, intangible awareness.

Anything that comes into your mind that you don't want there, you replace it with thoughts of Him.

Anything that comes against you, you take it to Him.

Anything that battles against you, you take it to Him.

This sounds so simple, and it is - but it's not always easy. And sometimes there's a delay between the time of the thought and when you take it to Him.

I believe you can have that in your life, if you so choose; you set your mind on it, you practice it intently, and you do it with Jesus.

Currently, most of the time, I am pretty consistently able to take each thing to Him in that way, but it was hard to get to that place.

It's taken discipline, focus, and effort. There were days when it didn't work. For a few hours I would worry or stew or ruminate. But then I finally got my eyes back on Him.

It took a decision. It often took changing scenes; if I'm somewhere, I would go somewhere else. I would take a walk. I would intentionally talk with Him. I would intentionally praise Him. I would intentionally pray in the Spirit.

If I don't know what to pray, I pray in tongues. If I'm stressed, the fastest, easiest way for me to enter into complete calm with Him is to either (or both) remind myself audibly that He is in control, He is peace, He is my peace, He surrounds me, He's in me, He's right there with me; and/or I pray in tongues and in the Spirit.

During that time with Him I return to a place of calm, a place of being open to Him and hearing Him, and I often receive clarity during that time about what's next.

This regular, daily, continuous, day after day after day time with Him, conversing with Him, sometimes journaling, sometimes just talking, sometimes the semi-structured conversations I've outlined earlier, sometimes just walking with Him, sometimes just silence, has transformationally grown me closer to Him.

Connection Space:

Take a few minutes to just consciously put your mind back on Him.

Perhaps you have sinned or fallen back, and you've taken it back to Him or a brother or sister in Christ and confessed.

You know you are right with Him, but perhaps there's an urge or a tendency to just focus on where you messed up.

He's forgiven you, you are righteous in His sight, so you might as well be able to walk in that!

Take a few minutes to worship Him, to talk with Him.

To re-center your eyes on Jesus!

Oh! What a sweet time!

PART 6: FEAR, ANXIETY, AND OTHER EMOTIONS

25

Anxiety and Worry

You can have a strong desire in your heart, activities and practices to engage with Him, and even a schedule to make sure you stay on track, and yet there are countless distractions, emotions, enemies, and thoughts that can strongly pull you away from intimacy with Jesus.

We can be overcome with anxiety and worry, misled by our feelings, overcome with emotions, feel like He isn't listening or is far away, or be distracted by sinful or just irritating thoughts that go through our minds, especially when attempting to spend time with Him.

An important part of my own journey has been not only embracing the time and activity with Him, but also managing these negatives that fight to pull me away from the intimacy He is building in me.

When you have overcome the general tendency to worry and internalize anxiety instead of releasing it to Him, when you can resist the sinful or distracting thoughts that come your way, and when you are not evaluating reality by your feelings, it makes your journey to closeness with Jesus so much easier!

Overcoming Anxiety and Worry

Stress and anxiety are significant blocks to growing closer to Jesus. If we are worried when we are praying, we are distracted and don't focus on Him. More than that, worrying and stress make it hard to feel close to Him, they make it hard to be close to Him, and they make it hard to trust Him.

At first glance, it might appear that worrying about what's happening in our day, the overwhelming circumstances, or the people and situations in our lives that are stacked against us, would simply be a challenge on our side of the equation, and we can still get closest to Jesus while holding the worry and stress. The presence of the stress isn't the problem so much as our worry and anxiety over the negative circumstances or fear. We must release the stress and anxiety to Him if we want to grow closest to Him.

Consider this, written by Peter:

Casting all your care upon him; for he careth for you.

Be sober, be vigilant; because your adversary the devil, as a roaring lion, walketh about, seeking whom he may devour:

Whom resist stedfast in the faith, knowing that the same afflictions are accomplished in your brethren that are in the world. (I Peter 5:7-9)

The Bible not only tells us to cast our cares on Him, but it gives real advice for resisting the forces that lead to our anxiety and worry.

The enemy, the adversary, the devil, lays traps for us with the afflictions that come against us, and even some that we bring on ourselves.

Peter states that we aren't alone - the same afflictions and stresses that you are dealing with, other people around the world are dealing with.

As harsh as it might sound, I'm not the only person to go through a devastating divorce (and she would say it was devastating and very painful for her as well; both parties in a divorce, regardless of contribution, effort, or ability to work through the complexities of internal emotional processing, experience pain). I'm not the only person to have been molded by parents and life and reaction into an avoidant people pleaser, I'm not the only person to struggle with food or drink or social scrolling, I'm not the only person to struggle to balance a budget or make enough money or put enough away. I'm not the only person to spend years in foster care, to nearly die from starvation, to make really bad life choices, or to ignore the Lord's warnings.

And you are not the only person to go through what you are going through. Yes, it's painful. But you aren't the only person. I'm not the only person.

Interjection: one of the most valuable things for me during my most recent trial was attending a few groups with people who were going through something similar. The camaraderie was powerful. But a word of warning: some people weren't growing through the experience, so over time just as being with them was powerful at first, helping me realize I was not alone; when some others in those groups were not growing through their situation, I began to feel that was holding me back, so I moved to groups of people who HAD overcome. Get comfort and camaraderie, but beware that you don't trade in one struggle [feeling like you are the only one] for another struggle [griping about how bad things are instead of getting help or fixing them].

Let's take a look at a few real-world situations of stress during the ministry of Jesus.

The first is when Lazarus was sick and then died.

Now a certain man was sick, named Lazarus, of Bethany, the town of Mary and her sister Martha.

(It was that Mary which anointed the Lord with ointment, and wiped his feet with her hair, whose brother Lazarus was sick.)

Therefore his sisters sent unto him, saying, Lord, behold, he whom thou lovest is sick.

When Jesus heard that, he said, This sickness is not unto death, but for the glory of God, that the Son of God might be glorified thereby.

Now Jesus loved Martha, and her sister, and Lazarus.

When he had heard therefore that he was sick, he abode two days still in the same place where he was. (John 11:1-6)

This is such a rich passage! These people are near and dear to Jesus. Lazarus, Martha, Mary.

Notice that when Jesus heard that Lazarus was sick, He waited two days. The stress of His friends' sickness was palpable, Martha and Mary were surely worried, and yet Jesus waited two days.

It then seems that by the time Jesus got to Lazarus, he had been dead now for 4 days:

Then when Jesus came, he found that he had lain in the grave four days already. (John 11:17)

Martha and Mary were so stressed.

Martha meets Him on the road:

Then said Martha unto Jesus, Lord, if thou hadst been here, my brother had not died. (John 11:21)

Mary is distraught and weeping:

The Jews then which were with her in the house, and comforted her, when they saw Mary, that she rose up hastily and went out, followed her, saying, She goeth unto the grave to weep there.

Then when Mary was come where Jesus was, and saw him, she fell down at his feet, saying unto him, Lord, if thou hadst been here, my brother had not died.

When Jesus therefore saw her weeping, and the Jews also weeping which came with her, he groaned in the spirit, and was troubled. (John 11:31-33)

Mary was weeping. The Jews around her were weeping. Jesus groaned in the spirit, and was troubled.

Jesus was in personal pain over this situation. His heart went out to Mary and Martha. He felt the pain in the house. Even though He was God in man, He felt deep pain over Mary and Martha's pain (even though He knew He would raise Lazarus from the grave).

What can we surmise about this?

When I am going through pain, Jesus feels for me. He might even groan in the spirit, even today. Jesus might be troubled by my pain.

When you are going through pain, Jesus feels for you. And He might even be groaning in the spirit over your pain. And He might be troubled by your pain.

Consider what happens next:

And [Jesus] said, Where have ye laid him? They said unto him, Lord, come and see.

Jesus wept.

Then said the Jews, Behold how he loved him! (John 11:34-36)

Jesus is apparently, or at least those around Him believed it to be so, weeping for Lazarus himself. Even though He had the power to raise him from the dead!

The story closes as Jesus raises Lazarus from the dead:

Jesus therefore again groaning in himself cometh to the grave. It was a cave, and a stone lay upon it.

Jesus said, Take ye away the stone. Martha, the sister of him that was dead, saith unto him, Lord, by this time he stinketh: for he hath been dead four days.

Jesus saith unto her, Said I not unto thee, that, if thou wouldest believe, thou shouldest see the glory of God?

Then they took away the stone from the place where the dead was laid. And Jesus lifted up his eyes, and said, Father, I thank thee that thou hast heard me.

And I knew that thou hearest me always: but because of the people which stand by I said it, that they may believe that thou hast sent me.

And when he thus had spoken, he cried with a loud voice, Lazarus, come forth.

And he that was dead came forth, bound hand and foot with graveclothes: and his face was bound about with a napkin. Jesus saith unto them, Loose him, and let him go.

Then many of the Jews which came to Mary, and had seen the things which Jesus did, believed on him. (John 11:38-45)

This is so rich and full of meaning. Jesus is still groaning in His spirit when He goes to the grave to raise Lazarus from the dead!

I submit to you that even though Jesus was/is God, that was a deeply troubling time for Him. And yet He persevered, relying on the Father, keeping His eyes on the power of the Father.

As our ultimate example, I believe if we can adopt the attitude, with all of our trials, that Jesus had in this situation, we can experience significantly more victory over stress and anxiety.

Here's a simpler case:

And when they had sent away the multitude, they took him even as he was in the ship. And there were also with him other little ships.

And there arose a great storm of wind, and the waves beat into the ship, so that it was now full.

And he was in the hinder part of the ship, asleep on a pillow: and they awake him, and say unto him, Master, carest thou not that we perish?

And he arose, and rebuked the wind, and said unto the sea, Peace, be still. And the wind ceased, and there was a great calm.

And he said unto them, Why are ye so fearful? how is it that ye have no faith?

And they feared exceedingly, and said one to another, What manner of man is this, that even the wind and the sea obey him? (Mark 4:36-41)

Notice when the disciples were totally overcome with fear when the storm was raging, Jesus didn't tell them it would be okay, and that their stress and anxiety was alright. Instead, He calmed the storm. And He told them to "fear not." He commanded them to not be afraid.

Any situation or circumstance that comes against you is no more real or powerful than that storm that threatened the disciples' lives, and yet Jesus not only had control over the storm, but He commanded the disciples to "fear not."

Jesus was aware of the storm when He went to sleep in the rear of the boat. Jesus is aware of your storm. Jesus was aware when I felt totally helpless to help someone else in their pain. Jesus was aware when I made some wrong choices that led to long-term disastrous consequences. Jesus was aware when I was afraid to go to sleep at night, and awoke scared and worried. He knew my storm was there, and yet He didn't just make it disappear. He let me go through the storm, with His Presence.

If He had taken the storm from me, I wouldn't be writing this book because I wouldn't have the experience with Him to share the victories within. Sure, I could have had the testimony, "Jesus calmed my storm," but I wouldn't have grown the way I have.

Mark 4:40 says *And he said unto them, Why are ye so fearful? how is it that ye have no faith?*

He didn't applaud the scared disciples for their fear. He didn't assume they could just carry their fear. He asked them, "why are you so afraid?" He asked them, "where is your faith?"

Jesus assumed that faith would overcome their fear.

Is that storm - with possible impending death by the boat capsizing - any worse than our current worries? A bill that is late, a person that is angry with us, our own mistakes, a long day of stressful conversations, are any of those qualifiably different from this storm example?

I don't think so. I know that in the midst of our own pain, we often think it's the hardest thing anyone can ever go through. If you are going through a divorce and someone else is being beaten and abused, and someone else is starving to death - those are all very bad situations. And yet, for the person in it, they often believe their situation is the worst.

The disciples believed their situation was dire. The fear that accompanies your situation is similar to the fear that the disciples experienced and it's similar to the fear that someone in a different stressful situation is experiencing.

So if that fear is similar, and Jesus' response was, "what are you so afraid of, where is your faith?," is it possible that's His response to our situations?

Even Jesus said, "take no thought for what you will eat or wear:"

Therefore I say unto you, Take no thought for your life, what ye shall eat, or what ye shall drink; nor yet for your body, what ye shall put on. Is not the life more than meat, and the body than raiment?

Behold the fowls of the air: for they sow not, neither do they reap, nor gather into barns; yet your heavenly Father feedeth them. Are ye not much better than they? (Matthew 6:25-26)

I think on one hand, it's easy for us to say, but Jesus didn't know how it is today. They didn't have such complicated lives with gym memberships and mental health subscriptions and social networking obligations. They didn't have credit cards and road rage and people who take too long in line at the big box store.

Or did they?

They had to walk to the well each morning to fill their pot with water, and bring it back home, listening to the village gossip and griping and bitterness.

They took their problems to the local rabbi or priest and he gave them Bible verses to memorize.

They had elaborate social structures, who got to sit in the village gate and weigh the problems of the community, who had to get their water at the well at noon time instead of morning because she was so shamed by her inability to settle down with one person (possibly because she had childhood trauma that set her up to pick the wrong guy again . . . and again . . . and again because they *didn't* have mental health counseling).

They didn't have credit cards but if you borrowed against your land and didn't pay it back you lost your land and went to jail. They didn't have road rage . . . or did they? Can't you see the camels jockeying to get through the eye of the needle gate before it closed at sundown, so the robbers wouldn't rob them blind while they were stuck outside the gate after dark?

Instead of a long line at the big box store, they had to jostle and push and yell to get the best piece of meat at the butcher, because they didn't have electronic numbers to pick to keep everyone in line.

This might feel sacrilegious or sarcastic, and yet, I'm not so sure they didn't experience a similar level of stress to what we have now. It just looked different.

Jesus knew what stress was. He couldn't even preach in his hometown, because his hometown villagers couldn't believe the illegitimate son of the local carpenter could possibly heal people. Talk about insecurity and trauma!

So when Jesus says, "take no thought" . . . or "why are you so afraid? Where is your faith?" I don't think He was speaking out of immaturity or cluelessness, I believe He was serious and that He knew His way worked.

Without making a list of 100 stresses in my own life over the years, I've experienced many of the common stresses I've listed below:

People who are more concerned about what you wear to church than your heart.

People who are more nosy about what you do because they want to know how much money you make so they can criticize how much you feed the poor.

When you have legal problems.

When the car won't start and you have to get to work.

When your children won't listen.

When your spouse won't get counseling.

When you won't get counseling.

Bills to pay (late sometimes).

Taxes to pay (late sometimes).

People who post hateful things about your work.

When you don't think you need counseling and you continue to treat your spouse poorly.

When you don't know how you are going to make payroll.

When you don't know how you are going to fire the person who is destroying your company.

When you are totally overwhelmed by all the things you need to do today.

When you are totally overwhelmed by all the demands others have of you.

When . . .

When . . .

When . . .

And I haven't even touched the personal things like betrayal, child abuse, molestation, and I could go on and on.

Maybe you are going through something that's not on this list and I missed your torment.

Imagine it's on the list.

I remember during the heat of my own journey to understand why I failed at my marriage, I went to a group for people who were struggling with . . . problems like mine . . . and my situation was less-bad than every single other person's problems in the room.

I was humbled on the one hand. On the other hand I thought, these people have really big problems, why can't we solve ours and get along?

I write all of this to say, I may not have named or personally know the stress you are under. But I've experienced a ton of stress over the years, and the stress of the last year was nearly unbearable, comparably or not. It was nearly unbearable for me.

And yours may be unbearable for you.

But I can say confidently, Jesus took me all the way through.

I learned to "cast my cares at His feet," and simply let Him have them.

It did take mental discipline. You see, when you "give something to Jesus," for example, you say, "Jesus, I don't know what's going to happen with (whatever your biggest challenge is right now) and I don't know what I'm going to do, but I'm going to lay it at Your feet," and you say that at the altar or in your prayer time, but then five minutes afterwards you take it back, I believe that's a discipline thing.

One manifestation of the fruit of the Holy Spirit is self control. Self control is a close cousin to discipline. The Holy Spirit can help us have that discipline. I had to have discipline for days and days that added up to weeks and then months. It was hard.

And yet I can say, with the strength of Christ, I did it. For the most part! And when I didn't I said, "Lord, forgive me" . . . and I had more mental discipline.

And then even this morning during prayer my mind wandered and I worried about the slew of things I have to do today, the little tasks that add up and are super draining for me. Running errands, making decisions, wondering when someone is going to turn against me again, wondering if the pain is really gone. And yet, without this slip-up into stress, this chapter wouldn't exist. Because today was a fresh reminder of the difficulty of just trusting Him.

But without trusting Him, how close can I truly be? How close can I be to Jesus when my every other thought is, "How am I going to get through _____?," or "How am I going to deal with _____?"

I write all of that to hopefully emphatically express that I know how hard it is to NOT worry and be anxious.

And yet Jesus tells us not to worry, just like He says He'll abide with us, and just like He says to go ye into all the world and make disciples of all men.

He told us not to worry . . . so that we won't worry! He never asks us to do something we cannot do. We can escape worry. It requires a dedicated focus on Him, and it requires a level of discipline that when the worry returns, we give it right back to Him.

What does that look like in real life?

Sometimes to me it looks like starting with lip service: I tell Jesus I want to let Him take it. But I don't really release it. And he reveals that. And I give it to Him again. And again.

But consider this: as long as we keep focusing on the problem, we don't completely release it.

Sometimes I would give Jesus lip service: "I give this to You Lord," knowing I wanted to give it to Him, but having no reality of how I actually could release it. I mean, it's not like He was going to take that phone call for me, right?

But then I would commit - and do - with discipline, with strength of mind - a time of praise and worship. And when the thoughts of worry crept in, I ignored them and kept worshiping. And thirty minutes later, I wasn't focused on the worry anymore.

I found that the more I focused on Him, the more the problem receded into the background. The problem was still there. But it wasn't foremost on my mind.

Over time, He solved some problems for me. He fought battles and took things away. Some problems He gave me the strength to work through and taught me how to handle them.

Becoming Mature as a Person

That is part of how He matures us. The same things that would cause me stress and worry, many times because I wasn't responsible or proactive, He taught me how to sequentially and intentionally be proactive and take care of them.

And of course, you can't control other people. You can control your own response. You can control how much you allow them to fill your mind with their nonsense or toxicity.

Maybe with your own worries and problems, He gives you the peace and calm to get through the day to day currently. Maybe He also teaches you ways to reorder your life so it's not so prone to disaster.

That's one of the ways He's helped me. I'm a notorious procrastinator, I avoid conflict, I'd rather bow down and do things your way than advocate for my opinion. He's been teaching me how to reorder my life and see conflict and personalities and delay differently than I ever did. Yes, it's been a process.

Maybe you aren't a procrastinator or a conflict-avoider like me. Maybe you are on the opposite end of the spectrum, you do everything right now, with perfection - and demand that of others so you are always stressed that everyone around you is a procrastinator!

Maybe you have some other issue you deal with personally that has actually contributed to your current stressful circumstances. Sure, Jesus can take your circumstance away, but if something in the way you run your life is just going to attract the same thing again, then He hasn't solved the problem for you long run, He has just given you a short term fix.

Jesus can help me finish a project at the last minute, or apologize because I made a problem worse by avoiding conflict, and the "miracle" feels great in the short run - but true freedom comes when Jesus teaches me not to procrastinate, and how to advocate and speak up instead of ignoring difficulty.

Jesus can solve your short term nightmare, but if you don't let Him change your behavior so that you don't create the same nightmare again in six months, you don't have freedom.

Yes, you have miracles, but you don't have freedom!

A huge part of my own freedom has been learning to overcome the things about which I used to say, "that's just the way I am," and change that to, "that's how I used to act, and although it's not easy to evaluate things with a wise mind to find a more mature way of handling them, I'm going to do it anyway and step up and act differently."

I believe this is important to our development as a balanced Christ follower who makes an impact in the world, walks fully in the freedom Jesus paid for, and who is close to Jesus. Imagine how much closer to Jesus you can become when you've let go of some of your historical weaknesses and let Him mentor you to victory not just in the short term miraculous, but in the long term character issues!

> **Connection Space:**
>
> Let's try this out experientially.
>
> This may be the very hardest practice in the Christian faith! As hard as it is to consistently combat the "fiery darts" of the enemy, the unwanted thoughts that come into your mind; the reappearance of worries and anxieties may be even more difficult to combat!
>
> You may find yourself repeatedly, day after day, having to resubmit worries and anxiety to Him!
>
> Let's give it a try:
>
> Take something you are actively worried about now, and give it to Him.
>
> Lord, I give You this worry.
>
> I ask that You take it and cover it by the blood, just as You've covered everything else.

I ask that You take it from me, and that You give me comfort and peace in the midst of the stress.

I trust You to provide.

I trust You to guide me, give me wisdom, or remove the stress or anxiety.

In either case, I'm trusting You with this worry or anxiety.

I cast it on You, because You care for me.

Thank You for taking this anxiety.

Thank You for so completely caring for me that I no longer need to worry about this thing.

I ask that You will give me the strength to allow You to keep this!

Thank You in advance for removing the stress and anxiety.

Thank You, Lord Jesus!

Once you have released it to Him in this way, simply ignore it; use your mental shield of faith to avoid thinking of it again. But if it does come back to you, take it to the Lord again. You may have to do this repeatedly at first, but my experience is that over time it becomes easier to just "rest in the boat," and not be concerned with the storm outside.

26

Unwanted or Negative Thoughts

Eliminating Unwanted or Sinful Thoughts or Feelings

Do you deal with unwanted or random thoughts, sinful thoughts, or "fiery darts of the enemy?" Worry, stress, lustful thoughts, angry thoughts, sinful thoughts, the ones that pop into your head and if you just let them go they are meaningless, but if you entertain them at all, they grow. If you are like me, even if you don't entertain them you worry, "where did that come from?," "was that sin?," and on and on.

Or perhaps for you it's not thoughts so much as feelings. It might not just be random, sinful, or "fiery dart" thoughts that you want to get rid of. Perhaps there's an agitation or a frustration, or feelings of sadness or depression, insecurity or unworthiness. The enemy will send thoughts your way to distract you or derail you. Your own mind might just think things that aren't useful.

When we focus on those thoughts or feelings, whether they have come from our mind, or the enemy, they tend to get bigger or more frequent. Even the very act of trying to combat the thoughts to stop them results in focusing on them and they don't go away.

But if we can find a way that works for us to starve, ignore, or crowd out the thoughts or feelings, they tend to go away. Imagine replacing those thoughts with a different image, or allowing His peace to replace those thoughts. So instead of fighting them head on, we fight them through attrition or by replacement.

I think this is one of the concepts behind Ephesians 6:16: *Above all, taking the shield of faith, wherewith ye shall be able to quench all the fiery darts of the wicked.* The shield of faith is a defensive weapon, not an offensive weapon. By holding the shield of faith (mentally, with our faith given to us by God) we resist, block, or replace the "fiery dart of the enemy."

I started visualizing a consuming fire that would consume away the thought and any sin that might accompany it. Immediately when the thought comes in, I picture a consuming fire and I say, out loud or to myself, "consuming fire," or "Lord, please consume it in Your fire."

At first it was only effective at eradicating the thought in its infancy, but the thoughts continued to come back with their typical frequency. However, I was consistent with that for maybe 30-60 days and most of the unwanted thoughts stopped arriving. And when they do, it's so much easier to simply ignore them or visualize a consuming fire, and they are gone nearly instantly.

Picturing a consuming fire might not be effective for you. There might be another image that makes more sense. You can choose to think of Him, just spend time with Him, or develop your own mental picture that works for you, visualizing replacing the unwanted thoughts or feelings.

Connection Space:

Is there some feeling you are feeling today that you might normally want to get rid of?

Maybe it's agitation.

Maybe it's an irritation with something.

Maybe it's a feeling of depression or tiredness.

Now, instead of asking God to take it away, ask Him to give you calm and peace even with the feeling you have.

Lord, I feel _____ .

I want to also sense Your Presence.

May I feel Your calm and Your peace even as I feel _____ .

I know You are here.

You are right here with me.

You are calm.

You are peace.

And now I know that even though I feel _____, I know I am also more peaceful now, I feel calmer now.

Thank You Jesus!

I love You Lord Jesus!

>Thank You!

>Amen

>**My note:**

>Do you feel calmer now?

A sense of His peace?

>Even if your other feeling hasn't dissipated, your tiredness or your irritation, whatever it is, can you also sense calm and peace?

If so, it's an interesting sensation, isn't it?

>Allow yourself to sit with it a little!

>Now, my guess is that as you do, your original feeling will begin to dissipate.

>Time and distraction usually help with things like irritation, agitation, even tiredness or slight depression.

>But even if it doesn't, if you are sensing more calm, it's easier to get through the day (or the night!)

>Thank You, Lord!

Slaying the Negative

We cannot grow closest to Jesus when we are holding onto negative things like bitterness, resentment, hatred, anger, envy, jealousy, and even things like pouting and self-pity. Each of those things creates a wedge in your mind and in your spirit as you are drawing close to Jesus.

For example, you come to Jesus to spend time with Him, but you are harboring an active expression of envy about someone whom you have realized has something better than you in their life. I'm choosing a silly, yet realistic example for this, but any of the negative things operate the same way.

You open your time with Him in worship, but in the back of your mind, you are replaying the envy. Or the bitterness. Or the self-pity.

Regardless of the righteousness (or not) of the envy or the bitterness or whatever, that thing holds you back from being as close to Him as possible.

Just by its caustic nature of interruption, it will hold you back.

If it's a serious level of bitterness, for example, it won't just hold you back in this moment with Jesus, but it will seriously retard your growth with Him.

Jesus said this about unforgiveness:

And when ye stand praying, forgive, if ye have ought against any: that your Father also which is in heaven may forgive you your trespasses. (Mark 11:25)

He goes so far as to say that if you come to the altar and remember someone else has something against you, leave your gift at the altar and be reconciled, then come back to the altar:

Therefore if thou bring thy gift to the altar, and there rememberest that thy brother hath ought against thee;

Leave there thy gift before the altar, and go thy way; first be reconciled to thy brother, and then come and offer thy gift. (Matthew 5:23-24)

He spoke that in the days of physically making an offering to atone for our transgressions.

But consider that His heart would be the same today: if someone has something against you, be reconciled then come back to your time with Me.

Paul wrote extensively about putting off these seemingly little transgressions that make it hard to grow closest to Jesus:

Paul, in writing to the church at Colosse:

But now ye also put off all these; anger, wrath, malice, blasphemy, filthy communication out of your mouth.

Lie not one to another, seeing that ye have put off the old man with his deeds;

Put on therefore, as the elect of God, holy and beloved, bowels of mercies, kindness, humbleness of mind, meekness, longsuffering;

Forbearing one another, and forgiving one another, if any man have a quarrel against any: even as Christ forgave you, so also do ye. (Colossians 3:8-9, 12-13)

He says in Ephesians:

Let all bitterness, and wrath, and anger, and clamour, and evil speaking, be put away from you, with all malice:

And be ye kind one to another, tenderhearted, forgiving one another, even as God for Christ's sake hath forgiven you. (Ephesians 5:31-32)

And he says in Philippians:

Let nothing be done through strife or vainglory; but in lowliness of mind let each esteem other better than themselves. (Philippians 2:3)

Notice these are simple commands. Let all bitterness be put away from you. Let all wrath be put away from you. Let all evil speaking be put away from you. Be tenderhearted, forgiving one another.

I don't believe this has to be a complicated issue that involves months of contemplation and counseling to decide to let something go.

I also understand that long term, destructive behavior over time that is deeply embedded may require a deeper process.

In dealing with some of my own deep seated trauma roots, I went through significant counseling and hours and hours before the Lord.

So I understand that there are some issues that sometimes take longer to resolve.

Keep it simple. You've seen something on social that triggers you? Take it to the Lord or to the person and move on. Just because they won't stop or repent, that doesn't mean you have to hold onto it.

You can choose to forgive and be kind, even when they continue to be hateful and sue you. Again, I know personally that it's not easy. But as much as you have it within you, just do it!

Your relationship with Jesus will grow deeper as you do!

And of course, you have His strength and power and ability!

You have the fruit of the Spirit.

As you walk out the fruit of the Spirit, it displaces those negative thoughts and patterns.

> **Connection Space:**
>
> Lord Jesus, I come to You with (name it: bitterness, anger, unforgiveness, resentment, etc.)
>
> It's not easy to release this to You.
>
> It feels unfair that they don't have to follow through.
>
> But You've told me to let it go.
>
> To forgive.

To be loving.

So Lord Jesus I ask that You will show me how to release this.

I release the anger, the bitterness, or the unforgiveness.

I make a choice to forgive and to release.

I relinquish control over these negative feelings that hold me back from ultimate closeness with You.

Thank You in advance for showing me how to do this.

Thank You for taking these pains, and for helping me forgive and move on!

Thank You for loving me!

Thank You for making me whole again!

Thank You, Jesus!

27

Fear, Feelings, and Emotions

Friend, your entire life is part of your journey in growing close to Jesus.

Feelings and emotions are part of your life.

Imagine taking your feelings and emotions to Him when you are struggling with them.

Imagine you are hurt by someone, and instead of ruminating over it, and getting more and more hurt and upset, you were to take it to Jesus.

"Jesus, I bring You my pain today. This person did ___ and I was hurt by it. Lord Jesus, how should I respond?"

"Jesus, I bring You my pain today. This person hurt me in this way: _____. How can I process these feelings, with You?"

Imagine taking each feeling you have to Him and asking Him what He thinks of it.

You see, He feels your pain.

But He also doesn't want you to sit in it for years.

He doesn't want you to ignore your pain.

He wants to heal it.

For healing, you have to bring it to Him.

But you have to actually let it go, as well.

Here are some of the feelings you might deal with or need to process:

Fear.

Anxiety.

Worry.

Hurt.

Anger.

Betrayal.

Sadness.

Grief.

Pain.

Confusion.

Rage.

Disappointment.

Insecurity.

Ask Jesus to Come Alongside You

Imagine you take each emotion or pain you have to Jesus and ask Him to come alongside you.

Ask Him to join you in processing, feeling, or sitting with, the feeling.

Ask Him what He wants to do with it.

He may ask you to pray.

He might ask you to sit with it, to simply feel the feeling.

He may ask you to release it, even if you don't understand it.

He may ask you to talk it out, and then afterwards He might ask you to let it go.

He might ask you to look at it from another point of view.

Connection Space:

Consider a feeling or a state of emotion you are dealing with:

Fear.

Anxiety.

Worry.

Hurt.

Anger.

Betrayal.

Sadness.

Grief.

Pain.

Confusion.

Rage.

Disappointment.

Insecurity.

> **Take it to the Lord.**
>
> Ask Him to partner with you in understanding it.
>
> Sit with it.
>
> Allow yourself to feel the pain of the feeling or emotion.
>
> Sit with it.
>
> Ask Him what you should do with it.
>
> Ask Him if there's a new perspective you could take on.
>
> Ask Him to heal you.

By the way, if you've struggled with a certain emotion for years, you may have to use a process like this repeatedly for months or longer.

You may benefit from seeing a qualified counselor, or reading books on the subject, with an open mind.

You may need to spend more time with Jesus and the emotion or feeling.

Imagine taking each emotion or feeling to the Lord, each time it happens.

Hurt People Hurt People

There's a phrase I learned during my trial:

Hurt people hurt people.

I learned that so many of the people in our lives have hidden pain from their own childhood or from experiences throughout their life, and that hidden pain is reflected in how they react to ordinary situations.

Someone has gotten offended by something you said?

Maybe their father said that to them in anger, you saying it stimulated feelings of fear of their father.

Maybe their mother demanded they hide and cover their emotions, so later in life they either cannot feel emotions, or they hide from the pain of sharing them.

Maybe someone else traumatized them in some way and your innocuous phrase reminded them of something painful.

Maybe they don't even know it.

You certainly didn't mean it.

But that's their internal response.

And then they lash back at you.

And now you are hurt.

Hurt people hurt people.

If someone is rude to you, if someone is disrespectful, ask yourself, is it possible it's some pain in their own life?

Of course that doesn't mean if someone is perpetually rude to you, that you continue to stay in their close circle. It doesn't mean you don't address it.

But you can also have compassion for whatever might have gotten them to the place where they are rude or angry or hurtful.

Maybe you've hurt someone when you've been hurt.

You didn't mean it.

Or maybe you did.

Because you were hurt.

The silly thing about emotions and hurt is that we usually can't see what others hurt with.

If you express anger, you understand anger.

Maybe you can see the pain in someone else who expresses anger.

But if you don't express passive aggressiveness, or you don't express confusion, and someone else is passive aggressive or confused, you might judge them because you don't understand them.

And yet they are experiencing as much pain as you are but they are expressing it differently.

Fear

It's one thing to know that Jesus said, Fear not, for I am with you always, but it's another thing when you are facing an abusive person and they are threatening you physically or emotionally or sexually.

It's another thing to know Jesus is there, but when the mortgage is 6 months late because you were laid off and you've done all you can, and you are scared you are going to be homeless, that's down-to-earth fear.

Or maybe your fear is everyday, you fear going out in public, or you fear talking to people you don't know, or you fear . . . anything.

You know Jesus wants to partner with you, you know Jesus is bigger than the fear, and yet your body simply reacts with fear, even if you tell it not to!!

It's as if the fear is hard-coded in and in some ways it is.

Once you've had a bad experience that has hurt you, your brain [specifically your limbic system] hard-codes a defensive response, in its own effort to protect you.

So when something similar occurs in the future, your body displays an immediate fear response when that thing re-occurs.

For example, if you've been hit, the next time you see a hand raised, your heart beats harder in fear, and it happens in a split second.

It happens before Jesus calms you in the moment!

This can happen with anything that has instilled fear in you: any hurt, any emotional abuse, any unwelcome criticism, yelling, barrage, sexual abuse, even belittling or bullying.

Jesus can and will step into that with you - but you have to partner with Him proactively!

Through counselors and intensive study, He taught me why and how that fear response happens.

Once I saw that the fear response was automatic in the body, happening before we can even think it, I realized that that fear response had to be reprogrammed.

I initially tried some of the counseling solutions, but was frustrated that it was the only area in my recovery where I wasn't relying just on Jesus!

So I sought Him to show me how He could replace that fear response.

He showed me how I could partner with Him, using the techniques in this chapter, to replace that fear response (with His Presence and power and guidance).

Ultimately what provided the most powerful relief was relentlessly partnering with Jesus such that my internal peace level preempted the fear response.

This did not happen overnight and there are still times when I can strongly feel that fear response, but the more time I spend with Jesus, and the more peace and calm I walk in, the less I am finding myself overtaken by the fear response.

> **Here's an example of how you can invite Jesus to partner with you in overcoming the fear:**
>
> Lord Jesus, I bring You this fear.
>
> You know what I am going through with this fear.
>
> I am afraid of ___ and I'm afraid of _____.
>
> I am afraid You won't come through, I'm afraid of what will happen if _____ happens.
>
> But I ask You to come alongside me with this fear.
>
> I invite You into this fear.
>
> Help me to walk through this.
>
> Thank You for walking through this with me.

Once you've shared with the Lord in this way, take some time to praise and worship. If you don't have words, pray the Psalms. Or turn on streaming praise music online and sing along.

You can do this process for any fear or anxiety or stress or hurt. As with anything else with the Lord, He may heal things and fix things immediately. Or He may employ a process and time.

So often we focus on Jesus' immediate healings. And yet, He told the ten lepers to go to the priest . . and as they were walking, they were healed. The man to whom He said, pick up your mat and walk, I personally don't believe he was healed instantly, I believe he was healed as he went through the process of picking up his mat.

If you've had a fear response or an anxiety response for some time, let's say 10 years, yes, He might heal you immediately. But it's quite likely that even if He heals some component of it now, He will work out the complete healing in you over the next few months or even years as you take that fear to Him 25 times, 100 times, or 1000 times.

Other Emotions

Let's model some of the other emotions as well. Each of these negative emotions, such as anxiety (based on fear), hurt, stress, anger, etc., work in the body much same the way I shared about fear in that your body encodes a reaction to the trigger for that emotion, based on your life experiences.

My experience has been that relentlessly taking these emotions to Jesus has, over time, made it easier and faster for my mind and body to react in a healthy way, and not with the automatic fear-based trigger.

But I want to re-iterate that the physical response in your body is real, and you may benefit from counseling that helps you understand how your body specifically processes these emotions. Sometimes just knowing how it works, makes it easier to visualize the work Jesus is doing in you!

Anxiety:

Lord Jesus, I bring You this anxiety.

You know what I am going through with this anxiety.

I am concerned about ____ and I'm concerned about ____.

But I ask You to come alongside me with this anxiety.

I invite You into this anxiety.

Help me to walk through this.

Thank You for walking through this with me.

Hurt

Lord Jesus, I bring You this hurt.

You know what I am going through with this hurt.

I feel ____ about ____ and I feel ____ about ____.

I ask You to come near me with this hurt.

I invite You into this hurt.

Help me to walk through this.

Thank You for walking through this with me.

Stress

Lord Jesus, I bring You this stress.

You know what I am going through with this stress.

I feel ____ about ____ and I feel ____ about ____.

I ask You to come alongside me with this stress.

I invite You into this stress.

Help me to walk through this.

Thank You for walking through this with me.

Anger

Lord Jesus, I bring You this anger.

You know what I am going through with this anger.

I feel ____ about ____ and I feel ____ about ____.

I ask You to come alongside me with this anger.

I invite You into this anger.

Help me to walk through this.

Thank You for walking through this with me.

Every time the emotion or feeling comes back, go through the prayer process I shared earlier. Continue to spend time with Him. Let His Spirit overcome your fear.

When you walk in the Spirit you walk out of the fear or emotion. But it's an active walking. It's not a one time prayer, it's not just an intention.

It's walking step after step after step. That might mean prayer after prayer after prayer. Time with Him after time with Him after time with Him.

Connection Space:

Let's use this to create a template you can use to take any emotion to Him at any time:

Lord Jesus, I bring You this _____.

You know what I am going through with this _____.

I feel ____ about ___ and I feel _____ about _____.

I ask You to come alongside me with this _____.

I invite You into this _____.

Help me to walk through this.

Thank You for walking through this with me.

This gives you a solid framework to cover the important parts in your own mind and soul as they pertain to your struggle. It's not just the words, it's personal, it's intentional, it's genuinely asking for the Lord's help and presence.

Jesus wants to walk you through every single instance of pain or hurt or stress you are going through. He wants to heal you. He wants to help you. He wants to advise you. He wants to be present with you.

Another Word About Counseling

I'll say once again, this isn't easy to do if you've been exposed to deep trauma or pain in the past that has encoded itself in your mental processing. Jesus healed me, but part of the healing in this area was through human counselors, in addition to very consistently continuing to take the triggering situations to Jesus.

If you are dealing with something that feels bigger than you can deal with on your own, allow Jesus to lead you to the right counsel or help.

Just as part of my journey to closeness with Jesus was through people, whom He sent my way, different people who prayed for me or had words of encouragement for me in the spiritual, He also led me to several counselors who were critical in my journey, specifically in dealing with what's in this chapter about fear and anxiety, etc. So I would encourage you that just as you would accept help from someone who has been down the road ahead of you spiritually, be open to accepting help from someone qualified to help with these types of things as well!

PART 7: MATURITY IN JESUS

28

Where Are You, Lord?

Becoming Accustomed to His Presence

When we spend a lot of time with the Lord, we may have certain feelings or sensations that accompany that time.

That might be a sensed manifestation of His Presence, or it might simply be our own bodies' feelings and sensations that occur as we feel loved, accepted, and communicated with by Him.

Sometimes we become accustomed not just to Him in our lives, but also to the sensations that might accompany His Presence.

However, although we may sometimes sense His Presence, and our feelings are real, if we evaluate our relationship with Him just based on what we feel, we can become dismayed or even deceived.

True faith is walking with Him even when we cannot see Him, we cannot feel Him, or we cannot otherwise evaluate in the natural that He is there.

The Fallacy of Feelings

When we begin a new level of relationship with God, we enter a new understanding with Him, or we encounter a new level of His presence, sometimes that is accompanied by earthly feelings.

God created feelings for our good and for our use. Feelings are real, and they are a reflection of our current perception of events around us. Feelings on their own are not good or bad.

And by His great power and His great love, He gave us feelings to accompany certain experiences.

Feelings of calm, feelings of awe, feelings of ecstasy, feelings of love, happiness, contentment.

In the natural, those feelings occur and change over time.

Feelings are a reflection of our current perception of what's going on around us, or in us.

When we spend time with the Lord in a new way - perhaps that's walking in the woods with Him, a new praise posture, or a deeper intention in your awareness of Him - for months we may feel His presence in a fresh new way; there may be a new feeling associated with the time we spend with Him.

That feeling itself is not necessarily Him, that feeling is possibly the perception of our experience with Him that day. But our minds associate that feeling with "God." Over time, as we become attenuated to the new experience we no longer "feel" the newness, the freshness, of the new experience.

If we assume then that because we don't have that feeling anymore, that God isn't there, then we begin to feel lonely; we begin to feel as though God abandoned us.

But in reality, He's right there. He always was. The challenge is that we were ascribing our feelings to His presence, when indeed they were just . . . feelings.

I believe this is why so many times when we spend a lot of time with the Lord, over time we begin to wonder if He's not speaking as much. My belief is that He is speaking just as much, but because we were allowing our feelings to be the primary indicator to us that He was speaking, we aren't sensing His voice separately from the feelings.

Here's an earthly example:

If you ride a new roller coaster for the first time, you are likely to experience feelings at a deeper level: feelings of fear, anticipation, awe, an overwhelming sense of surprise or contentedness.

Those feelings are real.

They reflect your excitement and satisfaction with the roller coaster.

But if you ride that same roller coaster 100 times, do you experience the same feelings?

Probably not: fear: gone | anticipation: gone | excitement: reduced | overwhelm: gone

Has the roller coaster changed?

No.

Has the speed changed?

No.

Has anything changed about the actual ride?

No.

But the feeling of the roller coaster changes.

God created us as spiritual beings that live, operate, and feel in an earthly body.

When we enter a new level of spiritual experience with Him, sometimes we feel the same kinds of accompanying emotions that might occur on a roller coaster:

Feelings of fear, anticipation, awe, an overwhelming sense of surprise or contentedness.

We can associate those feelings with the new level of experience with God, and we can even believe that those feelings are God.

Those feelings reflect your excitement and satisfaction with the new level of time with God.

But if you spend that new level of time with God 100 times, do you experience the same feelings?

Probably not: fear: gone | anticipation: possibly gone or reduced | excitement: reduced | overwhelm: gone

Has the new level of time with God changed?

No.

Has the activity changed?

No.

Has anything changed about the actual time with God?

No.

But the feelings associated with the new level of time with God changes.

Some of what we experience with God is reflected through our emotions and feelings, and if we singularly evaluate our closeness to God based on how we feel, then we are incorrectly evaluating our depth of relationship to God.

If anything, our relationship with God will be amazingly increased with 100 times in His presence, just like our intimacy with the turns, twists, and dips of the roller coaster will be amazingly increased with 100 times around the loop, but in both cases, the feelings associated with it will be greatly reduced.

Connection Space:

Consider how you feel now.

Do you feel like God is here?

If not, do you know that He is here?

Can you see that even when you cannot feel His Presence, He is here?

Even when you don't feel something, He is here.

And He can speak to you even when you cannot hear Him.

It might be nudges.

It might just be a knowing.

You might have to just trust that He is getting through, in some way.

When you can disconnect feeling close to Him with actually being close to Him, you might be able to move much faster towards a constant awareness of His Presence.

You might be able to operate in a deep knowing, instead of a feeling.

Let's pray:

Lord Jesus, give us wisdom.

Give us the bravery to accept that You are speaking, even when we can't hear You.

Give us Your Spirit to know that You are there and You can speak, even when we can't feel it, even when there is no accompanying feeling.

Thank You, Lord!

We love You, Lord!

The Enemy Will Tell You God's Not There

The enemy will actually use the reduction in your feelings against you. The enemy will try to convince you that because you no longer "feel" the excitement when you've prayed in the Spirit for the 100th time, that it's no longer God, that it's no longer effective, that He has somehow left you, or forsaken you, or doesn't care.

But that would be like believing that the roller coaster is no longer a roller coaster because since you've ridden it 100 times and you know every turn and every dip, you no longer have the same feelings of fear and anticipation.

Of course it's still a roller coaster.

Of course God is still God.

Of course my 100th hour praying in the Spirit is just as powerful (if not more powerful) than my first - even if I don't feel anything special the 100th time.

I have read accounts of people spending as much as years trying to "find God" again after the feelings fade. They think, for years, that God is no longer there, because they can't feel Him.

The enemy tells you that because you can't feel Him anymore, He is gone and doesn't care.

And yet, He is just as much there as ever before.

Instead of worrying about whether or not He is there, assume that He is. Find different ways to connect with Him.

Elijah's Experience With Feelings

Consider Elijah.

Yesterday Elijah is hearing God clearly, he's challenging the prophets of Baal to get their god to burn their sacrifice, he makes his own altars, pours water all over them, God comes down, makes fire on all the water-drenched altars, Elijah kills all the false prophets, and he's on the top of the world. God came through and he's excited! He's been hearing God, He did what God told him to do, and he's on top of the world. (I Kings 18)

Max dopamine, top of the world experience, he's been running full tilt with the Lord, full adrenaline pumping for weeks, coffee-ed up, Victory is won . . .

Tomorrow he wakes up and . . . since the prophets are dead, he's not excited anymore. Job completed. Boredom sets in. He's just not feeling it. Not only does boredom set in, but the Queen decides to put an assassination order out against Elijah, so now he's bored, tired, not hearing God, running for his life . . . and feeling depressed and worthless. (I Kings 19)

There's no dopamine, the coffee's out, adrenaline is dried up, he's being chased by the same queen he just experienced Victory over . . . and he enters the worst days of his life. He's ready to die, he's feeling depressed, he tells God he's the only prophet seeking the Lord . . .

We've all been there before: big win yesterday, today we are down in the dumps. Part of that is our natural bodies' response: we've been running on cortisol and adrenaline because of the project, but once it's over our body stops producing those and other neurotransmitters. We feel depressed the next day. We are literally detoxing from our own bodies' neurotransmitters producing less because we don't need them today!

But because we don't feel good, we feel depressed, as Elijah did, and we think God must not be here anymore. We can't hear Him. We can't sit still long enough to hear Him.

But did God change?

No.

Did God stop talking?

No.

Did God stop loving us?

No.

The only thing that changed is our feelings!

Our circumstances change, and we think that God's not here.

Our feelings have changed.

We become bored, and we tune out.

The queen is chasing us, and we become scared.

We experience trauma, betrayal, anger, loss . . . and we become depressed.

And our old ways of talking with God . . .

Aren't working for us.

Not because God isn't there.

Not because God doesn't care.

Not because God doesn't love you anymore.

But simply because we don't have the feelings we had in the past, or we aren't hearing Him the way we heard Him in the past.

Connection Space:

How is God speaking to you now?

How do you remember Him speaking to you in the past?

What has changed?

What are possible ways He is speaking to you currently?

Are you missing or discounting some of them?

Let's pray:

Father, show me how You are speaking to me.

I want to hear Your voice.

I want to hear the Holy Spirit.

I want to listen, I want to hear You!

I want to trust that You are near, even when I don't feel You, even when I've become accustomed to Your Presence and then don't sense You as strongly.

Thank You in advance for speaking clearly and for showing me how You are speaking to me now!

In Jesus name,

Amen

Solid Relationship With Him

Build a relationship with God that's so secure, so deep, that when you get bored, when life throws you a curveball, when you are so stressed that you can't hear God's still small voice, you simply know He's there, and you keep moving forward.

Just like Elijah, we may be seeking Him in the fire . . but we don't feel Him there. We may be seeking Him in the earthquake . . but we don't feel Him there. Instead, He's in the still, calm voice.

In my own experience, over many years, I've experienced Him in different ways. But the most recent, memorable experience for me has been during this most recent trial. For months and months, I would praise and worship and kneel and cry and I had intense feelings, and I heard God through them.

But over time, I began to have less of an emotional reaction to the time in praise and worship.

At one point, I was spending a significant amount of time - hours - praying in tongues. Wow! I felt so close to Him! I felt like He was moving things in the heavenlies (I still believe He was!).

I prayed prayers that were intense and I experienced the reality of God speaking into my heart.

But over time I began to "feel" less in situations like those. At first it was disconcerting; am I listening, what am I doing wrong, God?

Then I began to more quietly lean into Him. Softly praying. Softly praying in tongues. Taking Him everything.

A deeper awareness of His nudges when I'm speaking with someone: don't say that, Sean, don't talk about that, Sean, share this, Sean.

A much deeper calm. Instead of as much of a palpable "feeling" that He is there, I have more of a calm, "knowing" that He's there. He's in me, He's next to me, and the knowing of it is real, it's visceral. But it doesn't carry the same emotional feeling that it used to.

Does that mean God's not here with me? Does that mean God's not speaking to me?

No, God is more real to me now than ever before!

God is here, God is watching me write these words.

God is so close to me.

I know He's here.

It's almost impossible to share the intensity of my belief, my knowing that He's here with me, He's guiding me today, He guided my interactions and the people who were impacted by His words through me even in the last few days.

And yet as I stand here writing, I don't have a "feeling."

If anything, I'm simply very calm.

So if I were to evaluate my current closeness with God by how I feel right now ... I might think He's not close.

But I know that He is!

As you spend time with Jesus, you may experience some spiritual highs, you may experience some moments that feel ecstatic, you might experience things that "feel" good - and all of that is well and good and it's part of the (roller coaster!) ride - but when the dust settles, when you've prayed 100 times, when you've been to the top of the mountain and experienced Victory -

And you wake up the next day and don't feel His presence -

Learn from Elijah, learn from this book, learn from life, learn from Jesus Himself:

He didn't go anywhere.

He's right there.

He's in the still, small voice.

> **Connection Space:**
>
> Take 5 minutes, and engage with Him.
>
> Evaluate the way you sense or feel His Presence now.
>
> Or consider what you don't feel in this moment, that perhaps you've felt in the past.
>
> Closeness. Calm. Peace. Ecstatic. Nothing. Overwhelming. Underwhelming. Less than before.

How do you sense or feel God now?

Is it more of a tangible feeling and can you truly sense that He's in the moment?

Or is it quieter, and you simply have to lean into the calm and know He is there?

If you are journaling yet, write down these thoughts.

Take them to the Lord:

Lord, I feel _____. What do You want me to know about how I sense, or don't sense You, now?

Listen. Wait.

Ask, How do You want me to deal with this feeling?

How do You feel about this feeling?

Listen to Him. Wait for Him.

Don't just quickly get up or read on.

Sit in silence for a few moments or a few minutes.

Know that God is there, Jesus is there, whether you feel Him or not!

29

Maturity With Jesus

From Principles to Maturity

Not only do we have access to a deep and personal relationship with Christ, dwelling in Him and He in us, but there is a deeper level of spiritual maturity available. In fact, it's not only available to us, but we were created for it, we are being equipped for it, and it's for the unity and the development of the body.

We are instructed to move past the principles of the doctrine of Christ, and move towards perfection (completeness):

Therefore leaving the principles of the doctrine of Christ, let us go on unto perfection; not laying again the foundation of repentance from dead works, and of faith toward God,

Of the doctrine of baptisms, and of laying on of hands, and of resurrection of the dead, and of eternal judgment. (Hebrews 6:1-2)

The author of Hebrews is saying that those things listed, which are pretty deep indeed, are simply the principles of the doctrine of Christ, and that we can now go on unto perfection. The original Greek for "perfection" was "teleiotes" which has a meaning of completeness or perfection.

It happens to be the same word as Paul used in Colossians 3:14:

And above all these things put on charity, which is the bond of perfectness.

Charity of course being deep, caring love; he is saying that love is the bond, the uniting agent of perfectness.

And that verse is immediately followed by a verse that speaks deeply to the concept of peace, which is an expression of the fruit of the Holy Spirit, and is a state of mind we receive when we are in perfect union with Christ, dwelling in His Presence, and He in us!:

And let the peace of God rule in your hearts, to the which also ye are called in one body; and be ye thankful. (Colossians 3:15)

The writer of Hebrews writes in the context of the believers being stuck in the first principles, and needing milk, not strong meat:

For when for the time ye ought to be teachers, ye have need that one teach you again which be the first principles of the oracles of God; and are become such as have need of milk, and not of strong meat.

For every one that useth milk is unskilful in the word of righteousness: for he is a babe.

But strong meat belongeth to them that are of full age, even those who by reason of use have their senses exercised to discern both good and evil. (Hebrews 5:12-14)

He concludes that strong meat belongs to us who are mature, and by reason of use (practice) our senses are exercised to discern both good and evil.

It's obvious there is a foundational level of our faith with Jesus that's wrapped up in the basics.

And there is also an advanced level of maturity that is marked by love, that is the unity of completeness or perfection, and is closely related to having the peace of God ruling in our hearts!

The writer of Hebrews goes on to say:

And we desire that every one of you do shew the same diligence to the full assurance of hope unto the end:

That ye be not slothful, but followers of them who through faith and patience inherit the promises. (Hebrews 6:11-12)

The example of inheriting the promises he gives next is the faith of Abraham!

I want to encourage you in that now that you have received the practices of drawing close to Him, connecting with His Presence, walking in the Spirit and not fulfilling the lusts of the flesh, slaying the negative thoughts as they come, dealing with feelings, overcoming anxiety, and so on, that it doesn't all become a routine implementation of a stale and religious process.

Instead, assuming that you are walking in everything so far, that's not the end goal or the final accomplishment.

Paul writes:

Not as though I had already attained, either were already perfect: but I follow after, if that I may apprehend that for which also I am apprehended of Christ Jesus.

Brethren, I count not myself to have apprehended: but this one thing I do, forgetting those things which are behind, and reaching forth unto those things which are before,

I press toward the mark for the prize of the high calling of God in Christ Jesus. (Philippians 3:14-16)

The prize of the high calling of God in Christ Jesus is not the religious implementation of activities that keep us from sin, allow us to feel or even be close to Him, or any other adherence to principles, but instead it's the final culmination of our eternal relationship with Christ!

To me this next passage tells us not only our position in Christ currently in our faith, but also by virtue of the words "in the ages to come" indicates that the "exceeding riches of his grace in his kindness toward us through Christ Jesus" is eternal in scope!

And hath raised us up together, and made us sit together in heavenly places in Christ Jesus:

That in the ages to come he might shew the exceeding riches of his grace in his kindness toward us through Christ Jesus. (Ephesians 2:6-7)

We are not just going through the motions of living a good life, even connecting with Jesus for any earthly reward or satisfaction (although that's present and real), but we are currently living out the first segment of our eternal place with Christ, sitting in heavenly places, and being the recipient of exceeding riches of His grace!

So in light of all of these verses (and frankly, so many more like this hidden in the New Testament), what's the next step towards spiritual maturity?

When we have laid the foundation of His life dwelling in us and us simultaneously connecting with Him; we are walking in the Spirit and all that entails, both the slaying of the flesh and the fruit of the Spirit; and we are living out the spiritual practices of communication with Him, such as praise and hearing His voice, talking with Him, and praying in the Spirit; we can step into a depth with Him that is constant and ever-present in nature, constantly communing with Him and experiencing His Presence and peace continuously.

In that depth of relationship, not only will we grow closer to Christ Himself and become more like Him, but we will also begin to draw others closer to Him, passing on the truths He's given us, operating in our gifts for the growth of the church body, and living a life of love that is the unity that holds our completeness together with our purpose.

Connection Space:

Father, thank You for the foundational elements of faith in Jesus that You have grown in me.

Thank You for the sanctification that is being walked out in me as I walk in Your Spirit.

Thank You for making me fit for Your use.

Show me how I can walk in deeper maturity with You.

Thank You for loving me so much, and for making a part of Your mission on earth!

In Jesus name,

Amen

Pray Without Ceasing

The phrase "pray without ceasing" in I Thessalonians 5:17 is clear and direct. For years I've made an effort to pray without ceasing, but because for me prayer was concentrated words and specific conversation with the Lord, it was very hard. No, not just very hard - practically impossible. It was always a genuine attempt at something that I hoped to one day be able to do - and yet now when I consider it I realize that my meaning of it makes it practically impossible unless you quit life, quit people, and just pray all the time.

In the context of what we've studied in this book, which of course includes a lot of prayer, but also includes a deep closeness developed with the Lord, let's read part of the passage in which the phrase "pray without ceasing" exists (even this passage is a continuation of a prior set of practical instructions for living life and getting along with others):

Rejoice evermore.

Pray without ceasing.

In every thing give thanks: for this is the will of God in Christ Jesus concerning you.

Quench not the Spirit.

Despise not prophesyings.

Prove all things; hold fast that which is good.

Abstain from all appearance of evil.

And the very God of peace sanctify you wholly; and I pray God your whole spirit and soul and body be preserved blameless unto the coming of our Lord Jesus Christ. (I Thessalonians 5: 16-23)

The directive "pray without ceasing" did not stand alone when it was originally penned!

If we consider that we are called to rejoice, and pray, and give thanks, and don't stop the Spirit and don't despise prophesies, and finally may the God of peace sanctify you and may your whole spirit and soul and body be preserved blameless, we get a much richer idea of what our continuous communication with Him looks like!

It's a much bigger picture than even including praise and worship and tongues and thanksgiving in prayer. It's a lifestyle of continuous awareness and communication with Him, combined with thanksgiving and reliance on the God of peace to sanctify us!

Now with this expanded concept of our daily peaceful life, one that is full of the fruit of the Spirit, where there is joy and peace and gentleness and longsuffering and more, and that has rejoicing and thanksgiving and prayer, imagine living a full day just like this!

I believe that's the full context of "pray without ceasing!" It's a continuous awareness and communication with Him, submission to Him, and reliance on Him; and it's full of the complete fruit of the Spirit!

Could we be aware of His presence constantly? Could we, between every activity, acknowledge His presence? Between every conversation could we acknowledge His presence? Could we be aware of His presence constantly, even during our activities? Maybe at first it's an effort, maybe at first it requires a reminder or intentional diligence, but over time it becomes so natural that it barely requires thought, to just know that He is there, that you are in submission, and that you rely on Him.

How do we get here? Planned time with Him is the first step and the foundation. Making a concerted, intentional effort to spend time with Him between activities increases our time with Him, and our awareness of His presence. Then it becomes easier to be aware of Him during those activities as well. The more time I am spending with Him, either in planned set-aside time, time between activities, or throughout the day and my activities, the more I am constantly aware of Him and able to be communicating with Him.

Additionally, the trials and daily challenges have kept me reliant on Him constantly. Each time I take a challenge to Him instead of solving it on my own brings a deeper expression of conscious awareness of His presence in my life. If I take a challenge and solve it on my own, I'm not utilizing His presence or His power, and I'm not praying without ceasing. But if I receive a challenge, or I am daily enduring the impact of a trial, and instead of trying to solve it on my own, I am completely reliant on Him, this amplifies the level of conscious awareness I have of His presence and His activity in my life. Contiguous with my conversation with Him, this brings me significantly closer to the ideal of "praying without ceasing."

Perhaps the hardest place to remain in constant awareness or prayer is that of the good times! It's counterintuitive, because certainly initially when we are celebratory we are giving Him credit and we are communicating with Him and aware of Him. But over time, if there are no challenges, and life and circumstances are going well, it's easy to drift from constantly thinking of His impact, presence, and power in our lives. As we drift, we move further from the ideal of "praying without ceasing" and start losing the constant awareness of His communication and presence with us. So it's during these easy times when we might have to make even a greater effort to remain in connection with Him!

The more aware that I am of Him, when something comes up, such as an interruption, a reason to get irritated, a reaction to a judgment or a criticism or an annoyance, the easier it is to take it to Him immediately. That adds to the consistent awareness with Him.

I do believe this takes time (as in months or quarters, not just hours) to attain, so if it feels unattainable at first, that's okay. Know that it gets easier. It certainly has for me.

I also believe it takes intentional effort. Not effort in terms of working hard to have it, but effort in terms of intentionality, returning to awareness of Him when you lose it, and an awareness of how much time we really have throughout the day between conversations and activities.

Connection Space:

Let's consider that you want to be praying without ceasing.

Imagine you have a deep awareness of Him right now, and in the back of your mind, you are conscious of Him, and you are open to any thoughts He has for you.

You are submitted to any desire or nudge He gives you.

You are open to talking with Him about anything He wants.

If someone asks you something, if you consider a decision, you are silently taking it to Him.

This may not be an involved process, but can almost be a sensing of the thought of taking it to Him, as you develop this practice of being in constant communication and awareness of Him.

Lord Jesus, I want to pray without ceasing.

Please show me what that means experientially.

Is it exactly what I'm understanding here, or is there another nuance You have to it for me?

Please guide me in becoming more open, more aware, and more constantly communicative with You and Your Spirit!

Thank You Jesus!

The Purpose in the Trial

Just having a deep relationship with Jesus doesn't miraculously take your problems away. Yes, He does miracles and sometimes He takes the situation away. But if He doesn't, he is right there with you. Always. And the wait may be for months on end, it might be years-long. He promises to be right there with you; He promises you "I am with you always, even until the end of the age" (Matthew 28:20b). He promises His burden is light and His yoke is easy (Matthew 11:30), but He does not promise to take the problems of life away or to remove us from the world (John 17:15).

I challenge you to persevere. You don't have to do it all. It won't happen overnight. It won't happen without mistakes and trial and error, and failing and apologizing and learning and testing and pressure and time and frustration.

You may be continuing to wrestle with the value of the trial you've been through that has been part of growing closer to Him. I want to encourage you next that your trial has value, and that not only does it bring you closer to Jesus, it also gives you the strength, maturity and character to bring His light and presence to others who have been through what you've been through.

James tells us:

My brethren, count it all joy when ye fall into divers temptations;

Knowing this, that the trying of your faith worketh patience.

But let patience have her perfect work, that ye may be perfect and entire, wanting nothing. (James 1:2-4)

Counting it all joy is difficult when we are going through a tough situation. But the logic in that passage rings so true: "the trying (testing) of our faith works patience."

And James draws a line from developing patience to a place of becoming "perfect and entire." This might feel like a stretch, and yet in our trial, as we go through and suffer, and we become patient through it, in that patience is birthed a deeper relationship with Christ, a deeper compassion for others going through something similar, and a constancy with Him that is rooted in real-world trust and reliance that can only come through walking through a trial together!

Paul takes this a little deeper:

And not only so, but we glory in tribulations also: knowing that tribulation worketh patience;

And patience, experience; and experience, hope:

And hope maketh not ashamed; because the love of God is shed abroad in our hearts by the Holy Ghost which is given unto us. (Romans 5:3-5)

The trials we go through season us with patience and experience, and as we emerge on the other side, they give us hope that we can share with others.

Although I wish there had been an easier path through my life so far, and I would take back the pain I've caused others, I wouldn't change my own struggle, pain, or hurt, if it meant I couldn't have the relationship I now have with Jesus.

I relate it to the journey of Joseph: without being sold into slavery by his brothers (talk about trauma), without becoming excellent in his work in the house of Potiphar but then being betrayed and lied on by Potiphar's wife, without landing in prison and becoming the #1 prisoner in charge of the other prisoners, without having to wait two additional years after he asked the butler to mention him to Pharoah, without all of that pain and travail, Joseph never could have become the second in charge in all of Egypt. He never could have brought the world through the seven year famine, he never could have said to his brothers, with love in his eyes, and in his heart, with complete forgiveness: "you meant it for evil but God meant it for good . . . I will take care of you and your little ones [for life]." (Genesis 37, 39-45)

God's call to ministry has been on my life in a known way at least since I was about 12 years old. He re-affirmed that call a couple years before my marriage.

But because of my stubbornness, my inability or unwillingness to see the trauma and my flawed response, I wasn't ready for ministry then. I wasn't ready, like Joseph wasn't ready when he received the dream of his father and mother and brothers bowing down to him, and shared it with them.

Twenty years ago, I would have ruined any ministry He gave me, through ineffective stress coping, my inauthenticity, and my untruthfulness to avoid criticism, judgment, and pain.

But today, after suffering through and emerging from the pains I've shared here, drawing close to Him, and He drawing close to me, I believe I'm ready for a new season.

I wouldn't be here without the deep travail of my last season.

Is there something God is preparing you for, through your current trial? Are you fighting your trial instead of leaning into it, letting

God heal you, draw close to you, and make you into the person He originally designed you to be before life, parents, the enemy, or your choices, sabotaged it?

Is it possible He is burning away the dross in your life, like He did in my life?

Is it possible He is returning you to your original condition with Him, before you were even born?

If any or all of that is true, would it be worth it to you - as it has been to me - to emerge from the rest of the journey of pain He is allowing you to go through - with complete reliance on Him, a deep personal, communicatory relationship with Him - and the ability to live out His original call on your life; like Joseph was able to finally do as second in command in Egypt and provider of his brothers and their families, and as I have been released to do, perhaps even starting off with the writing and publishing of this book?

No matter who has hurt you, harmed you, betrayed you, or destroyed you, He can redeem you from it all, change your heart and make it original, soft, and open.

And no matter who you have hurt, harmed, betrayed, or destroyed, He can forgive you of it all; He can redeem you from it all, change your heart and make it original, soft, and open - and give you a second chance to live the life He intended for you, as He has given me a second chance to do life right and do it His way instead of my way.

My hope and prayer is that you can draw close to the Lord and develop a deep meaningful relationship with Him.

If you are going through the trial of your life, allow the pressure to aid you in drawing closer to Him.

If you are not going through the trial of your life, I encourage you to deeply lean into Him as if your life depends on it, as so often we only grow during the tough times, not because we can't grow during boom times, but because we don't focus and we don't have enough urgency and pain. Growing close to the Father, Jesus, and the Holy Spirit is worth ANY effort!

> **Connection Space:**
>
> Trials are never easy or they wouldn't be trials!
>
> As you consider the trial you are going through or have emerged from, are you able to see that you've grown in ways you couldn't have grown otherwise?
>
> Is your trial able to inform others in a way that allows them to grow faster, perhaps without enduring your pain and your trial?
>
> Take it to the Lord:
>
> I know I may not fully understand this trial, but thank You for the fruit of the trial.
>
> Thank You for molding me into deeper relationship with You, and for making me into a useful vessel in Your Kingdom and Your plan.

Please show me how I can walk out the rest of this trial in more grace, and to more benefit to others.

What else do You want me to learn through this trial?

Is it time for me to release more of what I've learned so far, to others, even before I complete this trial?

Show me Your wisdom, Your way, and Your love for me and others, through this trial.

Thank You for Your abiding love, always!

Amen

Maturity for the Development of the Body

The improvement of our own selves and our relationship and purity before Him is not the final end-state of maturity with Christ! When we draw close to Christ, when we are aware of His Presence and leading in our lives, when we are walking in the Spirit, and when we are trusting and resting in Him, we have become the type of vessel that is fit for the Master's use not just for our own communication and enjoyment with Him, but for the contribution to others' maturity as well.

Paul in this next passage indicates that we each are "given grace according to the measure of the gift of Christ" and we are each given some measure of capacity as apostles, prophets, evangelists, pastors, or teachers. Each of us should play at least one of those roles in the body of Christ.

And the purpose of it is expressed in verse 12, "for the perfecting of the saints, for the work of the ministry, for the edifying of the body of Christ;" it's the culmination of ultimate maturity in Christ!

There is one body, and one Spirit, even as ye are called in one hope of your calling;

One Lord, one faith, one baptism,

One God and Father of all, who is above all, and through all, and in you all.

But unto every one of us is given grace according to the measure of the gift of Christ.

Wherefore he saith, When he ascended up on high, he led captivity captive, and gave gifts unto men.

And he gave some, apostles; and some, prophets; and some, evangelists; and some, pastors and teachers;

For the perfecting of the saints, for the work of the ministry, for the edifying of the body of Christ: (Ephesians 4:4-8,11-12)

We already have the basics, the foundational elements of our faith, we have moved from milk to meat, by reason of use discerning good and evil, and we are personally growing close to Him.

But then as we move from personal growth to empowering others, the activities of apostle, prophet, evangelist, pastor, and teacher are "for the perfecting of the saints . . . for the edifying of the body of Christ:"

This reminds me of this powerful verse:

For we are his workmanship, created in Christ Jesus unto good works, which God hath before ordained that we should walk in them. (Ephesians 2:10)

God has already ordained us for good works of ministry, edification, and contributing to the growth of our fellow believers into perfection. His work in us is not just for our own personal salvation and eternal relationship with Him, but it's to contribute to the spiritual development of those He has already ordained for us to help!

Paul goes on to say that our works as apostles, prophets, evangelists, pastors, and teachers (or our role in those capacities, no matter how small), continues:

Till we all come in the unity of the faith, and of the knowledge of the Son of God, unto a perfect man, unto the measure of the stature of the fulness of Christ: (Ephesians 4:13)

And one main reason for this is:

That we henceforth be no more children, tossed to and fro, and carried about with every wind of doctrine, by the sleight of men, and cunning craftiness, whereby they lie in wait to deceive; (Ephesians 4:14)

So not only are we growing in the practices of growing close to Christ, walking in the Spirit, and leaving our old way of life behind, but we become impervious to the cunning craftiness of the world that might deceive us into letting go of the challenge of being a brilliant light on a hill for Christ!

But speaking the truth in love, may grow up into him in all things, which is the head, even Christ:

From whom the whole body fitly joined together and compacted by that which every joint supplieth, according to the effectual working in the measure of every part, maketh increase of the body unto the edifying of itself in love. (Ephesians 4:15-16)

These final verses summarize it all, that the purpose of it all is the edification of the body in love!

Our salvation and personal relationship is with Christ personally, but it's part of a grand plan of the Father for us to be unified in growing close to Christ together, not just as individual units!

So as much as the principles in this book have been focused on your personal growth with Him, and rooted in the very practices He's taken me through not just over 40+ years, but very deeply so during the 18 month trial, their additional purpose is to prepare you (and me) for the growth and edification of others, not just ourselves!

Connection Space:

Let's take this connection space to take time with the Lord and ask Him how you are participating in the edification of the saints, of those around you who could benefit from the spiritual maturity you've gained recently.

What has your growth has been over the last few months or years?

Where have you grown in His gifts?

Where have you stalled, and need to push harder into His grace?

(Not to push harder to make something happen on your own, but to more intentionally connect with the gifts He has placed in you.)

How would He have you minister to others?

How can you pass on some of what He's recently taught you?

Where do you fit into the body of Christ?

How does walking in your gifts to help others, help you remain focused on connecting with Him?

Which of these gifts do you feel you most identify with: the activities of apostle, prophet, evangelist, pastor, or teacher?

If you could choose one gifting where you would be most comfortable, which would it be?

What can you do today or this week to impact just one person in that way?

Let's pray:

Lord Jesus, thank You for Your grace in my life, for drawing me close to You.

Thank You for what You've grown in me recently.

Thank You for giving me gifts I can pass on to others.

Thank You for the ministry You have placed in me.

Thank You for making me Your workmanship in Your way!

Please give me wisdom to know where You have gifted me, so I can operate in Your gifts!

Please give me opportunities to share what You have poured into me.

Please help me to be aware of those opportunities.

Please give me the grace and the ability to carry out anything You have prepared me for!

Thank You for aiding me in becoming a useful vessel in Your Kingdom!

I love You Lord and thank You for Your ministry to me, and making me useful in Your Kingdom!

Amen

30

Always in His Presence

We've talked so much about the things we do to communicate with Jesus and experience His Presence. We've talked about setting aside structured time with Jesus. And we've talked about how we can experience His Presence at will, pretty much anytime.

We read in the Psalms how He is always with us:

Whither shall I go from thy spirit? or whither shall I flee from thy presence?

If I ascend up into heaven, thou art there: if I make my bed in hell, behold, thou art there.

If I take the wings of the morning, and dwell in the uttermost parts of the sea;

Even there shall thy hand lead me, and thy right hand shall hold me. (Psalm 139:7-10)

And in the New Testament:

For I am persuaded, that neither death, nor life, nor angels, nor principalities, nor powers, nor things present, nor things to come,

Nor height, nor depth, nor any other creature, shall be able to separate us from the love of God, which is in Christ Jesus our Lord. (Romans 8:38-39)

Nothing shall separate us from the love of God!

We can go through an entire day with an awareness of His Presence. And if we can go an entire day, we can stack days, and go for days or weeks or months or years.

You see, He's here anyway. He isn't more in my heart when I think about Him. He's here anyway.

He's with you anyway. He's with you right now as you are reading this. He's with you now, and He'll be with you in your structured time later, and He'll be with you during the next Connection Space.

So let's consider how it's possible to spend every waking moment with an awareness of Him.

Let's start with a conscious awareness of His Presence right now. He is here with you even as you are reading. Just know that. You don't have to speak anything, or do anything, you simply mentally think of His Presence within you and you just know it internally.

Notice that there was no effort or work involved in becoming aware of His Presence, even as you are reading. Perhaps you are even in the presence of others, or noise, or chaos around you. And yet you know He is here.

The actual step of connecting instantly with Him is effortless, because it's simply a matter of connecting with His Spirit that's already within you as a follower of Jesus. But even though it's effortless in terms of work, it does require your will and the act of intention. I think it's alot like faith. Faith itself isn't work, and yet without the mental step of choosing to believe in something that you cannot see or doesn't exist yet, it's not faith. It requires your will and intention.

Although there needn't be any striving involved in connecting with His Presence, there is work, effort, or intentioned awareness involved in setting your intention, choosing to connect, setting the time aside, and then staying free of distractions once you've connected with Him.

There is an intentional determination to spend more time with Him, a decision to prioritize time with Him over the many distractions of the day, and a commitment to learning how to stay in connection with Him even in the presence of others.

Now imagine that in the same way as you just became aware of His Presence, even as you were reading, you can do that at any time, during any activity. While reading, while driving, while cooking, when you wake up, when you are tired and prone to being irritable, when you are triggered and feel you are going to get angry, when . . . when . . . when . . . any time, any condition.

Once you can imagine that you are connected instantly, then each time you stop connecting, you can connect instantly again. You can connect instantly again so many times and so frequently, that over time you stay connectedly aware of His Presence more often, and for longer segments of time.

So, if that's the case, could you step into His Presence - simply connecting with the reality of His Presence inside you - so frequently that the times begin to overlap?

If you are connecting with Him so frequently that the times overlap, how close are you getting to connecting with Him constantly?

Of course we know that we will fall out of it from time to time, but I suggest to you that just as Paul advised us to "pray without ceasing" (I Thessalonians 5:17) and to be "always abounding in the work of the Lord," (I Corinthians 15:58); I believe we can set as a goal or a standard to connect with Him as much as possible, and if not constantly, as close as we can to constantly, with His grace and power in us!

Distractions from His Presence

Let's talk about distractions and how they pull us away from awareness and connection to His Presence.

Consider a time when you sense His Presence. Maybe it's 5 minutes during a quiet time. You are totally focused on Him. But your phone rings or you feel compelled to scroll. You take your focus off of Him and into the distraction. You've lost the awareness of His Presence.

Notice the loss of the awareness of His Presence was not because He was no longer there, nor was it because your desire to spend time with Him was lessened, but simply because an external distraction filled your awareness and displaced your awareness and connection with Him. In this case, the problem isn't in connecting with Him, the problem is in the interruption of the distraction.

So imagine you were to remove some of those distractions for longer periods of time. And you experience His Presence for longer.

Not because you had to work harder (or at all) to get into or stay in His Presence, but simply because you eliminated the thing interrupting or blocking His Presence once you are already there!

Could you imagine experiencing totally focused time with Jesus for 30 minutes, if distractions were removed or ignored?

I shared with you earlier about my own experiment of imagining a consuming fire each time an unwanted thought came into my mind. That was highly effective at reducing the amount and intensity of unwanted thoughts coming in. Now that they are significantly reduced, I will normally circumvent new distracting thoughts quickly by either ignoring them or mentally thinking of a "shield of faith" that repels the thoughts, taking a cue from this verse:

Above all, taking the shield of faith, wherewith ye shall be able to quench all the fiery darts of the wicked. (Ephesians 6:16)

If that's not effective, I will then imagine the consuming fire, or picture His blood washing over the thought.

Each of these visuals gives the mind an alternative thought to replace the unwanted thought.

There is a moment of mental decision and discipline to simply ignore the thought.

His Holy Spirit gives us the capacity to bring every thought into captivity to the obedience of Christ:

Casting down imaginations, and every high thing that exalteth itself against the knowledge of God, and bringing into captivity every thought to the obedience of Christ; (II Corinthians 10:5)

I'm not saying it's easy. It's taken a significant amount of discipline, focus, and effort to train my mind to repel thoughts with faith and to take every thought into captivity, but it's been worth it. And it's by His power, not mine, anyhow!

Presence With Him While With Other People

We are called to love people, to edify people, and to take care of certain people in our lives; and we can remain connected with Jesus while we are doing that.

Of course, there is a time and place for getting alone, for getting away from people. You may need the emotional space or the emotional rest. You may need to rest for emotional or spiritual bandwidth. And no matter how much He has called us to minister to others, He created your body and mind with limitations.

So considering that it is normal and necessary to separate from people for rest and dedicated time with Him, when we are with other people, we can still experience the Presence of Jesus. You see, the Holy Spirit is with you always. You simply have to be aware of Him there, and you can engage with Him and He can be a part of every interaction with other people.

Imagine that when you are with people, He is right there with you. He's the third person in the room. If you are in a large group, He's your sidekick; He's right there with you, even with the other people present.

You'll recall I shared about the time the lady whose shuffling and plastic crinkling while I was writing distracted me, and frankly annoyed me, and I was initially irritated. I saw that distraction as an interruption to my work, and it was. The error on my part was not in recognizing the distraction from my work, the error was in stepping out of the peace of walking in the Spirit. Initially I saw the distraction of the noise as an interruption, a break in my work. But once I saw the person accompanying the noise and distraction as a person who actually was hurting and struggling at that moment, I saw it as an invitation to minister to her, and in doing so I drew strength from Jesus Himself.

Instead of an interruption, it became a refreshing moment of potential ministry. Once I had the mental reframe, I made the conscious decision to treat her as if our interaction was really important, perhaps even orchestrated by God.

You see, in theory I want the interruptions, I want people to stop me and ask for help. But it's so easy in the moment - focused while writing, focused while meeting a deadline, focused while processing some prior emotion, even focused while connecting with Him! - to reject the interruption because it's not convenient - even though we want to help others!

How many times do we ask Him to send someone our way whom we can help? To whom we can offer advice out of our own experience? But many times they don't appear or need help when we are sitting and waiting for them; instead they appear when He sees they need help, or their pain becomes so great they reach out.

And once He ordains that time, or the person's need is realized, we have to quickly realize the power of the moment, and set aside our desires for a time, and lean into the opportunity He has provided, even if it's not instantly convenient!

You can be aware of Him and interacting with Him, while you are interacting with other people.

You can continue in connection and presence with Him during communication with others, just as you can continue conversation with someone in the natural when a third person walks in the door and sits down at your table. It is like Jesus is at your table, always.

Staying in His Presence

We've just considered several ways of expanding the time you spend in His Presence: increasing the time you intentionally set aside to be with Him, reducing the distractions that pull you out of deep communion with Him, being actively aware of Him while interacting with others, and continually staying in constant awareness and reciprocal communication, even if at only the thought or spirit level.

So with all of this in mind, how can you purposely spend more time in His Presence, throughout the day, even if it's not structured prayer time or quiet time? How can you have more awareness of His active Presence for more minutes of every hour?

We've seen how quickly you can enter an awareness and connection with His Presence. You can stay in that awareness and connection for minutes at a time, for hours at time, or even days at a time. But it starts with a moment, and that moment turns into minutes, and then those minutes turn into hours.

As you increase the minutes, and you increase the hours, you will be able to spend more and more time with Jesus!

Imagine that over time, you begin stacking the time with Him. Not only the constant awareness and communication, but the tangible and intentional time with Him.

Moments here, moments there, that add up to minutes of precious time with Him, even while with people or doing other things.

When you are walking somewhere for 10 minutes, instead of instinctively pulling your phone out, connect with Jesus for 10 minutes.

Add to that the constant intangible awareness, just as you know that right now He is with you and you can share any thought with Him now, and you can be aware of any thought He has for you.

When you consistently connect with Him in these ways, you begin to get a sense of always being with Him. You begin to spend more and more time with Him and less and less time on the trivial things that pull your attention from Him.

You can have as much time with Jesus as you want! And don't be discouraged when it takes time. It does take time. Part of the effort to stay aware of Him and to be aware of Him more, is focusing your attention on Him. Anytime we increase our focus or attention, there's an experience curve involved. It takes practice, repeated effort, and intention.

But it's so very worth it to be aware of Jesus much more during the day! The more hours in the day I can be aware of how close I am to Him, the more I hear Him, the more I listen to Him, the more I do His work, and the more I impact others!

Connection Space:

Consider if you want to be aware of Him more.

Tell Him what awareness you want with Him.

Tell Him how much closer you want to become to Him.

Ask Him for His help, His direction, His focus.

Consider what times of the day you can incrementally add distraction-free time with Him.

Consider how you can be prepared to practice being aware of and close to Him even during time with other people.

It might start small and be small interactions at first.

Lean into your awareness of Him in your conversations, in your struggles, in your arguments, in your discussions.

Lean into your awareness of His Presence as you are alone, and as you are with others.

Continue Connection Spaces

The spirit of the Connection Spaces throughout this book has been to foster a sense of stopping what you are doing and spending a few minutes with Him.

I encourage you to continue the practice of taking several times during the day to Connect with Him.

Those can be hour long quiet times or praise sessions, they can be 5 minute Connection Spaces, or anything in between.

You can do this anytime.

When you want to.

When you are tired.

When you are irritated and just need a few minutes.

When you need time with Him.

When you are happy and calm and everything is well.

When you need a lift.

When . . .

When . . .

When . . . anything.

Imagine a day with 10 Connection Spaces . . . one each hour during the day.

Imagine a week with 10 Connection Spaces each day.

How much closer would you grow to Him with 10 Connection Spaces each day?

The Connection Spaces are simply a tangible way to visualize taking a small segment of time and attention and placing it on the Lord, through the day.

The Quiet Times or Worship Times or other times you set aside are intentional times and spaces where you engage with Him.

The time you spend with Him can be more frequent than just Quiet Times, Worship Times, and Connection Spaces.

You can talk with Him between every work switch you do, you can talk with Him between conversations, if only for 30 seconds.

You can talk with Him throughout the day - constantly carrying on conversation with God, and listening for Him.

The more fully immersed in His Presence that you become, the more His Spirit will become real to you, and the more you will find yourself walking in the Spirit with less effort.

> **Connection Space:**
>
> Imagine you have a one minute break.
>
> Take something to the Lord quickly.
>
> Lord, what do You want me to know about this?
>
> Lord, how can I walk more deeply in Your Spirit right now?
>
> Lord, is there anything You would say to me now?

Or just worship Him for 30 seconds:

Lord, I worship You!

Thank You for powering my day!

Thank You for being here with me, and ahead of me!

Thank You, Lord!

Trusting Him

As we rely on Him, and trust Him more, we grow closer to Him.

Where was Jesus when the storm was raging around the boat, and the water was filling the boat from the storm? He was sleeping. That's right, sleeping. Not just ignoring the storm - but knowing that it didn't matter, knowing that He was fine, knowing that it was just a storm, knowing that when the disciples freaked out and woke Him, He would say just a few words and the storm would stop.

Should we treat our storms any differently than Jesus treated that one?

During the worst of my own storms in the last year, Jesus led me to do just that: Rest in the storm. Sleep in the storm.

In growing close to Christ, we learn to rely on Him for everything: our sustenance, our life, our emotions, our help, our rescue.

It's a constant abiding with Him.

It's a constant turning to Him in every need and every circumstance.

It's a complete reliance on Him for every need, whether spiritual or emotional or wisdom-based or any other need. Recognizing Him as the Source of everything.

During some of the darkest days of my recent trial, for several months, I cried out to the Lord and He simply had me wait, to trust, to do nothing, to let Him do His thing.

I believe He showed me glimpses of what He was doing behind the scenes, and He asked me to pray, pray in the Spirit, and just depend on Him.

I cannot help but think that the trust I have in Him now is related to the deep dependency I had, the trust I had, the complete surrender and submission to just let Him do His thing, His way, during those critical months.

It's during the time of real and intense battle or struggle that the real growth occurs. It's during that time when true dependence emerges, and can continue to grow past that time.

This element of complete surrender, complete submission, is critical to the process of growing closer to Him.

Without dependence, you simply wouldn't be as close. The deeper that reliance and submission is, the closer you can be to the Father, Jesus, and the Holy Spirit.

The more you can actively take your current troubles, challenges, even goals and projects, to Him, the more you can submit to Him. His Spirit can help you through everything, no matter how mundane.

The more you deeply rely on Him, the more you completely submit yourself and your circumstances to Him, completely releasing and letting go, the closer you can grow to Him!

> **Connection Space:**
>
> Let's make this real:
>
> Take 5 minutes, and engage with Him.
>
> Take your greatest challenge, attack, or stress to Him.
>
> Ask Him: "What do You want me to know about this?"
>
> Listen.
>
> Let Him answer.
>
> Ask Him: "What do You want me to do with this?"
>
> Let Him answer.
>
> Listen.
>
> Don't just quickly get up or read on.
>
> Sit in silence for a few moments or a few minutes.

Immediately In His Presence

As you are going through the activities I've shared, and growing closer to Jesus, you may find that you feel as though it takes some time to enter His presence, or to fully enter your time with Him. It certainly was that way for me for a long time, and even today there are times when I feel it takes time for me to fully engage.

However, I had a realization about God that's had a profound impact on how quickly I can enter His presence, or more correctly, connect with His Presence Who is always dwelling in me, and I'll share it with you here.

This is the realization: We experience God now. Today. We don't experience God yesterday, and we don't experience God tomorrow. In fact, we cannot even experience God one second ago. Or in one second. NOW is the time when we can experience God.

When we intentionally step into the Spirit realm, simply with our intent, we are immediately communicating in the Spirit. When we intentionally silence ourselves so that we can hear God, we can hear Him in this second only. Of course, seconds can add up. But the actual experience of God is right now, in this second.

The way to get into this second with God is intention. I must ignore what's around me, and simply be with God NOW.

Hereby know we that we dwell in him, and he in us, because he hath given us of his Spirit. (I John 4:13)

If we dwell in Him and He dwells in us, that implies constancy. He doesn't move in and out each day. We don't move in and out of Him each day. We dwell in Him and He dwells in us, so He is constantly here, and we can be with Him now.

It's not something we have to work "up to," although it gets easier with time to instantly connect with Him.

If you, right now, set a laser-sharp intention to simply exist with Jesus - who is in your heart, in your entire body right now if you follow Him - to simply exist with Him, to connect with Him, then right now you can experience God.

Try it.

Set a laser intention to focus on Jesus, close your eyes, and just be. Be with Jesus. Sense His presence. He is here now.

You can "dwell in him" now. You can be in His presence now. In fact, He is right with you now, even if you can't sense Him. Step into that awareness.

Over time, you can shift into that awareness right in the presence of others. Right now I'm writing in a public square, people all around me, and I sense the presence of Jesus right now as I'm typing. He is here with me, and I can sense it partly due to my intention. Perhaps practiced intention, but intention nevertheless!

Once you have this deep realization that He is right there, always, it's easy to go to Him in an instance.

We don't need an hour, or even 15 minutes set aside.

We can touch base with Him in a second.

We can spend 15 seconds with Him.

We can constantly commune.

Or check in throughout the day.

This realization that He is so close, right here, right now, has been so powerful to me.

Because it's freed me from feeling like if I haven't scheduled this deep time with Him, that I am missing something today.

Yes, I might feel I have missed Him in the moment ... but I don't have to live with it, carry it around all day.

Instead, I can spend time with Him now.

I can sense Him here as I'm writing.

Perhaps you can sense Him here as you are reading.

He is here with me.

He is here with you.

Connection Space:

Imagine you are in His presence now – how would that be?

You are in His presence now – you don't have to get to His presence, He is right here, right now.

He is in you.

Completely.

Fully.

All of you.

Not just a corner of your heart.

But all of you.

Turn to Him, take a moment, maybe even close this and take it from here just with Him personally.

Lord, You are here with me.

I know You are here.

If you can sense Him, tell Him, Lord, I sense You here.

If not, that's okay.

He isn't physical and the spiritual doesn't always have a physical sensation.

Lord, I sense You here.

Lord, I feel _____ about knowing You are this close.

Perhaps ask Him something:

> Lord, how do You want me to connect with You here?
>
> When do You want to talk with me?
>
> Right here.
>
> Right now.
>
> In an hour.
>
> In a moment.
>
> All day.
>
> Enjoy this time with the Lord.

His Presence Infills You

Jesus is peace.

If His Presence fully fills you and engulfs you- then you can live in perfect peace and perfect love.

His Presence in our life isn't some far away concept, a God that we do certain things right for and then He rewards us in some way.

Instead, since His Presence is in us, and since He is in us, fully in us, fully infusing us, we will be what He is.

Just as if you drink a very cold glass of water, on a hot day, you begin to feel cooler.

You drink another very cold glass of water, as the first one is going into your veins, and you can feel the cold getting to your head, you are beginning to cool off.

You have another glass of very cold water. And now you are beginning to feel cooler ... cold even.

Why has this happened?

It's because your body became fully infused with the cold water.

God's that way.

When He fully infuses us with His Peace, it gets into our head and our heart and our veins and our arms, and we experience His Peace.

We practically become His Peace.

He is love.

Perfect love and complete love.

Beloved, if God so loved us, we ought also to love one another.

No man hath seen God at any time. If we love one another, God dwelleth in us, and his love is perfected in us. (I John 4:11-12)

So when we are completely filled with Him and His love, we will become loving. We will become love.

From a prayer of Paul:

That Christ may dwell in your hearts by faith; that ye, being rooted and grounded in love,

May be able to comprehend with all saints what is the breadth, and length, and depth, and height;

And to know the love of Christ, which passeth knowledge, that ye might be filled with all the fulness of God. (Ephesians 3:17-19)

When Christ dwells in our hearts, we are rooted and grounded in love, and when we know His love, we are filled with the fullness of God!

Indeed all of the fruit of the Spirit:

But the fruit of the Spirit is love, joy, peace, longsuffering, gentleness, goodness, faith,

Meekness, temperance: against such there is no law. (Galatians 5:22-23)

Every expression of the complete fruit of the Spirit.

Every result of His life in us.

Imagine that with the fruit of the Spirit, our constant connection with Him, and His Spirit indwelling us, this summarizes our Christian walk:

And above all these things put on charity, which is the bond of perfectness.

And let the peace of God rule in your hearts, to the which also ye are called in one body; and be ye thankful.

Let the word of Christ dwell in you richly in all wisdom; teaching and admonishing one another in psalms and hymns and spiritual songs, singing with grace in your hearts to the Lord.

And whatsoever ye do in word or deed, do all in the name of the Lord Jesus, giving thanks to God and the Father by him. (Colossians 3:14-17)

He literally indwells us, and as we walk out His life in us, the fruit in our lives is incredible!

Connection Space:

Let's take a moment to acknowledge His Presence, to lean into His Presence.

You are here with me now, Jesus, even if I can't sense it.

And yet perhaps even as I am speaking these words . . . and I'm reflecting on the conversations I've had with You . . . I know Your Presence is here.

And knowing Your Presence is here is powerful.

I know Your Presence is here.

And I'm trusting that I have Your Presence.

And that over time, I'll be able to sense Your Presence better.

I ask, Lord, that You will give me an awareness of Your Presence, of Your Abiding Presence that's right here, with me!

Lord, thank You for being more than a distant God, thank You for being God right here, right now, even in me.

Connecting with my spirit, hearing my words as I say them.

And I'm growing in confidence that Your Presence is here.

You are really right here, right now!

Thank You Lord for Your Presence!

Thank You for dwelling in me, and giving me this abundant life in You, and that overflows to others!

He Is Always With You

As you press in and continue to spend time with Him, you'll develop a deep knowing and connection with Him, an inner sense of peace that He is in control, that He cares for you, that He will never leave you, and that He is guiding you.

Jesus Himself said:

Peace I leave with you, my peace I give unto you: not as the world giveth, give I unto you. Let not your heart be troubled, neither let it be afraid. (John 14:27)

In my own journey, the activities helped to lay the groundwork to get away from the rest of the world and lean into Him, but the actual relationship with Him is very deep and personal.

Through this last round of crushing crisis He developed in me a strong peace that was present even when circumstances were very very bad.

When the storm was raging outside, He showed me how to "sleep in the boat" like Jesus did when the storm raged, and His disciples were scared, but He was just sleeping, completely at peace.

I received this image of being in the eye of the hurricane with Him, the winds and rains might be 180 mph at the eyewall, but I was in the eye of the hurricane, at complete peace.

Even if the storm moved to the right or the left, the eyewall didn't hit me, as long as I stayed in the center of the eye, moving as the storm moved, but remaining centered in the eye, with Him.

That's the peace that passes all understanding.

I know that I don't have to understand what He is doing to rest into it and simply wait on Him.

I don't have to see the work He is doing, but I do have to wait for Him to do it. Some work on the inside of us takes time even when there is no apparent effort.

Consider this directive from Paul:

And let the peace of God rule in your hearts, to the which also ye are called in one body; and be ye thankful. (Colossians 3:15)

The word "let" implies that we must let, or allow, it to happen. We must allow or lean into His rest in order to fully experience it.

Jesus said:

Come unto me, all ye that labour and are heavy laden, and I will give you rest.

Take my yoke upon you, and learn of me; for I am meek and lowly in heart: and ye shall find rest unto your souls.

For my yoke is easy, and my burden is light. (Matthew 11:28-30)

When I rest utterly completely in Him, learning from His meekness and humility, instead of striving in accomplishment and pride, I receive His peace and presence. His way is easy, and His burden is light, and when we carry no more than He gives us to carry, our walk is light and fulfilled!

I want that untethered, deep, abiding, completely fulfilling and peaceful relationship with the Father, Jesus, and the Holy Spirit, and it's lived out every day both in our singular and personal experiences, with our earthly relationships, and the communities in which we exist.

I have an awareness of constantly being plugged in to Him. Which makes sense, because He lives in me. He's always here. His presence is always here. And I can connect with His presence any time I want.

It is a state of being, a mental state of mind that is constantly conscious of being in contact and communion with Him - as if I were separated in a monastery, and yet I'm not. I'm going about my day, meeting with people, working, recreating, etc.

If I'm close to Jesus, and spending enough time and process with Him, I'm peaceful. When I'm not spending enough time with Jesus or not relying on Him completely, I'm not peaceful.

Give yourself grace! Don't give up because you don't "feel peace" right away. Trust Jesus. Trust the process. Trust that even when you don't "feel peace," you are still growing closer to Him.

Enjoy that closeness with Him!!!

Connection Space:

Take a moment to visualize that peace.

Feel that peace.

You've prayed into it, you've read about it.

Now simply claim it:

Lord Jesus, thank You for the peace You have placed in me.

Thank You for Your peace that passes all understanding.

Thank You that You are growing that peace in me.

Thank You for Your peace!

I can sense Your peace now,

Thank You, thank You, thank You!

Experience This With Jesus

Over the years, Jesus has grown in me a deep awareness of His Presence, He's carried me through multiple life challenges, and He's been right by my side for over 40 years.

He's shown me peace, He's shown me His providence, and He's shown me His Presence, even during the toughest times.

Although for years I worked hard during prayer, striving to please Him, working hard to live the Christian life but always struggling with something, He has transformed my life from one of stress and anxiety, spinning my wheels in relationship with Him, to a deep, abiding relationship. I can now just be in His Presence.

This verse has become so real to me:

Be still, and know that I am God: I will be exalted among the heathen, I will be exalted in the earth.

The Lord of hosts is with us; the God of Jacob is our refuge. Selah.
(Psalm 46:10)

It used to be so hard for me to just be in His Presence. But now that I've immersed in His Presence so much, and I've experienced His work so deeply in my life, He's placed in me a level of peace and joy that makes it natural to just be in His Presence!

I can be walking or standing or sitting or lying down; I can experience His Presence during worship, with community, or even as I'm writing.

The closest we can be is in His Presence. Us in Him. Him in us.

There is no closer that we can be.

If you are born again, Jesus is in you.

You simply know it, walk it, connect with Him.

He's already there, so there's nothing we have to do to get more of Him.

We become aware of His Presence, and as we become aware of His Presence we can access the reality of it.

You can close your eyes and instantly be aware of His Presence. You don't even have to close your eyes, and you can know He is with you. It's not a matter of Him just being with you, but of you also being aware of Him being with you.

You can sit here and be in His Presence. Be in the Presence. Where you are, where you go, He goes.

When we love Him, when we seek His face, when we separate from our earthly desires, when we desire Him and we are completely immersed and connected with His Presence, such that we carry His Presence into our next task, our life becomes so much easier.

When I rest completely in Him, simply doing what He has given me for the day, and not worrying about anything outside of what He's given me, including tomorrow, I have peace. He knows my beginning from my end, He has a perfect plan for my joy, satisfaction, and His impact on others through me.

You can rest in Him completely in this way, simply doing what He's given you for today. He knows your beginning and your end; He has a perfect plan for your joy and peace, and He is ready for you to grow exponentially closer to Him!

Connection Space:

In this Connection Space, let's embrace His Presence within you.

You know He's there, He's always with you.

Lean into the awareness of His Presence within you.

The God of the Universe is communing with you.

The Spirit of Jesus, alive in you.

The Holy Spirit, ready to communicate with you.

He's always there, but we aren't always aware.

Be aware of His Presence.

So close.

So real.

Living and thinking and existing even as you read these words.

Alive.

Powerful.

The mind of Christ.

Access to the deep things of God.

Knowledge to aid and edify others.

Compassion to love them with the love of Christ.

All of Him within you.

Let's pray, Lord Jesus,

I love You.

Thank You for Your Presence and Your Spirit within me.

Thank You for being so close to me, so readily available for comfort or support or knowledge or power.

And yet so intimate, loving me with all of Yourself, Your love embracing me now.

I love You Lord!

Amen

31

Stay Close to Jesus for Life

The Lifelong Walk

I am feeling a bit melancholic today as I write this. It's been 4 months and a day of writing, and I'm finishing it up.

I think of all the topics that could have been included: spiritual warfare, victory, healing, ministry, loving others, taking care of the temple (our bodies), and so on. But they didn't fit strictly under "growing closer to Jesus," so I left them out.

And yet, as I contemplate them, with the exception of small details, if we walk out the spiritual walk with Jesus that's in the pages of this book, those things will fall into place.

You see, when we walk in the Spirit, we walk in fruit that contains all of these qualities:

Peace, joy, love, gentleness, faith, humility, patience, goodness, and self-control.

If we truly walk in all of those things, every hour of the day, just about everything else takes care of itself. We trust Jesus to heal when we pray. We love others but with boundaries like Jesus did. We minister to others, but with wisdom, like when the disciples brought on deacons to help with the serving of the food, so they could devote time to study and preaching. Warfare is simple: stay close to Jesus, and let Him fight the battles. Stand strong as in Ephesians 6.

A book about Victory would contain many of the same elements as this book, except with a focus on the end goal of Victory.

A book about Freedom in Christ would be mostly what's in here, with more reminders about staying free!

When we have a deep relationship with Jesus as the core element, with Him as the goal, not Victory as the goal, not ministry as the goal, not even love (gulp) as the goal . . . but Jesus in me, living in me, through me, with me . . . then everything else falls into place.

I could write a chapter about guarding against falling away, there are so many scriptures that warn against falling away . . . and yet it's so simple: just draw close to Jesus every single day, and you won't fall away.

Keep Him close.

He loves you so much, but He won't force Himself to be close. We have to lean in. Daily. Perhaps hourly. Or dare we say, constantly.

I think back on the mistakes in my life that led to poor choices and decisions 20 years ago that ended in divorce and pain and regret, and I've dissected forks in the road, what could I have done differently here, there, everywhere.

I conclude that if I had simply kept Jesus close (and first) the entire time, the choices would have been different. The mistakes wouldn't have happened, or if they had, they would have been exposed and rectified quickly.

I contemplate keeping my eyes on Jesus, the author and finisher of my faith, and keeping Him first. We are looking to Him first, we are looking to Him for decisions, and answers, and our life path.

I think of looking for guidance, asking Him to guide my steps . . . and if I simply stay close to Jesus, of course I'm receiving guidance.

I think of asking for wisdom, which He says He will give us liberally if we ask, and I have asked, and He has given, but I also think, if I stay close to Jesus . . . I'll live in wisdom.

In fact, the fruit of the Spirit exemplifies wisdom!

Every answer to life is in the Bible. I've included a lot of scripture in this book so that everyone can see where the concepts are rooted.

If we keep close to Jesus, search out the instructions that are in the Bible, and fellowship with other believers who can encourage us and offer godly advice and perspective, the rest of our life goes so much smoother.

He gives us answers to fix our mistakes. He gives us answers to direct our paths. He gives us answers to set our feet right. Even in the most complicated situations.

I've used the phrase "18 months" so many times in this book. But 4 months later, as I conclude the words in this book, it's nearly two years.

The 18 months were long, and grueling, and no, I couldn't see the light at the end of the tunnel for much of the time. But the freedom I've lived in these last 6 or 8 months or so after most of the realizations in this book is so real. It's not just spiritual. It's not just a feeling. It's not just knowing Jesus is close, and that He's first.

It's knowing that He got me through the worst storm of my life. He did miraculous things, not just in my life, my heart, my soul, my communication, my mind, but also externally, in bringing peace to chaos and even changing circumstances around me.

I don't know the storm you are going through. The solutions to my storm were not in any book. I read portions of possibly 20-30 books on communication, marriage, emotional wounds, and healing; and although bits and pieces were here and there, most of the healing in me came directly through Jesus and the people He surrounded me with. God intervened.

And yes, I had to take action. He showed me the steps, and I took action.

In your situation, you've perhaps searched books, videos, talked with people, and there's no clear easy pathway out. But Jesus knows the answer, He knows the way.

But you may have to take action, guided by Him.

Draw close to Him, grow deep in relationship with Him, ask Him to take you all the way through, keep your eyes on Him and let Him take you all the way through. And when you come out of the valley, you'll be able to pour into others who are going through something similar!

Closing Thoughts

As we come to the close of this book, I want to thank you for spending this time with me. This has been a reflection of my own journey, and I'm so grateful you've taken this time!

I truly believe that as you lean into the practices, presence, and relationship you will grow closer to Him.

But it is a journey that's lived out day after day, month after month, and year after year.

Based on my experience, as you grow closer to Jesus, your peace and calm will become evident to the world around you. You will naturally begin to operate in the fruit of the Spirit. You will begin to impact others' lives even as you grow closer to Jesus.

I've discovered that growing closer to Jesus isn't a one way flat ramp that gets you 1% closer each day.

It's more like a roller coaster: you have a great experience today, and then the rails rattle tomorrow, and you slow down at the peak, and then gravity takes over and you are plunging to a new low.

And I've learned that relationship with Jesus isn't something you store up, meaning you spend more time with Him today so you need less time tomorrow.

Yes, there is a cumulative effect of His Presence and even being able to step into a rhythm of closeness and peace with Him, and that cumulative effect builds over time. But it is a relationship, and it requires frequent communication and time to sustain.

When times are good, you may need to make more of an effort to spend time with Him. It's easy to fill our schedules with things and people and even ministry, and when times are good, we feel better about doing the things, especially if they appear to be for God, than when times are hard.

But when the hard times come and stress goes up, the first thing you want to do is make sure you spend enough time with Him.

Do it first. Not last! Make Him the first resort, not the last resort.

When you begin to feel stressed or overwhelmed, take it to Him. Spend time with Him. Walk with Him. Talk with Him. Pray in tongues.

The more time you spend with Him, the better everything is, hands-down.

When you are tired, it can feel even more burdensome. You don't have the words. You don't have the energy to talk with Him. That is a great time for praying in the Spirit or praying in tongues.

Every day for 18 months I had to spend time with the Lord or I wouldn't have made it through. Even as I am writing this book, if I didn't spend serious time with the Lord, it wouldn't be in your hands right now.

The journey is long, but He is faithful.

There were times during the worst of it when I spent 5 hours with Him. There were times when it was an hour or two and my soul begged for more.

And there are times like today when I've spent an hour with the Lord, wrestling with different things.

At the end of the day, what's important is extreme reliance on Him. It doesn't look the same every time. But in every situation, battle, bleakness, poverty, scarcity, pride, sin, desperation, tiredness, exhaustion, the answer is reliance on Him.

It's not even just the things in this book. They are just an outline, a framework, helpful tools.

It's reflecting on the God of the Universe, Holy, Holy God.

It's communion with Jesus, the author and finisher of our faith, majestic and regal, sitting at the right hand of God, making intercession for us.

It's constant communication - both talking and listening - to the Holy Spirit who lives in you.

The practices offered in this book are simply a window into my own experiential relationship with Christ, and not exhaustively every single practice any Christian does in their journey with Christ.

I've spoken with, read about, and read from others with intimate relationships with Christ and none exactly mirror what I've shared here. Nor could I see myself with the exact intimacy with Jesus by following their set of practices.

God is infinite and relates to each of us in a way that's as unique as the fingerprint on our hand, or as the facets of a gemstone.

What I've written here is not "the" way. It's what's been effective for me and my personality to draw close to Him.

I encourage you to experiment and see what works for you in your unique relationship with him.

Take what you've read here, and don't allow it to just be theoretical, to just be interesting, but instead to become a part of your daily life.

I would also suggest that if something didn't resonate with you . . . maybe you don't want to pray in tongues, or maybe you don't like journaling, don't let those few things that don't resonate stop you from embracing the activities that would draw you closer to Him.

Having a relationship with Jesus isn't about a set of activities or practices, it's about drawing close to Him, relying on Him, trusting Him, confiding in Him, and walking with Him.

This book is just a fragment, a shadow of what's in the Big Book, the Bible. You can read the Bible from cover to cover repeatedly, and never discover everything about God and Jesus and the Holy Spirit. There are many books written on faith and hope and relying on Jesus and even closeness to God and yet all of them together don't completely reveal all the truth about Him!

I've simply given you the best of the realizations that helped me draw closer to Jesus during my time of trial, and that are enduring now, during my day-to-day life, recovering from the impact of the trial, and honestly, working to get this message out to the world.

But with everything you've received here, it's about drawing close to Him. Daily. With all your heart.

The final thoughts I want to share with you are:

1) Don't give up. Stay in the game. It's a long game. Play daily. Spend time with Jesus every single day. When it's tough, go to Jesus. When you don't know what to do, go to Jesus. When you have it all figured out and you get into pride, go to Jesus. Take everything to Jesus consistently, repeatedly, and without giving up.

2) Remember this is not about what to do: praise, worship, tongues, reading the Word, conversations. Instead, it's about relationship with Him. The "to-dos" are simply there to aid you in staying close to Him.

3) Lean in and embrace closeness to Him. The closer you can grow to God, to Jesus, to the Holy Spirit, the easier everything becomes. You get answers faster, you get clarity faster, you live in more peace.

4) Consider making a daily practice of having several "Connection Spaces" each day. You can re-use the ones in this book, write your own, speak your own, or download new ones at the website.

Every time you face anything challenging, worship God first.

Anytime you have a celebration or a thanksgiving, worship God first.

Create an environment of praise and thankfulness and joy in your life.

Spend time and attention delighting in the Lord, His Presence, His Providence, and His attributes.

This powerful verse contains so much deep meaning:

Delight yourself in the Lord, and he will give you the desires of your heart. (Psalm 37:4)

God repeatedly provides blessing for those who praise Him, who keep their eyes on Him.

He gives peace, He gives stability, He gives a future and a hope.

What He gives us is inexpressible, it's inexhaustible.

In His presence is great calm and peace.

We have to keep our eyes on Him.

Or return our eyes back on Him every day, every hour, if necessary.

He loves you beyond measure.

He forgives you beyond measure.

He accepts you beyond measure.

He cherishes you beyond measure.

He guides you beyond measure.

He restores you beyond measure.

He wants the very best for you.

But He won't force it on any of us, because He gave us free will and power over our lives.

So when the going gets rough, keep your eyes on Jesus.

No, it's not easy.

Yes, it might take months or even years.

When you've done all to stand, stand.

Patiently waiting for the resolution.

Patiently waiting for His solution.

Knowing He's right there with you.

He's right here, right now.

He's with you and for you.

He indwells you.

He's living in you.

His life shines through you.

His life is lived through you.

The Holy Spirit lives in you.

You are His and He is yours.

Rest in His peace.

Rest in His presence.

Jesus loves us so very much.

He created us for communion with Him in the garden.

He wants to have a personal relationship with us.

And He gave us His Holy Spirit - God Himself - so that we have God inside us.

This is the Jesus we serve.

This is the Jesus we know.

This is the Jesus of this book.

Immerse yourself in His Presence, in His ways.

He is limitless.

Enter limitless relationship, enter limitless existence!

Close to God. Close to Jesus. Close to the Holy Spirit.

Close.

Let's enjoy one final Connection Space together!

Connection Space:

Jesus, thank You for the time I've gotten to spend with Your readers and followers. I've had a great time writing these words that I truly believe are from You, and I'm so grateful You entrusted them to me.

The time we've had together as I've been writing has been so sweet. I feel like even writing this has helped me grow closer to You, to understand more of You.

I lift up to You each person reading these words, that You will give them wisdom and guidance to adapt what they've seen here to their own individual relationship with You.

I ask that You will continue to draw both me and them closer to You as well.

Thank You again for this time together.

I cannot even begin to imagine what the next level with You must be, and I'm looking forward to it!

I love You Lord!

Amen

-- Sean

A Personal Note

Friend, thank you for reading this book.

As I've shared, this is a reflection of my current relationship with Jesus, the Father, and the Holy Spirit, and I hope that it inspires you in some way to draw closer to Him.

Although I've shared it before, not everything in here will likely be a fit for you, your personality, and your own relationship with Jesus.

Take what you need, and add or subtract as necessary.

Writing about some of my own personal challenges, sins, and mistakes has been incredibly therapeutic.

Prior to this last year or so of my life, most of the mistakes I've shared here, and nearly all of my early life history, I had shared with practically no one. I had a deep fear of judgment, not being accepted, and honestly, embarrassment over having grown up the way I did.

Yes, I was embarrassed for the mistakes my parents (and their parents before them) made that led me to experience what I did, and my nature wanted to simply hide it from the world. But in hiding it, I developed a pattern of hiding everything.

Revealing some of these things in small groups and therapy was helpful and freeing, but writing about it here, knowing that you and many more will read these words, judge me, accept me, or any combination of the two, has been exceedingly powerful in my own journey to emotional freedom.

The process of putting these things into print, and of course having to organize my thoughts into coherent sentences and paragraphs, was incredibly clarifying.

I would write something, and in a few days re-read it, and realize that the words I used didn't exactly express my thoughts or feelings, so I would make the changes necessary to exactly express the intended meaning.

The same was true for the spiritual elements. So much of what I wrote about I internalized, I lived out, but I didn't have the words to effectively share it with others, or even to perhaps fully understand it for myself!

So writing it out for you, the reader, and having to make it clear because I wouldn't have the luxury of explaining it with more words as if we were talking, has improved my own understanding of the depth and intricacies of my relationship with Christ!

Thank you again for reading this book. I hope that as you implement what I've shared and take it to the Lord for your own personal clarity and depth, He blesses your relationship with Him greatly!

To your relationship with Jesus,

Sean Mize

A few guidelines to grow by:

Look to Jesus first in everything.

It's better to slow down and be sure you are walking with Him, than to rush ahead and waste days or even years.

Know that God knows your spiritual make up better than any pastor, friend, or acquaintance, and He is the Master Engineer in your life.

But also know that He uses imperfect people in our lives to show us things, reveal our flaws, sharpen our minds, and grow us closer to Him.

He wants to use you to impact others in the ways you've been impacted.

He wants to use you to help others who have been through what you've been through.

Jesus loves you completely, always and forever.

Jesus is more concerned with growing close to you than you building a kingdom for His glory.

But once you have a deep relationship with Him, He'll likely call you to "feed my sheep," as He called Peter.

It's a beautiful thing to walk with Jesus, and walk alongside others as they walk with Jesus!

Additional Reading

I've selected a few books that can take you deeper on some of the topics taught.

4 Keys to Hearing God's Voice, by Mark and Patti Virkler

Empowered by Praise, by Michael Youssef

Holy Spirit: God Within You, by David Diga Hernandez

Living Fearless: Exchanging the Lies of the World for the Liberating Truth of God, by Jamie Winship

Exploring Worship: A Practical Guide to Praise and Worship, by Bob Sorge

Worship: The Ultimate Priority, by John MacArthur

About the Author

About Sean Mize:

Sean Mize is a follower of Jesus first, who has walked a long and deep journey of emotional pain and hurt, success and failure in business, relationships, and faith. He's encountered trials, made momentous mistakes, and been completely transformed by the blood of Jesus. Sean wants the words of this book to make it so much easier to draw close to Jesus so that you can have intimacy with Him, get faster relief from the current pain or trial you are enduring, and even position yourself to take the gift He has placed in you, and reveal it to the world.

To receive more faith based training from Sean, visit ClosetoJesus.com

www.ingramcontent.com/pod-product-compliance
Lightning Source LLC
Chambersburg PA
CBHW011613290426
44110CB00020BA/2573